Liam Canniffe was formerly an Irish diplomat who served on three continents. His foreign postings included the Irish Representation to the European Union in Brussels, Consul General in both Chicago and Boston and as ambassador to Nigeria and other countries in West Africa.

Liam also served on the Northern Ireland desk during the troubles in the 1980s. He was the adviser to both the Foreign and European Affairs Committees in the Irish parliament and following his official retirement he was appointed as adviser to the Irish Co-Chair of the British Irish Parliamentary Assembly.

In recent years, he has written several volumes of poetry.

To my father and all those other young men and women
who sought justice and freedom.

Liam Canniffe

TRANSITION

A Novel Set in a Time of Change

AUSTIN MACAULEY PUBLISHERS™
LONDON * CAMBRIDGE * NEW YORK * SHARJAH

Copyright © Liam Canniffe 2023

The right of Liam Canniffe to be identified as author of this work has been asserted by the author in accordance with sections 77 and 78 of the Copyright, Designs and Patents Act 1988.

All rights reserved. No part of this publication may be reproduced, stored in a retrieval system, or transmitted in any form or by any means, electronic, mechanical, photocopying, recording, or otherwise, without the prior permission of the publishers.

Any person who commits any unauthorised act in relation to this publication may be liable to criminal prosecution and civil claims for damages.

This is a work of fiction. Names, characters, businesses, places, events, locales, and incidents are either the products of the author's imagination or used in a fictitious manner. Any resemblance to actual persons, living or dead, or actual events is purely coincidental.

A CIP catalogue record for this title is available from the British Library.

ISBN 9781035819935 (Paperback)
ISBN 9781035819942 (ePub e-book)

www.austinmacauley.com

First Published 2023
Austin Macauley Publishers Ltd®
1 Canada Square
Canary Wharf
London
E14 5AA

To Frances and my family for their forbearance and encouragement and Tony for his insistence and support…

Prologue

Sometimes we see ourselves in the faces of those, who, at another time and place would be considered enemies. Why? It is difficult to say. Perhaps they may remind us of someone we knew from the past, who had befriended us in some way or had helped when our needs were most. Or maybe a fraternal bond is formed with a fellow human being, who like you, has walked the same ground, experienced the same abominations; survivors from hell, a brother from the same horror trenches of a Great War. Or maybe it's just that in our innate and complex human nature we sometimes come to the aid of another human being simply because he or she needs our help.

Introduction

As an island to the north west of Europe, Ireland had not suffered the endless invasions as had the rest of Europe. The principal early invasion had been by the Celts who arrived around 500 B.C. The Romans who invaded Britain did not come. The next major invaders were the Normans, but not until the 12th century AD. The Vikings had come, but mainly to pillage with only a few settlements.

Post-Norman arrival the Gaelic order survived however in most areas outside Dublin (the "Pale") until the defeat of the Great Northern Gaelic Chieftains at Kinsale in 1601. After that, despite continued fighting by the Irish over the next century, the country was virtually under the English Crown from the 18th century. A good deal of the southern part of Ireland was settled early on by the Normans but they quite quickly integrated with the local population, mainly because they were Catholic and so the transition was almost seamless.

After Kinsale however, the northern part of the country was heavily settled with Protestants primarily from Scotland and Northern England. The Williamite and Cromwellian wars were mainly Catholic versus Protestant in nature and the defeat in both cases of the former ensured that the Protestant minority not only were given the land formerly owned by Catholic Irish or Normans but also given a privileged position as the established authority in Ireland, subservient to the Crown. The English establishment thus ensured, as it did in all of its colonies, that its policy of *'divide and conquer'* was firmly in place.

While the English policy had the desired effect of ensuring that the local establishment would control the original natives, because it also continued to divide the communities, there were continued revolts and rebellions every century. Penal laws against non-established religions, Catholics and others, coercion laws and economic acts in favour of English trade during the following centuries only helped to keep the desire for independence alive.

Even though the members of the local Dublin parliament, which was subject to the crown and Westminster, were only drawn from the Protestant ascendancy it nonetheless contained individuals such as Henry Grattan who sought emancipation for Irish Catholics and free trade for Ireland with Britain. Its abolition in 1800 under the Act of Union ensured that the Irish henceforth would be subject to the needs of England rather than Ireland.

Catholics were not allowed to enter Westminster until after the Catholic Emancipation Act of 1829 and then after Catholic voters were reduced by increasing the rateable valuations of those eligible five-fold.

During the latter half of the 19th century Irish Parliamentarians, particularly Parnell, sought to have a separate Irish Parliament, accepting that it would continue to have ties to Westminster particularly in Foreign and Defense affairs. While liberal politicians such as Gladstone were prepared to accede to this, the conservative Tory party with ties to the Protestant Unionists in Ireland fought vehemently against it.

However, with the Liberals under Prime Minister Asquith, depending on the Irish Parliamentary Party to remain in Government, the Home Rule Bill was introduced in 1912 and despite extreme Unionist protest, including the creation and arming of the Ulster Volunteer Force and a mutiny of British Army Officers in Ireland, the bill passed into law by 1914. Because the war intervened its introduction was postponed until after it was over.

Reacting to the Ulster Volunteer Force (UVF) the Nationalists set up their own force called the Nationalist Volunteers (NV). While no action had been taken against the UVF even when they imported a large quantity of arms, similar leniencies were not shown to the NV when they subsequently imported a far less quantity and quality of arms.

On the promise of Home Rule after the war, the leader of the Irish Parliamentary Party, John Redmond, encouraged the Irish to join the British Army *'in the fight for the freedom of small nations'* and many answered the call. Up to 250,000 Irish from around the world took part, of whom up to 50,000 were killed.

Meanwhile among the National Volunteers a more radical group calling themselves the Irish Volunteers emerged. They refused to follow Redmond's exhortations. These were mainly members of the more radical Irish Republican Brotherhood which was formed in the latter part of the 19th century and wanted total Irish freedom. They saw an opportunity to force the issue of separation during the war and a rebellion against British rule in Ireland took place in 1916. Because of a lack of preparation, coordination and indeed popular support the rebellion was confined only to Dublin and had no chance of success. It was quickly put down and the British Military Commander in Dublin executed the leaders shortly after.

The revolutionaries had little or no support for the uprising from the average Irish person in Dublin or indeed in the rest of the country. Many of the families in Ireland at that time had a son or some relation fighting for their lives near the Somme. The summary executions of the leaders however, who were locally regarded as mere misguided mystics and poets, revived the latent bitterness against the Sassenach deep within the soul of Catholic Ireland.

At the end of the Great War and its enormous upheaval in Europe, the general elections in Britain resulted in a landslide victory for Sinn Fein in Ireland. The Sinn Fein (Our Selves) Party was founded in 1906 by Arthur Griffith and had attracted a young energetic group to its basic goal which was independence from Britain. It had spoken against the Home Rule Bill introduced in 1912 as not going far enough. Even though Griffith had not taken a role in the 1916 rebellion Sinn Fein became the name most referred to in relation to the rebellion.

Later in 1918 it vehemently denounced conscription and rapidly took over the mantle of Irish nationalism from the old Home Rule Party which had failed to deliver the promised Home Rule. The British reaction to the advancement of Sinn Fein, including the jailing of a number of its leaders including Eamon de Valera on a trumped-up charge of a 'German plot', only assisted in increasing its popularity among nationalist Ireland.

In January 1919 Sinn Fein formed a separate parliament in Dublin, called the Dail, with Eamon de Valera as its president and issued a declaration of Irish independence. Only the four north-eastern counties of Ireland with a strong two thirds protestant/unionist population returned majority unionist representatives. Unionists continued to attend Westminster and demanded that the Government in London would ensure the Dail was not permitted to function. The Dail was outlawed by Britain in September 1919.

The beginning of the War of Independence can be traced back to an attack at Sodhedburg in Co Tipperary in April 1919 on an explosives delivery where two police officers were shot dead by the Irish Republican Brotherhood (IRB). That action did not have the approval of the Dail. However, the attacks continued and were directed mainly against the Royal Irish Constabulary (RIC).

The justification for this was that, as the force was made up of Irishmen enforcing British law on an Irish population, they were acting as traitors against the Irish people. RIC retaliation gave a certain legitimacy to the attackers who eventually came under the name of the IRA after the Dail approved the name change of the Irish Volunteers to the Irish Republican Army. The members of the IRA still retained the name Volunteers.

Though the "troubles" had begun in 1919, it was 1920 before they began to seriously take off. Not all parts of the country were affected by IRA activities and they were in the main concentrated in certain parts of the country, primarily Dublin, Co. Cork and Co. Tipperary.

Initially the British Government was determined to treat the issue as police rather than a military matter and the RIC were given the task of dealing with it. As time moved on it became too much for them as a number of officers, who were unprepared to take on their own kinsmen in what was obviously a political issue, left that force.

The Government next reinforced the RIC in two phases in 1920 with paramilitaries drawn from veterans of the British Army. However, when parts of the country became ungovernable, the British introduced martial law in mid-1920 and the British Army became more involved.

The IRA had very limited numbers on active service, only 9,000 to 16,000 in the whole country during the War of Independence. This could have been expanded by many times more but it did not possess the weapons to do so and so the war was waged on the back of what arms the IRA could capture from the security forces. However, through guerrilla tactics, marshalled primarily by Michael Collins from Dublin, that limited number of fighters was able to show Britain's inability to control the whole country without large amounts of troops and a heavily armed expanded police force.

Dublin

Michael Collins not only coordinated the total IRA activities but as Minister for Finance in the new Dail, set up and oversaw the use of a Loan Fund to run the new administration. These roles involved him in *funding* and equipping the IRA. *He* also was instrumental in escalating attacks on British security forces in Ireland and ensured that the situation would cause sufficient difficulty for the British Establishment that they would have to retaliate harder or come to the negotiating table. Remarkably, while he was constantly on the ground and was known to the British to play a vital role in the IRA, he remained elusive during the Troubles and was never captured.

Cork

While the hostilities broke out in 1919, it was not until 1920 that they became more widespread and more serious in that county. RIC barracks in certain areas, particularly in Cork, were attacked and the smaller ones destroyed. By early 1920 the countryside in West Cork became almost a no-go area for small patrols of security forces.

Chapter 1
Joe Ryan

Joe Ryan, a native of Bandon, came from a tradesman's family. He had two other brothers. His father died when he was only nine. His mother in those harsh times had to struggle to keep the family together and ensure that there was a roof over their heads and food on the table.

Joe was an excellent student and excelled at math and English. However, because of the poor economic circumstances, his mother being the only real breadwinner in the family, he was unable to progress further than primary certificate level at school.

He and his brothers took on apprenticeships in the town which paid nothing. He did not allow this to deter him however and he made full use of the local library to continue his education.

In late 1915, Joe, without first telling his mother what he intended, following the example set by his older brothers, volunteered for military service. He had done so as he believed the justice of the war and he was influenced in particular by John Redmond, the leader of the Irish Parliamentary Party at Westminster. Redmond had encouraged Irish men to join to emphasise Ireland's solidarity with Britain in its time of need as well as demonstrating that the new emerging Ireland wanted to show solidarity with small nations by coming to Belgium's aid.

Primarily however, he wished to show Britain, and perhaps especially the Unionists in Ireland, that Ireland could be trusted as an ally after it received Home Rule from Britain, which had been passed by Parliament and was awaiting final clearance and implementation after the war.

Joe was also driven by the need to relieve the economic situation at home where because of the paucity of the job situation in the town he could only find non-paying apprenticeship work. Because there were no outgoings in the army, he was able to have most of his pay diverted to his mother. He was just 16 years old, like so many others who joined.

His mother was distraught. Was it for this she had devoted her whole life after the early death of her husband? Nothing could be done to reverse the situation. He had signed up—she was just a poor widow woman with no connections.

He was inducted into the Munster Fusiliers who saw action in Gallipoli, the Middle East, as well as on the Western Front. After initial perfunctory training Joe was sent with his Battalion to France. He had shown early on that he was literate, intelligent, athletic and dexterous and consequently he was selected for the engineer's corps. In France, he received further training in signals and was promptly sent up the line.

Trench warfare primarily consisted of defence, bombardment, attack and counter-attack. Gains made on either side were miniscule between 1914 and 1918 and the war was primarily one of attrition. It became obvious early on that the side that could endure the most would win, unless a major break-through could be achieved. In the circumstances, the tolerance of the populations on both sides to major loss, while not publicly debated or indeed mentioned, was understood by politicians to be a key factor in which side would be victorious.

Conscription was introduced in mainland Britain but not in Ireland because of the sensitivities there, particularly after the Rising in Dublin by the Irish Republican Brotherhood at Easter 1916. The casualties of the War even at that time were enormous. It is estimated that the first Battle of the Somme alone from July to November 1916 resulted in 450,000 British casualties, 200,000 French casualties and 500,000 German casualties.

As in all wars the side with the superior strategies would invariably win. For those strategies to be implemented effectively reliable intelligence plays a vital role. Consequently, both sides from early on in the Great War paid great attention to equipping themselves with the best intelligence possible. On the Western Front most of this intelligence gathering was concentrated on ascertaining the strengths of either side, both men and equipment, all along the line that divided them, stretching from the English Channel to Switzerland.

That intelligence was gathered primarily by photos obtained by military aircraft flyovers or by the signals corps using sightings from their elevated positions or as in most situations on very flat terrain of the Northern French and Belgian borders, (where the British were located) by extending trenches out into

No Man's Land and even during cover of darkness crawling out as near as possible to the enemy lines. There in that hazardous occupation Joe Ryan carried out his duties with others diligently and, despite the selective targeting of the signals soldiers in there, most often, precarious positions by German machine gunners and sniper fire, unlike 70% of his colleagues, he survived physically intact until 1918.

During that time, he received rapid promotions, first to Corporal and then to Sergeant, due to his abilities and resourcefulness, but primarily because those positions became available all too regularly in this dreadful arena. In late 1917 he was recalled to Dunstable in England for specialised training in signals and intelligence. He returned to the Front in 1918 and was wounded during the spring counter-offensive against the Germans, which, after the introduction of the US forces, was the start of the turning point of the war.

Joe was still recovering from his wounds when the war ended in November 1918. He was, with the bulk of the British Forces, demobbed soon after and returned home to civilian life some months after when he recovered from his wounds.

Back home there was a subdued welcome for the returning troops outside their immediate families. The aftermath of the 1916 Rising and Sinn Fein's outright victory in the December 2018 Westminster General Election had changed irrevocably the mood in Ireland and ensured that in those parts of Ireland where Sinn Fein held sway British rule would be opposed in every way possible. While initially Joe had regarded the 1916 rising as a stab in the back for the Irish like himself who were fighting for small nations in France and could not understand why this had taken place, he like other Irishmen at the Front were dismayed by the executions of the leaders in such a pre-emptive way by the military in Dublin.

Like Redmond he wanted to show Britain and the unionists that they had nothing to fear from an Irish parliament. He had moreover committed himself to fight and would continue to do so if for no other reason than that he had lost so many friends and colleagues already to give up now would be tantamount to denying their sacrifice.

Besides the non-recognition of what he had gone through during those past awful four years his membership of the British Army was even resented by some of the locals back home. It was a very heavy load to carry. If he had come from a unionist background he would have been received back home as a hero. He had come back to nothing. Not only had he lost a good number of his friends in the war, his two brothers, one in the navy the other in the army, had not survived.

Joe did not allow this to deter him. He had fought against the odds for four years and had not given up. He would not change now. He had plans and he was determined to put them into practice.

Joe wasted little time in settling down to civilian life and within a short number of very active months he was running a lucrative business in the town. He had a pleasing personality, knew everyone in the town and crossed all barriers between rich and poor, loyalist and nationalist, protestant and catholic. Because of his War background he was even welcomed into the British Army Barracks in the town.

He knew some of the Officers and NCOs by first name and was often invited into their respective Messes. In particular, because of his wartime experiences, he was friendly with the NCOs who were attached to the communications side and would call in to their office when in the barracks. He was an expert in their equipment, due to his training in Dunstable and was happy to share his superior knowledge with them when asked.

Chapter 2
Geoffrey Eastbourne

Geoffrey Eastbourne, the only child of a Lord and Lady Eastbourne, grew up with enormous social privilege but little emotional support from his parents. They had a large mansion and tracts of inherited land in the country and a substantial house in London. He saw very little of his parents who were quite often absent and he was left to his own devices with the servants in whatever house he happened to be located at the time.

His parents were both people of a world that existed at the end of 19th century Victorian England. Life was complex, cruel and mean for those who not only did not have advantage but also even for those with it, who did not strive to take every conceivable gain from that advantage. Children were to be seen and not heard. To ensure that Geoffrey was brought up to understand his place he was given the warm luxury of master and the cold privation of isolation.

When he was five, he was sent off to public school some distance from them and came home only at holiday time. Lord Eastbourne was not as hard-hearted as his wife but he had been brought up in a similar fashion and saw it merely as the correct way to raise a young man. Both his parents consequently showed him little interest, apart from what appeared to be a remote obligation to give him material things and a proper education.

He had a governess from early on but whatever benefits she brought with her in the way of imparting knowledge and the proper behaviour of children, affection was certainly not one them. All of her social skills, or at least the limited degree she unfortunately possessed, were totally reserved to flatter his mother and, when she was not around, to coquettishly smile at his father.

Geoffrey, lacking confidence and initially an inability to fit in, found a late 19th century/early 20th boarding school a very difficult and cruel place. He was regarded and treated by the teaching staff as a boy of little ability who would never amount to much: the prefects and senior boys bullied and abused him: and he had no real friends in his own term. He tried hard to make the rugby and cricket teams, but from early on at school he was never given a real chance. His real abilities were hidden because he had never been given an opportunity to develop them. Consequently, his academic and social advancement were stymied from the start.

His only solace at that time was vacation periods when he could return home to the constant smile and genuine affection of Nannie Kate. So long as she was there, he could endure any hardship and accept the intolerance and cruelty of non-acceptance by an unwelcoming world.

He did however, learn in time to play the game, to feign acceptance of the status quo. Nurtured by Nannie Kate he was in essence a kindly soul and he responded positively to any little kindness shown to him.

When he had finished in Public School, his parents, particularly his father, expected that, like him, Geoffrey would go up to Oxford University and finish his education before he went into some business his father would establish for him and also perhaps win a seat in Parliament. Unfortunately, this all proved to be in vain as Geoffrey not only emerged with no grades but also with an unhelpful, unprepossessing letter from the school's headmaster at what might be described as a character reference, which his father had demanded from the school.

That episode resulted in a blazing row with his father who felt Geoffrey had let the whole family down. To compound Geoffrey's misery, his mother Lady Georgina, true to form, did not offer any support for her son. Rather she derisively questioned why Lord Eastbourne should have expected much from Geoffrey. Did his father not realise that he never showed much enthusiasm for anything and anyway he was always such a dull boy. "It's about time you realised Geoffrey will never amount to anything."

As always Geoffrey had to turn to Nannie Kate for comfort and support.

"Never mind, my dear, dear boy, a hiccup like this is merely a fallen hurdle on the way to the finishing line. There will be many successes in your life ahead, and you will look back and see how wrong they were about you. Your parents are too busy to see the goodness and the abilities that you have latent in you. Put this day behind you and march on.

"You and I know you can succeed. In time you will show them how wrong they were in not understanding that. You have greatness in you but, more importantly, above that you have a generosity of spirit that will always win through. And remember you are loved."

Lord Eastbourne, ever since the boy's birth, had built up expectations for his son. He had believed Geoffrey would not only carry on the high regard in which the family were held for generations past but would even further enhance its name and fortunes. He had to come to terms with the choices that were now open to him. At that moment he believed that his heritage, which had lasted from the Middle Ages, might even come to an abrupt halt.

In the circumstances Lord Eastbourne felt he would have to reassess his position. He needed time to decide how to plan for the future and the handicap fate had bestowed on him. Distance would have to be maintained between himself and Geoffrey until such time as he could plan for his admission into family matters, where Geoffrey's inadequacies could be as opaque as possible.

Consequently, he could not now countenance having Geoffrey near him in any of his endeavours. What would his friends and associates say? The boy would not only be regarded as incompetent and useless: worse he would reflect damagingly on the family and certainly on Lord Eastbourne himself. His standing, which over the years he had given so much time, effort and finances to build, would be blunted in an instant if he allowed Geoffrey to be associated with him in any way.

Using his high offices and demanding repayment of favours done in the past Lord Eastbourne had Geoffrey enrolled at Oxford, although little was expected by way of return from Geoffrey.

Geoffrey found however, that University was far easier than boarding school and he actually began to fit in. But then the war had begun and was already in its second year when the pressure came on him to make his contribution to the war effort. His father, who saw little of him now, expected no great change. Accordingly, he did not need to have his father's desire to hide him from his society pointed out to him. He thus voluntarily relieved the situation he found himself in by declaring that he would enter military service.

It was the early months of 1916. The Great War was taking its toll on manpower and the Army was only too willing to accept recruits, particularly those from noble backgrounds who would be expected to enter as officers and give leadership and enthusiasm to the regiments they joined. "Backbone" and "battles won on playing fields" were very much ingrained in the thinking of the establishment at that time.

Lord Eastbourne, if he thought about it at all, believed that for many reasons this was a very good solution to an immediate difficulty. His son should serve at a time when the Empire needed him and anyway, he would preserve the standing of the family by doing so. Had not his forebears won great fortune at Blenheim and Waterloo among other great battles?

If the dangers Geoffrey faced and were well understood after two years of bloodletting that the world had not seen since the Middle Ages, his father did not dwell on them. "Noblesse Oblige" and "call of duty" were foremost and the only consideration. By this one noble gesture Geoffrey had redeemed himself, if only temporarily.

The family and Lord Eastbourne could bask in the knowledge that they were part of the great struggle on behalf of the Empire. For the first time in years Lord Eastbourne felt inordinately proud of his son and wished he had known him better. He at that moment realised that if he had shown more interest in Geoffrey in his formative years, he perhaps could have helped him achieve greater things. Unhappily he did not share this feeling with Geoffrey and they parted with a mere handshake and an admonition to "do your duty, no matter what".

After a very short training course at the Royal Military College at Sandhurst, Geoffrey was assigned to the battalions of the Essex Regiment which were stationed on the Western Front. He arrived in France on 28 June 1916 and was in the trenches on 1 July 1916 for the start of the First Battle of the Somme. As 2nd Lieutenant he had command of a platoon and was ordered to take up position at 3.30 am. By 8.30 am the advance was called and the worst day in the history of the British Army for casualties commenced. However, because of congestion in No Man's Land the inevitable slaughter of the Essex was delayed until 10.50 am.

Leading from the front Geoffrey, with pistol in hand, urged on his troops to almost certain death for him and those with him against the German machine guns, from which the bullets with sickening rapidity seemed to pierce the air around them like driving sleet. When they were stopped in mid NO Man's Land minutes later, he could only see seven men of the 26 he had started out with. His whole company had fared no better, as did the British advance all along the line.

The madness of that attack against an enemy, which was deeply and indestructibly dug in and which had far superior fire power than the British troops who charged against it, could only be compared to hopelessness of the Charge of the Light Brigade. The difference in the final outcome though was enormous. While in the latter battle the British lost hundreds of brave men following the orders of an idiot commander, at the Somme they lost tens of thousands and that only on the first day.

At the end of the day the British had gained only three and a half square miles of territory and had over 57,000 casualties. They were forced to dig in where they were and continue the attack.

Geoffrey's battalion suffered such heavy losses that it had to be amalgamated with another which had similar losses. The battle dragged on for months until November 1916 and was a very expensive lesson in how to conduct war for the British, who had failed to use enough bombardment to pulverise the Germans and take out their barbed wire prior to the attack. They also delayed the advance too long after the bombardment stopped, allowing the Germans to prepare their machine gun positions for the attack.

Geoffrey grew up very quickly in the trenches and learned that empathising with his troops was just as important as leading them. Most of those around him were younger than he and had never before left home. He found his métier in understanding their needs and where possible showing he was mindful of the atrocious conditions they were living under.

He manfully set time aside to ensure the wounded were seen too. He also wrote to the parents and loved ones of those who had perished under his command, inserting comforting words in a small effort to ease their pain and show his respect and solidarity with them in their grieving.

He was one of the few 2nd lieutenants who survived the onslaught that summer/autumn and he learned to accept death as inevitable and not fear it. Thus he lived through the war welcoming his R&R when it came but accepting his return to the front as part of the whim of authoritarian machinations, which the weakness of human nature and the times had imposed on men of his age.

He did not return to England during any of his R&R leave, feeling that he had no relationship with his parents and it would only impose a different kind of hardship. He wrote home irregularly as a duty rather than a need. He rarely talked about himself or least of all of the hardships of the Front. That he knew would not be acceptable from one of his backgrounds and anyway he felt it was not what they wished to read. Suffice to believe that they would require a communication from him from time to time to say that he was still alive and doing his duty.

They would need the information when the matter arose in whatever company they happened to be in at the time. *"Geoffrey wrote recently, said the war was going well. He's at the Front in France, you know. Seems to be acquitting himself as one would expect. Got a promotion in the field recently."*

Allowing the conversation to progress into more important and deeper political and topical discussion such as, *"—bloody thing seems to go on and on. —those awful Bolsheviks have blunted the effort against the Germans in the East and God knows what effect that will have down the road. It is difficult to see what the turmoil there will ultimately mean. etc. —revolting Irish—never satisfied. — can't understand why the Americans have not entered by now! Surely, they must understand that we are fighting for the peaceful co-existence of Europe and to prevent its domination by an ever-expanding Germany!"*

His father, from time to time, embarked on writing to Geoffrey to encourage him and show support and indeed even concern. However, when he reached the point of telling him that he was missed and prayed for he threw the unfinished letters into the waste bin and thought better of it. *"—not a wise thing to show emotion and paternal weakness at a time such as this when manly strength and fortitude were all that was called for."*

His mother, Lady Georgina, on the other hand, tiring of the *"war game"*, as she called it, as it *"grossly interfered"* and curtailed her normal social outings, took the infrequent letters literally and felt that her son was actually enjoying the excitement of the experience and "who indeed could not find life in France exhilarating".

However, it was not without some misgivings that Geoffrey stayed away. He missed Nannie Kate and regretted very much his enforced abstinence from her. She was the one person that sustained him in his darker hours in the Trenches where the interminable roar of the heavy artillery was punctuated by the moaning of young men, boys really, dying in agony on their own in No Man's Land away from the solace of family or friends.

He wrote to her, regularly opening his heart to her as he always did, knowing that she wanted to be as close as possible to him. He did not pity himself and filled his letters with as much humour as he could possibly dredge up from the hopefulness of his very much challenged humanity. She, understanding him like no other, replied weekly in similar fashion, giving him all the local gossip and the will to go on looking at a more positive future.

When the war ended, he returned home, having advanced to Major in the field and mentioned in dispatches, earning an M.C. for single-handedly taking out a German machine gun post which had stopped his company's advance. For a few days after returning home, he received something of a sub-hero's welcome from his parents, particularly his father. Within the week this soon faded as his future in the family interminable businesses and milieu came into question.

His mother, ever remote from him, felt he was totally unsuited to a career in business or indeed politics; his father had doubts and needed more time. Both outwardly showed their continuing disbelief in his abilities in ordinary civilian life—somehow the army was different and success there did not necessarily transfer into civilian life.

Geoffrey, as ever sensitive to the reaction of people towards him, took the hint and applied to remain on in the army. At that juncture the armed forces were being disbanded and only peacetime forces were being maintained. He was kept on at Colchester barracks "for the time being until something suitable could come up to allow him permanent appointment". He was however, reduced to Captain as his current grade *"was only a temporary field promotion"*.

He had to wait for more than a year in this capacity until he could find himself a post that would give him his permanency. Eventually through an acquaintance of his father he was introduced to the Colonel of the Essex Regiment who arranged for him to receive a posting in Ireland, "a quiet but pleasant outpost where he could enjoy life after his years at the Front".

Chapter 3

Joe Ryan had established himself in the town. His business was thriving; in just a little over a year from returning to Ireland after the War. It had been a big decision to start a business immediately, but coming after his experiences during the previous four years it posed no fears for him. He soon found a place to rent at a reasonable price in a good location in the town and with the little money he had saved, together with a modest loan, he quickly built up an electrical business.

Some years before the local miller had harnessed the river and was generating electricity for the town. All the businesses in the town were now on-line and over time many manual operated machines were being converted to use electrical power.

Additionally, even the most modest homes were slowly but inevitably using the service. Joe was providing the installation service for most of these new hook-ups.

The telephone and radio age had also arrived and Joe took advantage of his knowledge and business acumen to be one of the first to offer to service these new technologies. While as now these were mainly the preserve of the well-off in the community, he knew it would only be a matter of time before all these services would reach most homes.

Joe knew all of the locals in this small town and with his easy manner, good humour and dependability he was well liked there.

He found that his business was greatly welcomed by the other business leaders in the town, as he provided a much-needed local service for the up-dating they were just starting after the stagnant War years. He was particularly attached to John Walsh, an old established businessman in Bandon who had been friends with his father. John Walsh, who had no children of his own, became his mentor. He and his wife Mary welcomed him to their home often and he became a regular visitor there.

At their substantial house he met a young country girl, Ellen Griffin, who had become Mary's companion and acted as housekeeper for The Walshes. Her father, Michael Griffin, was related to John Walsh and they also had a strong friendship. Michael was a small farmer about 6 miles from Bandon. However, because of his involvement in Irish causes—he had been a Land Leaguer and a member of the Irish Republican Brotherhood—he had been in and out of British jails for 20 years and consequently his family suffered, not only from separation but also economically.

John knew Michael would not accept charity, even in his exceptional case, so ensuring that Michael's daughter was gainfully employed in a good family environment was an acceptable way of giving financial support.

Not that the Walshes did not benefit from this benevolent gesture: Ellen learned quickly and within months had transformed the house and become an exceptional cook into the bargain. Within a short space of time the Walshes realised that they, not Michael Griffin, were the real beneficiaries of this arrangement.

During his visits to the house Joe also fell under the spell of this beautiful and talented girl and before long they became very committed to one another.

Chapter 4

Geoffrey Eastbourne set out for Ireland not really knowing what to expect but pleased that he had a permanent post. His first port of call was at the battalion H. Q. in Kinsale in Co. Cork in Ireland. The Officer in Command received him well and told him to report to Major Percival. Percival, who was noted for his strategy and intelligence specialty saw from Geoffrey's records, which he had been given, someone who had the necessary qualities to fit in to his strategy section in West Cork.

Percival had made arrangements to have him assigned to Bandon, where the newly emerged Irish Republican Army was known to be strongest in West Cork. Geoffrey would soon learn that the situation he found himself in was not what he expected, if he thought about it in any great detail, and was certainly far, far different from his experiences on the Western Front.

Major Percival decided Captain Geoffrey Eastbourne would fit well into the strategic military plan he was working on for West Cork. He felt that as Captain Eastbourne had acquitted himself well in extraordinary circumstances and because he had experienced and survived the war without physical or apparent physiological damage, he could be expected not to flinch under pressure in the guerrilla war, which was now being waged in Ireland. Percival also felt that Geoffrey had interpersonal skills that would aid the strategy he was putting in place to defeat the IRA.

Percival had little regard for the Royal Irish Constabulary (RIC) nor indeed their Black and Tan backups. He felt they were incapable of having any real effect on defeating the rebels. The constabulary was now unable to send normal patrols outside the towns and even within some small towns and villages only in daylight for fear of the IRA; effectively conceding the countryside to the rebels.

First, they obviously were now despised by most of the Nationalist population and any knowledge they possessed was probably pre-insurrection and of little value in the current situation. Additionally, he believed that there were elements in the RIC who were agents for the IRA and therefore the force could not be wholly trusted with sensitive information.

He also had little time for the promised para-military reinforcements for the RIC from Britain, whom he believed would not be able to add much to the constabulary's efficiency in the face of the IRA problem. Percival was well aware that the British Government wanted to end the independence move by Sinn Fein and he understood that by removing the IRA from the equation the authorities would be able to deal effectively with the political problems in the country.

The IRA as a guerrilla organisation would have to be dealt with in a different fashion than that for which the army was trained. A new strategy was called for which would give them the upper hand. Understanding the value of intelligence in a war arena, which he saw was so important during the recent war in Europe, he embarked on a scheme of intelligence gathering as a central strategy in his campaign against the IRA.

Useful on the ground information would allow the army to both identify the activists and accurately predict their movements. To do this he needed specially selected officers within his regiment to take on the task.

Geoffrey Eastbourne, Percival believed, was the ideal officer for that task for a number of reasons. He was good humoured and above all he came from a noble family. (He, like most of the upper classes in Britain, believed matters requiring a higher understanding of priorities and order should only be dealt with by intelligent males who came exclusively from the upper-middle and upper classes.)

People, Percival felt, would be charmed by his manner in addition to his obvious aristocratic bearing. He perceived in Geoffrey an ability to win over people with his easy personality and his capacity to elicit useful information from these contacts.

Percival outlining his instructions said,

"Captain, I selected you for a special task. I need someone, not only that I can trust to do the job at hand, but particularly to be able to work on his own in the field, as it were. I need you to be my eyes, ears and indeed my extended hand in the most sensitive area of our operation."

Geoffrey, having come from the trenches in Passchendaele where the most 'sensitive' position was 'No Man's Land' and where he was all too aware of his good fortune, surviving while most of his fellow junior officers fell, wondered what he had let himself in for. He had no burning desire to return to those awful 'trench' days where he had left his youth and beloved comrades buried in the muddy fields of Flanders.

However, the die was cast and obey he must so he answered, "I am honoured that you believe I can be useful in your strategy Sir. I would be very interested in what you feel I can do to further that goal. What have you in mind for me Sir?"

"Captain, your base will be the Army Barracks in Bandon. As you probably know, that is the centre of the worst IRA activities in Southern Munster. I am currently very dissatisfied with the lack of intelligence coming from our resources in that town. The RIC intelligence is low-grade and not enough. What little useful first-hand information, mainly extracted from reluctant local nationalists, it is not therefore very reliable. Their more reliable intelligence is limited and comes mainly from the Anglo-Irish community. While it is useful and most times can be relied on, it is at best gleaned from what can be seen on the ground from a distance.

"Bear in mind, do not trust anyone with sensitive information but me—there are informants for the IRA in the RIC and they will use anything you give them for their own purpose and possibly at best muddy the pitch for us. I will bring them into the picture when I need their cooperation and that will be last minute and limited to what they need to know."

Geoffrey began to realise the extent of the task ahead of him. Coming as he was with no knowledge of the territory and moreover never having been to Ireland before he was not at all sure what to expect. Indeed, he had little knowledge of the Irish apart from the few Irishmen he had met in the Regiment and those he encountered from Irish regiments during the Great War. All he knew was that they were stubborn, extroverted, different and had a reputation for being great fighters.

Seeking to find someone at hand who would at least help him ease his way into the job ahead he asked,

"Who do I deal with at our Bandon post Sir?"

"Yes, I was coming to that. When you arrive in Bandon, report to Major Stewart the OC of the barracks. He will introduce you to your colleagues and provide accommodation and provisions for you.

"However, you are on your own otherwise. While he wants you to be his staff officer, I want you to work mainly on intelligence. Your first task will be to ensure that our own official information and that emanating from that post are secure. By this I mean also tightening up on not only official communications by also on all private and social correspondence and contacts made by the personnel at the barracks. This is important. I want absolutely no leakage whether through espionage or carelessness.

"In addition, and most especially, I want you to seek out contacts in the community who will have access to the type of information which can get us leads on IRA personnel and strategy. Primarily we need to know their leaders and active service people; but also, their activities. Where they are based; where they get their arms and equipment from; who are their superiors; who makes the decisions on engagement; what is their strategy short-term and, long-term, where they are most vulnerable, etc.

"I need you to find one or more people in the Nationalist community who you can persuade to give you information on the IRA: someone who can talk directly to people who are on the inside of the IRA organisation or at least who have a good knowledge of what they are planning. That will take ingenuity and persuasion plus a quantity of funds. The first two I believe you possess. The latter I will provide.

"In relation to any information, you receive about the IRA, I want you to report directly to me. Do not discuss this with anyone else unless I tell you to do otherwise. Remember intelligence is only useful if it is secure. It can only be relied on if the enemy does not know we have it. To ensure this, the lines of sharing that information must be as tight as possible. Hence you are the gatherer and I am the sole recipient."

Geoffrey's gut tightened as he attempted to digest the instructions given to him by the Commanding Officer. The first part of the orders was primarily administrative and anyway he hoped that much of what was contained in the Major's instructions in relation to information, both official and private, emanating from the barracks in Bandon was already in hand. If not, he should be able to ensure the necessary measures to do so would be put in place in a short space of time.

However, in relation to information gathering and especially the search for reliable useful informers was a daunting task, one he was very unsure that he would be able to carry out. Nevertheless, he could not let the Major share his hesitations. This is the Army and when you join the establishment doubt must be left behind with your civilian clothes.

In response to the Major's instructions Geoffrey wishing to be positive but with a certain degree of caution responded, "I shall endeavour to do my utmost Sir. On the point of communication, how do I reach you if you are here and not in Bandon? I presume you would wish any especially sensitive material passed to you immediately and verbally."

"Absolutely Captain, anything of a sensitive and immediate nature you are to convey to me personally and without any delay. I will ensure that adequate transportation is available to you to do so."

"I think that is all Captain. Good luck. Dismiss."

"Sir."

Geoffrey saluted and left. When he emerged into the open air, his mind was in a whirl. His assignment was way beyond what he had understood would be his role here in Ireland. When he took up the appointment in England, he assumed that his role would be merely a back-up one in support of the civil authority. He did not understand that he would not only be on the front line again, the civil authority having lost control, now facing a formidable enemy who were part of the overwhelming native population.

How different from the Western Front where he knew he was fighting for the people on whose soil he stood. How in the name of God was he to infiltrate the IRA? He, who knew nothing of the country or their customs, which even in his short time in Ireland he knew were so alien to him. Good Lord, he was barely able to understand them speaking English, they did so in such a fast singsong way. They also spoke in Irish, when they did not want the English, *'Sassenach I hear they call us'*, to understand what they were saying.

He left Kinsale for Bandon with a heavy heart. Reflecting on his current situation he could not help thinking *'God what a way to begin an assignment. Even facing the parents would be a great deal easier than this!'*

Chapter 5

Captain Geoffrey Eastbourne reported to Major Stewart in Bandon the next day.

'The OC in Kinsale instructed me to report directly to you Sir. He informed me that he had explained my role here and that you would understand."

Major Gordon Stewart, a long-time career officer had also served during the War in Europe, but unlike Geoffrey he had spent most of his time behind the lines at HQ acting as one of the Assistants in the Quartermaster General's office there. He was a genial type of man who would have preferred to have spent his later years in the Army back in Britain. However, after the war most of the Regiment, as indeed nearly the whole British Army, had been disbanded leaving only a mere core behind.

His former high-level contacts in the Regiment had either been killed in the War or else retired. He was therefore faced with the dilemma 'to Hell or to West Cork'. Having, in a sense, being near the gates of Hell just recently he had no difficulty in taking the alternative option.

Major Stewart rose from his desk and came around to meet Geoffrey, shaking him by the hand, invited him to sit down, got out two glasses and a bottle of Paddy Whiskey and poured for both.

"Good to have you on board Geoffrey. By the way in private please call me Gordon. I've seen your file and understand, notwithstanding your younger years, you've had more military experience than one spending a lifetime in the army pre-War. I also note that, like the rest of us, your rank was reduced as a thank you for living through that nightmare.

"The army has an invidious position here. It's strange to be in a part of Britain where our presence is not welcome by a large proportion of the population. I suspect like many of us you had little choice of where you were posted.

"Anyway, welcome to Bandon. I'm very happy to see you. There are not many of us and unfortunately the natives range from over-friendly to unfriendly if you understand what I mean. You will find you will be in barracks here more than normal, not because you desire it but because it is the safe thing to do."

"Thank you for the friendly reception, Gordon. I very much appreciate it and I would welcome your guidance in helping me settle into life here. It is my first time in Ireland, not my choice by the way, as you so quite accurately pointed out, one does not have much choice in that these days. Frankly I'm lucky to have been retained, not to mention demoted." Geoffrey added in his usual open way to those he felt he could trust.

Gordon Stewart, responding to that openness, came back:

"Funny old world. Just three years ago most would have given up anything to get out of military service, but now look at us hanging on by our nails. It's true what they say about long term slaves—they are more frightened of freedom than of remaining in servitude.

"Anyway, while here you can look forward to some pleasant aspects of your surroundings. The countryside around is rather stunning, when it stops raining, and the food is glorious.

"Unfortunately, in relation to the first you might find it hard to get to see it as these days one spends their short time in the countryside on the lookout for ambushes and snipers and the marvellous flora and picturesque hills and dales making great hiding places for the enemy.

"However, in relation to food you will find no better beef and dairy products anywhere. Additionally, once you acquire a taste for Irish whiskey you may not ever drink Scotch again, apart, that is, from the great malts. Coming from the Front and the two-continuing ration-bound Blighty you will doubly appreciate its bonus.

"You must come to dinner with us—currently my wife is visiting and she is an excellent cook. Our families usually do not accompany us here—not because we are concerned, they would be targeted in any way—the Irish and even the most vicious in the IRA regard women as sacrosanct and they have a special affection for children. However, in the situation we find ourselves in, at present at least, it is far too restrictive and there is always the danger of collateral injuries."

Geoffrey warmed to Major Stewart and his sense of dry humour. He was grateful for the friendly welcome and the opportunity to build on the new friendship.

"I'd be delighted to accept that most kind offer—that's provided your dear wife is not otherwise engaged and is prepared to spend part of her short stay here cooking and entertaining a stranger."

"I'm sure she'd love to meet you. There are not many things happening here on the social side and not being a resident, she hasn't got a wide selection of friends here. I will revert to you after I speak with her and fix a time."

Then, looking at the time, Major Stewart when on:

"Well, we better find a billet for you here. I hope you will find it comfortable. It's rather Spartan but then I expect it will be equivalent to the Savoy compared to the accommodation you endured at the Front."

"Yes, no matter what you have here would be heaven compared to the hell holes we had out there along the Messines Ridge."

Major Stewart, further easing Geoffrey into his new post, said that he wanted him to act as his Staff Officer and would not be asked to take on line duty. He also let him know he would not be interfering in what I understand you will be doing here for Major Percival and that Geoffrey would be reporting directly to Percival in relation to that.

He casually mentioned as they went to inspect the accommodation, "I have been instructed by the OC in Kinsale that you are here on a special mission and you will report directly to Major Percival. I am to assist you when you ask me to and provide any service I can. A word of advice. Major Percival has the ear of not only the OC in Kinsale but also, he is well got back in London. He is very ambitious and single-minded. Be careful how you deal with him."

Geoffrey, grateful for Major Stewart's words of warning and that he did not need to argue his independence, acknowledging the situation replied:

"I am very grateful for your guidance and hope I can speak freely to you during my time here. Regarding my role viz a viz Major Percival—yes those were my instructions also. I believe I will have much to do to read myself into the situation on the ground here and get to know the principal actors, as far as I can in the circumstances, before I even begin to be able to make a useful contribution."

Major Stewart looking straight at Geoffrey.

"I can guess what you are getting at, but like I said, I am here to help not to interfere."

Geoffrey glad to move on from the subject ended that part of the conversation by saying:

"I very much appreciate that offer. I will ask if I need you. Otherwise, I will not burden you with my comings and goings as I expect most of that, at the beginning especially, will be rather mundane and be of little, if any, additional value to your work here."

"Well let's go and see your quarters. As I mentioned before, I fear the billet is on the lesser side of adequate but unlike the Front at least you won't have to share."

"No matter what it offers I expect it will be like a couch in heaven compared to what we had on the edge of hell there."

Major Stewart led Geoffrey to the officers' quarters where he was shown into an 8 by 10-foot room with whitewashed walls, furnished merely by a single cot, a rough wooden small table and chair, a washstand and basin with a small shaving mirror hanging above it. There were iron hangers on the wall, which Geoffrey presumed were for his clothes.

Major Stewart, sensing this, added, "I have asked for a wardrobe for you and hopefully it should arrive soon."

Having been shown his quarters Major Stewart said.

"Now let me introduce you to your other officer colleagues here. I expect at this stage of the day a number of them will be in the mess hall. Currently there are three companies in Bandon. If reinforcements are needed, they come from Kinsale and of course, if need be, from Cork city.

"Here at present are Captains Charles Chilcot, and Edward Dawson. Lieutenant Adam Smith, 2nd Lieutenant David Blunt and Subaltern James Dunworthy. Like you Captain Chilcot and Lieutenant Smith were at the Front but I believe did not see as much action as you. Anyway, I'm sure they will tell you about it, or not, in due course."

Geoffrey made his introductions to his colleagues, had one drink with them and left 'to freshen up', not long after, taking his cue from Major Stewart as he left to go to meet his wife.

Alone Geoffrey felt reasonably pleased with the way things had gone on his introduction to the barracks. He particularly was thankful that the ranking officer there would allow him to get on with his tasks unhindered and yet he felt he could confide in him if need be.

Chapter 6

Captain Eastbourne appeared early for parade the next morning at the barracks. After breakfast, where he had taken the time to reacquaint himself with the officers, he met the evening before and meet those that had not been there at that time. He spent some time, mainly listening to their conversation—a mixture of banter and the happenings of the day before. They seemed to accept him without reserve and he felt he would settle into life in the barracks with little effort.

At the Barracks C.O.s meeting after he was again introduced and Major Stewart took the opportunity to outline his role at the barracks, instructing all of the officer's present to cooperate with Geoffrey when he asked for any assistance.

Geoffrey was content that his role was singular and he would not be required to take part in general duties, including patrols and other commands which would have taken him from his main task.

He had wasted little time getting down to his job. His first visit of the morning was to the Communications Hut where he met all of the men who were assigned to that duty. Staff Sergeant Turner introduced each man in turn and outlined each of their respective duties in the Hut. Geoffrey had made up his mind that he would start with the internal security as this would be easier to tackle. Then, when he had put his ideas in place there, he could move on to the external job, which undoubtedly would be a great deal more difficult.

"Sergeant Turner, I want you to outline the measures you are currently taking to ensure absolute security of the information that passes through this sector."

Sergeant Turner was shaken by the urgency of the request and while he had understood from what he had already been told that security would be high on the list of priorities he thought it would be dealt with in a gradual way and not the first item on the new officer's agenda. He had already decided that this highly experienced officer was someone to be respected and not ignored.

He would not be a spit and polish man. Rather he immediately knew the captain was a details man and would mainly expect that the tasks set would be carried out with efficiency and care. The Sergeant knew he would demand special attention to be given to the systems under their control and that no outside source would have access to the communication traffic which was coming in and especially leaving the Barracks.

Overall, Turner believed Captain Eastbourne to be a fair officer who would treat his men with respect and look after their needs if required.

"We already have strict rules in place, Sir, to counter any slip or laxity in dealing with the information passing through our post. Major Percival himself has spoken to us about that and we are mindful of the importance of security, especially in this region."

"I'm glad to hear that Sergeant, but nevertheless to satisfy my own mind and to see exactly what you put in place to counter any loss of information, I want you to take me through each sector pointing out the locks you have put in place for this safeguarding for our communications."

To ensure he understood all of the security measures and be totally familiar with them Geoffrey spent the rest of the morning with Sgt Turner and his staff going through each element of their procedures.

"Please explain that to me again."

"I think we can tighten that measure up more."

"Does that slow down the process and if so, is there a way we can keep the security at the same time as speeding up the transmission."

"I see you have a log for incoming communications and the dates and times are shown."

"I want you to do the same for outgoing calls and transmissions."

"The time should be recorded immediately when a transmission is made."

"I notice that clock on the wall is ten minutes slow by my watch. Correct it and ensure it is kept at the correct time."

"Who has access to this office?"

"The exact time should be recorded for each of the operators taking up duty here. I want that strictly adhered to—even if it means someone has shown up late for his duty."

"If there is cover for the late arrival, I will overlook non-habitual one-off transgressions. Those can be dealt with by you Sergeant. The important element is precise timing."

"Others, other than the staff working here, visiting the communications centre should be noted—and have business being here."

Ending his inspection and instructions, Geoffrey thanked the staff for their attention and said, 'carry on with your duties men.'

Speaking to Sergeant Turner he asked was there anything he wished to add.

"No Sir. Thank you for taking the time to speak to the men individually. I know they will have appreciated that. They can feel isolated in that office, where they spend hours at a time, often on their own. Your instructions were clear and we will ensure that the additional provisions will be carried out."

"One thing Sir, I am not sure if you were aware that we are expecting to have a new telephone system installed. I should have mentioned when we went through our systems."

"No Sergeant I was not. I take it that this will be a big improvement on the old system?"

"It is hoped that it will, Sir. The old one is unreliable and we keep on having bad connections and breakdowns. At times we would have been better off without it—it takes so much time to coax it into action and when it breaks down, which is often, it takes a great deal of time to find the problem.

"As a matter of fact, Sir, we are currently in the process of considering how we will install the system. The equipment is being delivered from Cork within a few weeks and we propose to engage an outside contractor to install it for us."

Geoffrey responding to this news, which he knew would have created a major lacuna in his knowledge if it had not come to his notice, showed some irritation. He said.

"Oh! I'm glad you told me."

Sergeant Turner, now concerned that the good rapport he felt he was beginning to establish with his superior would have been damaged, tried to defend his position while at the same time admitting his omission replied.

"Sorry, Sir, with the concentration on the procedures it slipped my mind and I had believed you would have been informed already."

Captain Eastbourne, satisfied that he had made his point, and not wishing to leave an unhappy Sergeant after their first encounter came back rapidly saying:

"That's okay Sergeant. I can understand that at our first meeting and my recent arrival here there would have been some slippage between what I know and what you think I know. In a sense it may be as well that that slip happened.

I should have made the point earlier but now that this has arisen, I want to make one thing clear.

"I need to know everything that happens on the communications side. I want to be aware of what is going on, not so much the routine stuff but the unusual. If something is happening out of the ordinary, I want to know. In a nutshell: I want no surprises."

Turner responding positively to what he felt was a let-off eagerly replied,

"I understand. That will be done, Sir."

"Who are the people installing the new System, Sergeant? Are they our sappers from Cork?"

"No, Sir. We hope a local business here in town can do the job."

Geoffrey was surprised to learn this, wanted to know more.

"Do we know these people? Do they have security clearance?"

"Yes, Sir. The owner of the business and the person who will be installing the system is one of our own. He is a decorated war veteran who held the rank of Sergeant before he was demobbed. He has already installed a number of electrical systems in the barracks and as a former Signals NCO, who was retrained in Dunstable in late 1917, he has been of great help to us here in teaching us some of the newer technologies."

"Thank you, Sergeant. I would like to meet him before he installs the system."

"I will arrange that, Sir."

Geoffrey was anxious to go into town to have his first recce as soon as possible. He thought, *'the sooner I suss out the town and get the lay of the land, the better.'*

'I need to be at least au fait with my territory here as quickly as possible well before I have to make my first report to Major Percival. I am unsure where to start in relation to selecting individuals who might give me the type of information, I need to find good contacts to build up my intelligence dossier.'

'I don't even know the ground rules here, as yet.'

'Still, first things first. I must ensure that I cover and secure the internal integrity of the barracks before I embark on my external quest.'

Later that same day Geoffrey made his first visit to the town. He found life in the town rather strange. While people were polite and amongst each other there was a noticeable warmth between some of them, there was also an atmosphere of tension and foreboding when members of the security forces were present. The British forces in the town were under constant threat from the IRA, which, albeit small in numbers, had the capacity to appear from nowhere and inflict casualties on the British Forces and suddenly disappear before reinforcements could be summoned.

A small percentage of the local nationalist population was either complicit in helping the IRA or too scared to oppose that organisation. Most of the nationalists did not condone violence but neither did they welcome the presence of the British Forces.

Among the places visited was the local hotel on the other side of town. There he met the owner Tom Good who seemed an amiable type and was quite helpful. After a perfunctory getting to know you type conversation Geoffrey asked Tom,

"Is there much social life in the town?"

"It's quiet for the most part of the year, particularly during the winter, but there is a golf club and a tennis club which might interest you."

"Are there any other social activities?"

"Well, the bars around town are sort of social centres if you like that kind of social occasion. The bar in the hotel attracts a number of professionals and businessmen who drop in from time to time and they make a convivial group."

"That sounds interesting. I wonder would they welcome me into such a group?"

"I'm sure they would. If you make yourself known."

"Would you introduce me to some of these people?"

"Certainly. By the way, are you a poker player?"

"Yes. Why?"

"If you are interested, we have a private game here on an irregular basis depending on who is available. As it happens, we are meeting for a game on Friday evening and we have a vacant seat if you wish to join us."

"Yes, I'd be delighted. What time should I be here?"

"7.30 we meet."

"Good I will be there."

Chapter 7
The Card Game

Like other games, where we put our skills and fortunes against opponents who believe they are equal or superior, there are winners and losers. Most times a loss is a temporary setback to be reversed at another time. On occasions though a loss can have far-reaching consequences, way beyond what was anticipated when the game began. This particular night was one of those.

For the young man that was seduced into the poker school that evening, little did he understand the dangers he was drifting into. Rather he saw it merely as part of the social scene—an opportunity to get to know and perhaps understand the locals. There was also the possibility that he, newly arrived in the town, would pick up some useful intelligence concerning the rebels who were engaged in attacks and ambushes against the British forces there.

Poker games were unusual in that while they were played in relative silence, particularly for higher stakes, you can discern quite an amount of insight into most individuals in the faces around you, if you are astute enough.

The game began early in the evening in a quiet small room in the local hotel at the other end of the town from his barracks. Standard poker, jacks to open, commenced with a reasonably safe three pence all in, open for half the pot.

There were five players. Geoffrey was the newest.

Geoffrey, shortly after arriving in the town, met Tom Good, the local hotel owner, and found him to be amiable and obliging. To get to know his environment as quickly as possible he had asked Tom to include him in social engagements where possible. When Tom had told him there was a vacancy in the card school next evening, if he was interested, Geoffrey had jumped at the chance.

The Players;

John Walsh, a local businessman, liked a poker game on occasions. He was shrewd and while, quite well off, rarely lost much money in any game.

Tom Good, the owner of the hotel, who played more for the amusement of the game and to socialise with those he found interesting, rather than for any monetary gain.

Robin Jefferson, an insurance agent who sold life policies and endowments to the general public which gave him a reasonably good income. He was known to be the local card shark. He lost no opportunity in taking advantage of a situation where he felt he had the upper hand, particularly against an easily outplayed and outwitted opponent.

Next was Joe Ryan, a young man like Geoffrey. Geoffrey had been told by Tom Good that Joe Ryan, on return from the Great War had set up a small successful business in the town. Joe was shrewd, but not fearful, and could read the cards well. Apart from Geoffrey he knew how each of the others would play and always set a limit to the amount he was prepared to lose before he sat down.

Geoffrey Eastbourne, having been at the Front and having escaped physically unharmed was used to risk at even the highest levels and now removed from the restrictions of the Victorian confines of upper crust England, Geoffrey felt liberated and confident.

The game began, as usual in these social surroundings, good humouredly and at a very relaxed pace. Drinks were served by a waiter from the bar while they played. At the start of the game some of the local gossip was discussed; nothing controversial. Politics was mentioned only in passing—wisely in these dangerous times—those it was very much on the minds of each one at the table. Mention was made of the IRA directed attacks against the RIC.

In the past months the IRA had been very active in the Bandon region and had attacked the RIC patrols and their barracks a number of times. The Army was not part of the main IRA action so far, as this appeared to be directed against the RIC.

Change was in the air, however. Everyone knew it. The 1916 rebellion in Dublin, had surprised even ardent nationalists. The sense of unfulfilled promise after the War added to the coercive nature of the British response to the rebellion and to the IRAs activities, was very much in the minds of everyone. The emergence of Sinn Fein in the 1918 Westminster General Election as the overwhelmingly majority political party in Ireland and its decision to set up an

Irish Parliament in Dublin was a challenge to British rule, the final outcome of which had yet to play out.

However, the present company, while not all loyalists, would have been regarded as most unsympathetic to violent nationalism. The presence of a serving British Army officer, particularly one new in this company, would mean that any real discussion on the topic would not take place that evening. It was a time of change, a time for hesitation, a time to rethink one's loyalties.

Consequently, for those who understood the hidden political scepticism and intrigues of a people, the majority of whom saw themselves as a colony rather than a nation, it was a time to keep one's political views to oneself. In any event, notwithstanding the foregoing, poker and controversial politics are not easy bedfellows.

The game continued with each player attempting to get the measure of the others. Caution was the main strategy, used by some to gauge the play of others and by others to coax unwitting players into false assumptions. Those experienced in the game and the company knew instinctively what to watch for. The neophytes! —well, they paid to learn. The very wise among them were able to make measured guesses as to the card's distribution, particularly as the game progressed and the cards remained unchanged.

Luck too played its part; as those who received great cards at times when others had high but lesser ones were consequently in a better position to take advantage of that boon. The problem lay in receiving an excellent hand of cards only to be pipped by another player whose cards were superior, particularly after the loser had bid up the pool.

As the night wore on and the players appeared to get into the rhythm of the game and their opponents, modest gains were made by those who had received the better cards. Some players were seen to hold hands long after it was mathematically wise to retain them. Others, more cautious, dropped out early if they had the slightest sense that their cards were not adequate i.e., a pair or better. Some made it very difficult to guess the value of their hands—being seen to bluff with little on occasions, but at other times when least expected to emerge with very strong hands.

One player, Robin Jefferson, in particular was such: on a few occasions he was caught bluffing in big pots. Geoffrey Eastbourne was particularly keen to ensure that Robin J was "kept honest" and he caught him bluffing on a number of occasions. Unfortunately, Geoffrey was both too young and inexperienced in this type of card school and he consequently failed to see that he was being led on by obvious "tells" to believe he had got the measure of Robin J. The others who had played with the latter on numerous other occasions were well aware of his wiles and could see that Geoffrey, who had been receiving excellent card hands all evening and was well ahead, was being led into believing that the table and evening were his.

The all-in stake had been raised to a half crown at midnight with no limit on opening or betting. By 1am Geoffrey was ahead by over 60 pounds most of which had come from Robin. So, when the latter suggested that they remove the coins from the table, Geoffrey was unperturbed and indeed felt that he could not deny Robin an opportunity to recover some of his losses for the night. Wealthy John Walsh and Tom Good, both of whom at this stage had lost little, did not demur.

Joe Ryan, realising that the game had turned into a much more aggressive "win or die" contest, was reluctant, but as he was winning about 5 pounds at that time he went along with the increase. Nevertheless, he resolved to change his play to a defensive mode and not to participate in rises unless the cards dealt to him could reasonably be felt to contain a winning hand. Joe was not a card shark but he had the ability to read the cards on the table fairly accurately and additionally could most often tell if one of the others was bluffing.

He had realised early on that evening that Robin had marked out the young officer as one who could be led on if he deemed his hand was sufficiently strong. He perceived that Robin had purposely lulled Geoffrey into a false sense of superiority by allowing him to win modest pots, giving off false "tells" which would indicate he was bluffing. Normally this card game was used as a social occasion with those participating losing or winning very little.

Tonight, was different, an edge had come into it between the new entrant who was unaware of what was really happening and the card shark who not only wanted to get his losings back but saw an opportunity to take advantage of an exuberant Icarus.

Thus, the night wore on stealthily, silent now apart from the calls, where in its quietness the unwary can so easily be confounded.

Encouraged by his earlier winnings and certain of his new found card skills young Geoffrey was more than willing to increase stakes where he felt he had the advantage of luck and enterprise. The game moved on for two more hours with the cards getting more difficult to interpret for some of the players as tiredness and early retirements (because of perceived poor initial cards) obfuscated the play.

At this stage John Walsh and Tom Good were down about 20 pounds each, Joe Ryan was up about 10 pounds while Geoffrey Eastbourne had lost all his previous winnings plus the 50 pounds he had brought to the table. At this stage he was playing with 30 pounds he borrowed from Robin Jefferson and was beginning to win some hands again. Robin Jefferson had reversed his earlier poor showing and was now up approximately 80 pounds.

At a point John Walsh and Tom Good suggested that they should play just one more round of hands and Joe agreed. The other two reluctantly had to concur – Geoffrey because he felt he could recover some if not all of his losses – Robin because he had the upper hand and knew he would not lose. At this time the table was open and there were no limits.

On the second last game all followed their hands, apart from Joe, who by now was playing very cautiously, as he realised that at this stage of the evening at least two of the players, for opposite reasons, could not be gauged easily. Because of the higher stakes and four in to see and raise, the pot was over 50 pounds before the final bidding took place. Geoffrey, who by now had borrowed a further 30 pounds from Robin, increased the pool by 50 pounds as he was confident of his very strong hand and had led the bidding from the start.

John and Tom bowed out at that and threw in their respective hands. Robin however, who had appeared unenthusiastic about the play earlier, surprised everyone by seeing the bet and raising it by a further 100 pounds. When Geoffrey said he had not got the money to see this raise, Robin said he would accept an IOU if he lost. Geoffrey accepted the offer and feeling supremely confident saw the raise, laying down a full house of three aces and two kings which he had been dealt cold.

All were shaken with disbelief, particularly Geoffrey, when Robin laid down four nines. Robin had bought three cards.

The game abruptly ended there. Robin was unable to conceal his self-regard for his card skills and his delight at getting such cards at a time when three other players had good hands and were thus kept in the game. However, everyone apart from Geoffrey knew that Robin, early in the evening, had marked out the newcomer as an easy mark in the game, who could be coaxed into unwise gambles. Geoffrey, who had returned from the Front Line with no injuries, would scarcely fear making a gamble with mere money.

Geoffrey was now however, in debt to the tune of 160 pounds. Robin Jefferson played poker to win and he was determined to get his pound of flesh. When the group broke up, he took Geoffrey Eastbourne aside and demanded payment. When Geoffrey asked for some time to pay, he laughed saying he should not have gambled if he could not afford to lose. Jefferson gave him one week to pay, threatening to inform his commanding officer if he did not do so. Joe Ryan, passing, overheard the conversation. He knew that Jefferson would carry out the threat if unpaid.

Joe left the hotel at the same time as Geoffrey. They walked together for a short time and said little. Joe nevertheless could sense that his companion was very troubled because of the debt. He realised that this would place Geoffrey in serious difficulties. He understood the honour code of the British Army, particularly in relation to its officer class. An officer's gambling debt must be paid—if not his shame would reflect on the regiment and that would not be tolerated. He would be reprimanded at least and possibly even cashiered.

On parting, Joe, on impulse, invited Geoffrey to call on him if he found himself with no other source for help. Exactly why he did so, he could never afterwards explain to himself. He had lived for years in a world without hope – where every day was counted as a bonus, if that is what one could call the hell he and millions of other young men had lived through. He had learned to live by instinct and reaction. There was little time for logic or reason. Thus, as he had done in the Trenches, he reached out to another human being in need.

On his way home he reprimanded himself for getting involved in something which was not of his concern. Why should he feel sorry for Geoffrey, who after all had entered freely into the gamble and losing all his funds had borrowed and borrowed and promised way beyond what he could afford to repay? Unless he had independent means, which from his demeanour it appeared he did not, the debt involved over six months of Geoffrey's salary. Moreover, he was the new enemy of his people. He was in Ireland, unwelcome, in the uniform of what had become the oppressor.

Chapter 8
Friend in Need

Geoffrey Eastbourne walked back to barracks that early morning a far different man than he had been just hours previously. How was he to repay the debt? He had less than 30 pounds in the bank. His pay (just over 250 pounds per year before deductions) was hopelessly inadequate in relation to what he owed and he knew no one in the Officer's Mess that he could call on to loan him that amount of money.

His father, vastly wealthy, would be the last person he would approach. Their relationship had ever been a very severe one. If it were for a purpose of extraordinary expenditure such as equipment or another item which could in his father's mind be considered legitimate, he would allow Geoffrey to send on the bill to his agent who would pay it. However, a gambling debt would not only bring a refusal but would add to his already poor opinion of his son.

On the Monday after the week-end card game Robin Jefferson made a point of calling on Geoffrey Eastbourne. After engaging in perfunctory conversation for a few minutes he came to the point of the reason for his visit.

"Geoffrey, I hope I won't have to remind you again that I want the 160 pounds by next week-end at the latest."

Geoffrey attempting to explain his current predicament:

"Robin, I need a good deal more time to get that amount together. As you know my home base is in England and I will have to revert to my bank there to have the money transferred. That will take some weeks. Being away from home, in Ireland for the first time, I am not sure of the logistics involved in all of this. There are bound to be some difficulties in transfers of monies from one bank to another, particularly as it's between the two islands."

Jefferson however, retorted, "You could get a loan from the banks here to tide you over until the transfer comes through. That should not be a problem for you?"

Geoffrey, replying said, "I have been to the banks and was told that they are unwilling to offer immediate credit because of my recent arrival here and I have no credit record in Ireland. Additionally, I have not had time to build up any friendships in the Barracks. Robin, please allow me some time to get the funds for you. You shall undoubtedly have the money. It is only a question of timing. Your forbearance would be greatly appreciated."

Jefferson shaking his head demurred saying, "I've given you sufficient time Geoffrey."

Geoffrey attempting to get some leeway added, "Robin please bear with me for a little longer. I am doing my best to put the amount together and it will take a bit longer than a week."

Jefferson however, never a man to give anyone a break, pressed his claim home by saying.

"I need the money now and cannot give you more time Geoffrey."

To let Geoffrey, know that he had no sympathy for him he added.

"Let me remind you that you borrowed 60 pounds from me, used that money to bump up that final pot and then went ahead and saw me for another 100 pounds, knowing full well that you did not have the funds to repay if you lost. You should have thought all this out before you started betting so heavily. You will well recall I had my money on the table and you would have had immediate ownership of it if you had been the winner that night."

Geoffrey, attempting to get something out of the dilemma he faced, suggested, "Look Robin, I will give you 30 pounds by the end of the week and the remainder in tranches to be paid in full by 3 months."

Jefferson laughed at the suggestion. A facetious sociopath he saw only his own needs and cared less about his fellow. He even went as far as saying,

"Geoffrey, how do I, or indeed you, know for sure you will be around in 3 months? Times are unsure and life can be short, particularly if you are in the firing line."

They stayed in this two-way conversation for a further ten minutes, Geoffrey saying finally that he would not be able to get all the funds together in the time given.

Jefferson now, as he had on Friday night, dealt the final blow to Geoffrey by telling him he did not care how he got the money he wanted by next week-end and if it was not forthcoming, he would report Geoffrey to his Commanding Officer for being unwilling to pay a legitimate gentleman's debt.

Geoffrey went back to his rooms in the barracks in a daze. In a strange way he found his present predicament traumatically far worse than any situation he had ever experienced either at home, at school or even when he continually faced death on the Western Front. For the first time in his life his honour was being questioned and his aristocratic upbringing and background imposed on him an obligation to acquit himself with dignity if he was to live up to that high standard.

Moreover, this was compounded by his current situation. As an army officer of standing, particularly in a hostile environment where the Crown was already under threat, his commanding officer (even a reasonable soul like Major Stewart) could not tolerate the insult to the regiment and Geoffrey could see that he would be invited to resign his commission. Such a situation would destroy everything he stood for and his family would disown him.

Geoffrey was receiving a trust fund of 500 pounds per annum from his father. He had already spent all of this year's allowance and it would be more than six months later that the next tranche would be available to him. Because of his lifestyle and that of a serving British Army Officer he found that sum together with his army salary barely enough to make ends meet. He was not extravagant but his status in life and the expectation that it might very well be short lived meant that he did not count money as an end in itself and had spent his family allowance even before he received it.

Consequently, that could not be called on to relieve his predicament. Calling his bank in London he was informed that he could extend him a loan on his allowance only if his father would stand as a guarantor of such a loan. Geoffrey would not approach his father for many reasons:

(a) he would have to explain his predicament to him,
(b) it would only convince his father that his poor opinion of him was justified,
(c) he was not to be trusted in any dealings the family were engaged in and finally and
(d) he would most likely be refused anyway, as an embarrassment and black sheep.

He knew his mother was no less antipathetic.

He had attempted to borrow funds from his fellow officers but they were no better funded than he and so apart from the generous, in the circumstance, promise of up to twenty pounds he was at his wits end. He felt he had nowhere to turn to.

Later that afternoon as he was walking in deep gloom through the town, he met Joe Ryan. He welcomed the opportunity to speak to someone and they stopped off at the nearby hotel in Shannon Street for coffee and a chat. The conversation was very friendly and as in many occasions when veterans of the Great War meet, and with no civilian present, their talk revolved round the many stories and remembrances of their time on the Western Front.

Early on after they sat down there was a realisation that in many ways, they had been not only comrades in arms but like-minded in relation to its awfulness and its senselessness. By the second drink Geoffrey had momentarily forgotten his immediate problem and felt at ease in Joe's company.

Joe Ryan, ever perspective, recognised a certain melancholy in him and remembering his difficulties with Robin Jefferson the previous Friday evening/Saturday morning he asked Geoffrey if Jefferson had approached him about the debt. Geoffrey, at a low ebb and feeling he could confide in Joe, told him what had transpired and said he was at his wits end in trying to come up with the money before the week-end. Joe, knowing Jefferson and his ruthlessness, understood that Geoffrey was in grave danger of being cashiered from the army if he did not pay his debt.

They talked about the problem for some minutes before Joe told Geoffrey that he would loan him the money to repay Jefferson. At first Geoffrey, knowing that the money represents a great proportion of Joe's funds (a modest home in Bandon could be brought for less than 200 pounds), would not at first accept but Joe persuaded him.

"Geoffrey you and I were prepared to put our lives at risk in the Western Front for one of our colleagues. What is money compared to that? Not coming from your world, I can't fully empathise with you, but nevertheless understand that your aristocratic honour puts you in what, for you, is obviously a worse than death situation and so I am not blind to your need. Anyway, I intensely dislike Jefferson and resent like hell his conniving and mean-spirited attitude.

"That game went too far. We have never before played for such high stakes. It is meant to be more of a social occasion rather than a gambling one. None of us apart from Jefferson felt good about how it turned out. As at the front, I will not leave a comrade at-arms behind, no matter what the cost."

Joe met Geoffrey the next day as promised and handed over 130 pounds. Joe asked for no conditions attached to the loan except to say,

"Pay me back when you can Geoffrey. I will not press you on time and will not mention it again."

Geoffrey again was reluctant to take the money.

"Joe this is too much to ask of you. There is no reason why you should want to help. It was my own fault and no one else is to blame for my stupidity."

Joe merely handed over the money and said, "Geoffrey if I were in a similar situation and you could help, I would expect you to do so. We do not have to be from the same background or indeed even the same nation to want to help one another."

Geoffrey promised to repay. Later that day he met Jefferson and handed him 160 pounds. Jefferson said nothing; taken aback that Geoffrey was able to gather the amount so quickly.

Chapter 9

Ellen and Joe unexpectedly visited her parent's place one Sunday when they met Sean Hales who had called on her father. Sean Hales was from the countryside nearby and was the Officer Commanding the IRA in the Bandon region.

After they had a light afternoon tea Sean and Joe took a stroll to the nearby village pub and over pints of Murphy's porter the conversation turned to the events of the day and particularly the more recent happenings in the district.

Sean Hales, an astute and savvy young man, had already made inquiries about Joe. Even though they both had not known each other well, they had a nodding acquaintance and anyway in a town such as Bandon not much escaped the enquiring minds, which abounded in these small communities.

Bandon had two very distinct communities, one Anglo-Irish Protestant, the other Irish Nationalist Catholic. You belonged to one or the other at that time, although with some Catholics not wishing to lose the connection with Britain and some Protestants wanting at least Home Rule if not independence.

Bandon was unique in Munster in that it had a large Anglo-Irish Protestant population. Indeed, it was founded about the time of the Battle of Kinsale (1601) by an Englishman named, Phane Beecher and it was settled by English "Planters" (i.e., those colonists who were rewarded by land or inducement after the Irish were defeated). It became a very Protestant town, particularly after the Cromwellians took it over and at one time Catholics were not permitted within the town walls.

The enmity between those within and those without was tellingly displayed in the earlier times on the entrance gates where a notice declared: "Turk, Jew, or Atheist may enter here but not a Papist."

Not to be outdone, one local Irish wag added: "Whoever wrote it wrote it well, For the same is written on the gates of Hell."

By the 19th century the Catholics had gained access to the town and that enmity had faded. However, there still remained the distance between the communities.

These differences were made manifest, primarily, though not exclusively, in the attachment each side had to their respective Protestant/Catholic beliefs.

Joe a Catholic, whilst having served and earned promotion and honour for exceptional service in the British Army during the War, was known by his friends to have joined to fight in that War for reasons that were in Ireland's interest rather than Britain's.

He was astute enough in a town of two halves to keep his political opinions to himself, particularly when more than half of his customers were from the Anglo-Irish Protestant side, as they were the ones who had owned most businesses and were also wealthiest. The majority population (included people from both sides), were, as of that time, not wealthy enough to up-grade to the new technologies.

Hales had also been told by Joe's prospective father-in-law, Michael Griffin, that he knew that Joe, while not being public in his beliefs was unhappy about the summary execution of the 1916 rebellion leaders by the British authorities, annoyed that despite the overwhelming election success of Sinn Fein, who demanded self-rule, the British Government was still dithering over Home Rule despite the passing of the act to allow that, which had been postponed until after the War, and furious over the coercive actions of the security services against the general Nationalist population.

Hales, who had to rely for the most part on young men who had no military training, was very much aware of Joe's skills in that regard and realised he could be a valuable resource if persuaded to help the IRA in their activities. Having talked around the matter for some time he came straight to the point.

"Joe, I know you are unhappy with the political situation in Ireland, especially after committing so much for that which was promised by the British Government. Are you prepared to take a stand to insist on Ireland's demands for self-governance?"

"Sean you well know that when it comes down to taking sides, I am four square behind the Nationalist position."

"How far are you willing to go to see that through?"

"I know what you are Sean and what you are asking. Let me be clear, I have seen death come to hundreds of young men, who should have just been enjoying the first fruits of their adulthood, blood wantonly spilt by weapons created for no other purpose but to tear apart every fibre of the human body and I have told myself I want forever to escape that hellish nightmare. However, I entered that madness for a reason that has not been fulfilled and so I am now in a situation where I cannot go back and yet am unable to go o'er."

"Then will you help us?"

Joe knowing full well what Sean Hales, leader of the local IRA, wanted could not commit himself without clearly stating his trench-earned deep dislike of violence answered: "Well Sean, I cannot be indifferent to the situation we find ourselves in at present and my sympathies are obviously on the Nationalist side. However, I have no desire to kill or maim another human being. I had hoped I would never have to go down that road again."

Sean, understanding where Joe was coming from but anxious to avail of his skills and experience persisted: "But you can help us greatly without having to get directly involved in the fighting itself. We are badly in need of inside intelligence into the British plans and their overall strategy. This applies particularly to the British Army, where we have no inside knowledge or access."

Joe having for months now, since the 'Troubles' began, asked himself where he stood in relation to all that was unfolding had to admit that, while he was unhappy that the violence had commenced, he was very much of the opinion that Ireland should have its freedom from British rule. Moreover, hadn't they been promised this before the War by the British Government, who was now apparently attempting to water down that promise?

One way or another, he could not now stand idle in the face of what was happening and let others carry the burden. Additionally, if he did not get involved in some way, he could not then have a say in any new Ireland which would emerge after the fighting was over. He was a pragmatist and a realist. He soon realised that Ireland had reached a stage at the beginning of the 20th century, where Empires were falling and new alliances being made, where nothing would remain as it had been.

Change had arrived and the future was at hand. He therefore replied without hesitation: "Sean I will see what I can do to help the cause. There are just a couple of conditions that I need to make before doing so."

"Maith an fhear tu, a Sheosaimh. What are these conditions?"

"The first is that I alone will determine how I will go about getting the intelligence you need. The second is that only you should know that I am doing so. If you have to refer to me when speaking to others, you should use only the name 'A' as in Apollo and then only sparingly.

"The third is that no reference should be made as to my background and therefore no reference to my connections with the British Army. The fourth condition is that unless all else fails and the need is most urgent, I will only report verbally with nothing in writing.

"The fifth condition is the method of reporting. It should be certain but secret, that is times and places with no obvious pattern and out of sight of any prying eyes. Anything which would create even the slightest doubt in the privacy of the meet should mean immediate abandonment of the rendezvous. If both do not show at the time appointed, then the arriver should abandon the meet without waiting around.

"The sixth condition is that nothing of material interest should be kept from me. To do my work I need to know. This does not mean that I have to be informed of all activities and indeed it would be better if I were not. However, if something is relevant to what I am doing then I should be told about it as soon as possible.

"All of these conditions have one central objective—to ensure the secrecy and security of the messenger, the contact and the message. It is a matter of trust. I trust you as indeed you must trust me in this enterprise. If you are caught, I must presume I would shortly thereafter meet a similar fate to yourself. The less the circle the less the risk."

"Joe, I have no trouble in accepting these conditions and indeed I am in agreement with you on their value and importance. Just one change if you accept it. The Director of Operations and Intelligence for the IRA in Dublin Michael Collins puts great store on intelligence and he has a voracious appetite for information on what the other side is thinking. You now that Mick comes from just up the road and he will undoubtedly ask me for your name and your background to help him judge the weight he will give to your reports. I would not be able to refuse him."

While Joe is considering this Sean adds: "I know I can get him to agree with your conditions and not divulge your name to anyone else. Additionally, I firmly believe that Collins would endure any torture before surrendering your or any other names to the British."

Joe, while not underestimating the persuasiveness of the British in extracting information from prisoners in wartime conditions, understood the logic of the leader in seeking to know the secret agent in order to evaluate the intelligence responded; "I accept that addition Sean, as it is not unreasonable and I trust Mick

Collins. On a lighter note, I should also hope that I will have more notice if he, rather than you, is caught so that I can get to hell out of the way."

Thus involved, Joe not only knew what information would be most useful to aid the struggle, but because of his training and experience in the War, knew exactly how to go about getting that intelligence. His freedom to visit the army barracks and socialise with the troops there, together with his knowledge and access to the communications centre made it all the easier.

He nevertheless knew full well that, in going over to the other side, if he had been discovered a fast death would be the best he could hope for. The one positive he believed he had going for him was that no one knew of his involvement, apart from Hales and Collins, both of whom he felt he could implicitly trust with his life even if they were captured.

Chapter 10

Joe Ryan had gained admittance to the army barracks in town since his return from the war. He was also asked to service some of the electrical and communications systems there because of his knowledge and skill in those areas.

Some months before, when he had been supervising the installation of electrical wiring in the cookhouse, he was asked by one of the Signals NCO's, Sergeant Tom Turner, with whom he was on first name terms, if he would be able to install a new telephone system. Joe had told him that he would if the equipment was complete as he would not have parts in his shop.

The Sergeant said he would have to consult with his superiors about it but felt they would ask him to do the job when the material arrived. Joe had also agreed to give the communications staff instructions on its use.

As always when he called to Communications Hut he was well received as one of their own, who not only was an expert on this modern technology but had also been trained in England to a high level in its use in wartime.

Joe had noticed that the codes the Barracks were using in their contacts with other Army establishments were the ones he was familiar with. He was pleased with that information, as, while he had on previous visits attempted to establish what were being used, they had always been locked away and consequently he was unable to access them.

This time he had been drawn in by the Sergeant to see the new telephone equipment which was located just beyond where the operators were working, and using the code.

"We're very pleased to get this new tech, Joe. The system we have at present is way pre-War and doesn't work half the time. The officers are continuously giving out to us for the problem and it's no good telling them it's not our fault."

"I fear that's the trouble with new technologies. Because it's so helpful and so fast, when it works, everyone comes to rely on it and when it is not there or not working properly, they find it hard to go back to the old way of doing things.

Anyway, blame must be given somewhere and unfortunately those of us who are in the firing line are blamed."

Pausing for effect Joe added to the laughter of the veterans present by adding: "I wonder where I heard that before."

"Thank God we can laugh about that now Joe." Tom Turner went on: "Hopefully this new stuff will be more robust and efficient; Major Percival is very keen on raising our standards and wants this up and running as soon as possible. How long do you think it will take Joe?"

"I will have to check to see if you have everything to do the job there. There may be additional parts that are needed to install the system. I will call round tomorrow and check. If I have the full equipment, I should have it up and running within a couple of days at most."

"Major Percival said he would be up to visit and wanted to be able to test it. Do you think it will be ready before the end of next week?"

"Certainly, I might have it done earlier if all the equipment is in order. Today is Thursday and I need to be here myself to ensure the work is set up properly. I will call around tomorrow morning to check the full extent of the material you have and if all is in order I will start right away. I need some of my technical men with me to help though."

Realising that the sensitivity of the new equipment would need special security he added immediately: "Will that pose a problem Tom."

"I will run it by the OC if you give me their names and any details you have on them and let you know. As you are aware, you have special clearance because of your record and previous service but we are careful, particularly in the current situation, about new faces."

"Good, I'll be here in the morning to examine the equipment and hopefully we can make a start if all is in order. I will give you the names and details then."

"Thanks Joe, we appreciate what you are doing for us at such short notice. We know you are very busy with electrical installations and even phones for business and even private homes. But you know how the officer ranks are about things they want done. It must be immediate and efficient—no excuses entertained."

"Tom, I won't let you down on this."

Joe was pleased that he was in a position to do them a favour. It would undoubtedly play a big part in his future friendly relations with this section of the barracks.

Staying for a cup of freshly brewed tea and talking of old times with a couple of the veterans present he had time to surreptitiously take in all that was being said and used in the communications centre.

During the tea break Sergeant Turner mentioned the arrival some weeks before of a new officer at the barracks. There had been little said about him other than him that he was a war veteran and had acquitted himself well in the fighting where he had spent most of his active time in Flanders in the trenches upfront. While now a Captain it was known that in the field, he had made Major and, remaining on, he like many others were given reduced status because of the enormous diminution in the numbers in the now "peacetime" army. Joe did not say that he had already met Captain Geoffrey Eastbourne.

Turner was somewhat apprehensive for a number of reasons:

i) as the new officer has communications as part of his duties, he would have to answer to him,
ii) it could be expected that coming from a constant long-term highly volatile war arena his demands would be high,
iii) with someone of that experience there would be no room for pulling the wool over his eyes and any attempt to do so could be expected to be dealt with severely and
iv) with less than 30% of junior officers on the Front surviving he must have been both lucky and skilful to have come through physically unhurt. Moreover, a large number of those who survived were left with mental scars, which were only revealed during stress occasions and as he would probably be in the first line of contact on some of those occasions, he would have to be careful how he handled the captain and take time to judge how far he could go in raising issues with him.
v) finally, as Percival was taking a very special interest in communications and as the captain had said he would be reporting directly to Percival he would have to watch his Ps and Qs.

Joe Ryan walked down the town towards home that evening, attempting to take in all he had learned that day. His thoughts ranged from the work in hand to the jobs he would have to postpone.

'That would take a great deal of diplomacy—it would be unwise to bite the hand that would feed him into the future and he had promised some of the businessmen in the town that he would shortly be getting around to their projects. Perhaps he should hire at least one more skilled worker. However, that would take time as he knew of no one around the town who could fit that position that was not already gainfully employed. He decided he would train two young men he had interviewed as they showed some promise. However, that he would have to make do with the staff he had for the moment.'

Having put that aside his principal concern was on his other task. From his return to Bandon after the War he had been welcome in the Army Barracks, where he had even been entertained in the NCOs Mess and even on occasions in the Officer's Mess. His wartime recognition and particularly his technology skills were well regarded and he was seen as one of their own.

Earlier he had an easy approach to that arrangement and, apart from the lucrative work it provided for his business, it was nice to share time and stories with men whose experiences were similar to his own – something he could not talk to the locals about, even his friends who were not involved, or indeed the many now who regarded those who fought in the war as being somehow traitors to the Irish cause in this new disposition.

In the new situation, post his arrangement with Sean Hales, he had to use his visits to the Barracks to pick up any information which might prove valuable to the cause. In that regard, his thoughts were very much tuned to what he had learned today:

A new telephone system, a new Captain in charge of communications, shrewd Percival taking a personal interest in communications and no doubt bringing the new Captain in for that purpose.'

Had he not been told by his contacts in the British Army that Percival had excelled in intelligence work during the War and now he has ended up here as the army's principal local strategist. No doubt he will endeavour to bring his talents in that field with him here and use them to best effect.

However, I will now know the full extent of the communications system which I will be instrumental in installing and hopefully pick up some more useful information during my time in that sensitive area.

Moreover, I will have to be extra careful. Percival's vast experience in this field would no doubt place special attention on any possible leakage of information from the Army or indeed from the other security establishments (RIC, Black and Tans, or Auxiliaries). While he could only monitor the latter group, he had direct control of the Army and I believe he will use that to its utmost.

Additionally, I will have to watch out for the new Captain who I guess will be no pushover. Furthermore, he will no doubt act as Percival's eyes and ears and would himself be engaged in attempting to suss out as much information on the IRA and its activities as he could gather.

Unfortunately, I am on my own now in relation to the task at hand and no one could or indeed should be asked to help in that endeavour. As a corollary I am fortunately alone in carrying out this mission, as I consequently do not have to mind my back, unless of course Sean Hales or Michael Collins are captured.

Nevertheless, I will now have to tread very warily.

Two words came to mind in this regard:

Opportunity and Vigilance.

Chapter 11

Joe Ryan visited the army barracks to meet with the officer who would give clearance for the contract for the installation of the telephone equipment. Arriving at the communication hut, he spoke with Sergeant Turner for a little while waiting for the officer to show. Joe showed no sign of recognition when Captain Eastbourne arrived.

Geoffrey was somewhat embarrassed at first, not knowing what to say after their first encounter at the card game and subsequently when he accepted Joe's generosity. Joe alleviated all of that awkwardness by ignoring that episode and dealing with Geoffrey as a valued client that he had met professionally for the first time.

Geoffrey was very grateful for Joe's discretion and the meeting was very professional. He was additionally pleased to have someone of Joe's obvious expertise nearby in the town to call on. Joe Ryan appeared to be exactly as Sergeant Turner had said, both an expert on electronics (an area in which Geoffrey had absolutely no expertise) and a reliable former solid NCO. Apart from Joe's generosity and the debt he owed him, as a former front-line officer he had already taken to the man who had experienced similar hardships as he did and who, like him, had seen most of his comrades die around him.

The average life of a Signals Operator in the forward trenches was, like his own rank at that time (Sub-Lieutenant), counted in weeks rather than months. Both were targeted by the boche snipers and for different but strategic reasons were seen by the General Staff as useful but disposable.

They discovered that they were operating in Flanders at the same time approximately in different sectors but all the old R&R locations they were able to recall, where, for short spaces of time, one could escape the constant proximity of death and the screaming of the injured and the ever-dreadful howitzers.

While so different—different nationalities, different backgrounds, different temperaments, different ambitions, different politics, different goals—they soon found that common bond that unites mankind—confidence that a fellow man, previously unknown to them, would stand by them in their time of need, willing to sacrifice anything, even life itself, to protect a colleague.

While with different ranks and fighting in different locations in the same arena of war, they had, during that most horrendous time, unconsciously formed a spiritually real fellowship—a brotherhood, which not even time would break.

Having established their introductions and their recent past similar experiences the conversation changed from a strictly official one to a much easier mixture of both Geoffrey's official needs and his personal desire to integrate, as far as was possible in the troubled circumstances, with the local citizenry.

For reasons of mutual advantage, though very opposite reasons, both men felt their acquaintance with the other could help their respective goals.

Geoffrey believes he could use his acquaintance with Joe Ryan to both help him meet other people in the town, socially and also get to know people through him who might be able to identify (knowingly or unknowingly) others who had connections to the IRA.

Joe Ryan on the other hand had no social reason to befriend Geoffrey, other than as an aid to his business. On the other hand, he immediately understood how valuable a guarded friendship would be with the very officer who is immediately responsible for security and information in the Army Barracks. He had apparently got over the first hurdle already in getting him to accept him as a former colleague and more importantly as someone he could trust.

Joe thought '*it would be too much to expect the captain to eventually even confide in me, however, the most important first step has been achieved—that he has accepted my bona fides and I will be able to enter the barracks freely and even enter one of the most security sensitive areas there, with no suspicion concerning my loyalty.*' He did not like having to use Geoffrey in this way but then he justified it by saying to himself, '*it is not him personally I oppose but what he stands for*'.

After Geoffrey had gone through the business of the phone installation e.g., time it would take, the advantages it would bring, security issues related to it, etc., he moved on to his second priority, introduction to the town and the people there who would welcome him.

At this stage, through Geoffrey's insistence, they both referred to each other by Christian names. Geoffrey asked, "Joe, I understand there are some sports clubs in the town? Not that I'm an ardent sports type but I would like to meet people and I suppose the best way to start would be through one or more of these or, if they exist, men's clubs? What do you think?"

"Yes Geoffrey, there are a number. There are no men's clubs that I can recommend for you. But you will discover however, that generally many of the social activities you might need can be found in the sports clubs. There are of course associations and outlets to be found in the Church organisations here in town. It depends of course which one of these you might have an affiliation with. In this town you will find nearly every one of the Christian Churches represented."

"Thanks for that information, Joe. Franky, I suppose my affiliation is with the Church of England, but I seem to have neglected that for some years now. I would be grateful if you could help in perhaps introducing me to someone in one or more of the clubs who might be interested in my joining."

Joe, without hesitating, replied; "Let me think which one would be best to start. I will come back when I have made some discreet inquiries. I don't want you to feel uncomfortable as you enter a strange town."

To reinforce his now fortunate friendship with a key individual who might, if he were to be extremely cautious, make his intelligence gathering more direct and meaningful, Joe added: "In the meantime, however, why don't you meet me tonight or Monday night in the local hotel bar, just nearby, and I will introduce you to some people you might find useful in making your way around the town."

Geoffrey immediately accepted and agreed to meet that evening as suggested.

They parted company at that—Joe to get on with his work on the installation of the phones—Geoffrey to call on the local RIC barracks to meet again with the superintendent in charge and this time, knowing more about the territory, spend more time to take a real reading of their capacity and commitment.

Geoffrey thought as he approached the police barracks:

'I will merely listen to what is said on this occasion. Bearing in mind what Percival advised, I must be cautious as to my role while ensuring that as far as I can insist that they keep us informed of any significant information they learn from time to time.'

Knowing policemen, he understood that they would most likely be as reticent in giving information as he was in parting with it. In time perhaps he could ensure that their advantage in parting with that information would outweigh their police instinct to withhold it.

Meanwhile back at the barracks, Joe found it hard to concentrate on his work thinking of all that had just passed, coming as it did, out of the blue. He was very pleased with his good luck, or what he hoped on reflection was good luck—'time will tell'—anyway he thought *'in for a penny, in for a pound'*.

Chapter 12

Later that evening they met as agreed at the bar of the Somerville Hotel.

"Good to see you again Geoffrey, what would you like to drink."

"I'll have a Scotch Joe. Although on second thoughts maybe I should try an Irish whiskey seeing that I'm in Ireland. I know that I had some before over in Flanders from a fellow Irish officer who was kind enough to share the last third of his bottle with me. At that time, I thought it was the best I'd ever had and I recall savouring each mouthful. But to be honest, as you well know, a treat like that was like water in the desert to a man who had lost his water bottle."

"It brings back memories. It's funny that in situations like we experienced it's the little things, especially when one's spirit is raised, that we remember most. Anyway, try an Allmans it's produced locally. It will have a stronger taste than Scotch but after you get used to it, I believe you will prefer it. John, can we have two Allmans with water"—before turning to Geoffrey saying, "or would you prefer soda with yours Geoffrey."

"No, water is great Joe, thanks."

"Here's to a pleasant and hopefully quiet posting for you here Geoffrey."

"I'll drink to that Joe."

Remembering, however, that he was here for more than social reasons he asked Joe, "Were you able to come up with any names I could approach to help me join a club here. The sooner I get my feet under the table here and settle in the easier my posting will be. I would welcome your guidance through—friends made in haste can at times become people you wish you had not associated with so easily at the start."

"I understand what you mean Geoffrey. I will bear that in mind and initially anyway, until you can sit back and determine the types of people you would like to befriend, I will be selective in the introductions I will make for you."

Joe had already decided on the first people he would get Geoffrey to meet—men who he knew would be friendly and useful in making connections with the

Anglo-Protestant side of the community, which would be very welcoming to Geoffrey. They would also be able to help him ease into many of the clubs he had mentioned in the town.

He had decided on the hotel bar for that purpose, knowing that he would find there, most evenings, at least a couple of the people he had in mind. This evening would be no exception to that observation.

"I see a couple of people who you should meet. As well as being friendly, I'm sure it will help to introduce you to others. Let's meet them."

"Tom, Jack, can I introduce Captain Geoffrey Eastbourne to you both? Geoffrey has been stationed here only a short time and has not had much time to fully acquaint himself with the town. Geoffrey, Jack Lee and you already met Tom. Tom and Jack are good friends. Tom, as you know, is the owner of this hotel—a good man, name and nature, to know and Jack runs a business in the town and is also secretary of the local Golf Club."

Geoffrey, immediately recognising the value of his getting to know the men and sensing a warmth towards him, he responded accordingly, "A pleasure to meet you, Jack. I have met Tom a number of times already and he has been kind to a newcomer. It's nice to meet people in the town. I'm a complete stranger to here as indeed I am to Ireland, it being my first time on the island."

Tom Good, always a gracious host and pleased to be helpful to a new prospective client, responding said, "Sure you're welcome here. Hope you will find us, at least most of us, happy to see you. Let me buy you a drink, indeed let me buy you all one. What will it be?"

The evening passed off very amicably and towards the close before Jack Lee left, he invited Geoffrey to meet him at the golf club early next evening to show him around. Geoffrey was delighted to accept, hoping of course that it might lead to his joining the club.

On leaving the hotel, he thanked Joe for his evening and particularly the introductions. Joe told him that he would arrange further introductions and try to get people like Jack Lee who would be able to introduce him to the other clubs.

Geoffrey, walking back to the nearby barracks, was very pleased with his evening and looked forward to the next day's meeting in the golf club. He felt very comfortable in the company of Jack Lee who, like Joe, was nearer his own age and hoped he could befriend him as he, being well placed, could make the introductions to the town society he would feel most comfortable in.

Tom Good, a much older man, was very amiable and easy to like, he instinctively knew he could rely on him. He was not unaware that he was in enemy territory and trust was a very valuable commodity. He had not missed the message hinted in Tom Good's first words that he would be welcome here by "at least most of us".

He thought, *'I have to walk carefully, taking one step at a time. Not everyone I meet will be as welcoming as those tonight. I was fortunate to have Joe make those first introductions. The first steps are the most vital. However, I must go on.'*

Apart from establishing myself in the town and learning to get to know the natives, I have a task at hand on which I need to begin work immediately. I must find people who can get me the information on the IRA and its activities that I need to fulfil my role here. That will require a great deal of thought and I expect a certain amount of risk. Then again, I did learn quite early on how to keep my head down in the trenches and how to zigzag when going forward on the killing theatre called "no man's land".

Joe, walking home, in the other direction, was caught between two worlds. The one of friendship and collegiality and the other of principal and commitment. He instinctively liked Geoffrey and together with their similar experiences at the Front he could not help having a special regard for him. That regard included a protective element and so he was somewhat of a dilemma as to his need to ensure the IRA's success while at the same time ensuring that he would not injure Geoffrey in the process.

That apart, however, he was pleased that he had now reinforced his relationship with Geoffrey and in doing so allowed for much easier access to the barracks, on the occasions in which he would visit, than he had previously. He could now not only install the telephone system with little oversight and in so doing perhaps figure out a method of gaining access to the conversations on it without the authorities knowing.

He now had to work on the other promises he had made to Geoffrey viz. introducing him to people he would easily find friendship with. Joe knew everyone in the small town in which he grew up. He would continue to select those who would quite easily fit in with Geoffrey, those who were pro-union rather than the vast majority who were nationalists.

Reflecting on the latter group he knew that while most had voted for Sinn Fein most of them would not have agreed with IRA violence. That position was, however, changing as the British authorities brought in more coercive regulations, including the talked about martial law, and particularly since the introduction first of the hated Black and Tan police reinforcements, who appeared to be able to flout the law without fear of reprimand.

As he reflected on the latter group, where his loyalties lay, he thought, *'I must also find some people from the Nationalist side to introduce to Geoffrey. I will have to carefully select. I have to tread a very fine line between those who thought against the union, would nevertheless wish to treat Geoffrey with respect and those who would see him as the enemy and use that position to cause trouble. It is not because I wish to keep him away from the cut and thrust of the reality of life in today's Ireland, it is because I do not want these people to queer the pitch, I am attempting to work in to achieve the goal which will be most important for the success of the independence mission.*

Additionally, I have to exercise care in relation to myself. While I have a great deal of friends in the town and the surrounding area, there are already troglodytes who see my service in the War as an outward sign of extreme pro-Britishness. They are not interested in understanding why many Irish people like me, who were members of, or supported, the Irish Volunteers joined the British Army to fight for small nations in the understanding that Ireland would have promised Home Rule after the War.

There is also an even greater worry that somehow loose lips might raise the question of where my loyalties really lay. I cannot afford to take that risk. I cannot have my back uncovered while I pursue my tricky and risky game of, dare I say it, "espionage".'

With those thoughts running through his head, Joe Ryan's mind went back again to the Front and his occasional lonely precipitous forays into "no man's land" at night to obtain more accurate readings on enemy troop dispositions to relay them back to Brigade HQ for logistics purposes.

Chapter 13

Next morning Joe Ryan and one of his employees (who had his security pass approved when doing other work in the barracks) were working on the new telephone system. This gave Joe total access to the communications hut and his expert knowledge of the systems which the British Army were using allowed him to quickly check out the communications equipment in use in the barracks. He was particularly keen on the codes the army were now using and he was pleased to confirm that the old simpler codes were still in use.

He had time to jot down some of the code while the operators were otherwise engaged. These together with the knowledge he had retained from the War—he had kept official papers including (surreptitiously taken when he was disbanding) parts of the code he had been using. They were taken at the time as a keepsake, thinking they would be irrelevant now that the War ("the War to End All Wars") had ended.

Later in the morning he was joined by Captain Eastbourne who was interested in how the work was progressing. Addressing Joe in a formal way in the presence of his troops Geoffrey asked:

"Hope everything is going well here Mr Ryan. I'll be very pleased to have the new system up and running. I used the old one yesterday and frankly the telegraph would have been ten times more efficient and indeed even faster."

"We're making steady progress, Captain. The hope is we should be finished here today if we work into the late evening which I would like to do, provided that can be accommodated by your staff." Joe had already run that by Sergeant Turner and had got his approval. Joe wished to ensure that he would keep very much in with the Sergeant and the staff operating the Communications Hut.

They would be his main point of contact on a continuing basis if he wished for any reason to gain access to the hut. He had of course to ensure the permission of the captain to cover all sides, while at the same time he showed his willingness to work late on Saturday night to complete the job.

"That will be no problem, Mr Ryan. There is always someone on duty in the Hut anyway, so it will not involve any additional duties. That is of course unless you need extra bodies to help you with some tasks to complete the job? Can you foresee any problems, Sergeant?"

"No Sir. None at all. As you say Sir, it will require no additional duties for us unless Mr Ryan requires our help."

"Then Mr Ryan we would indeed be grateful if you could finish the job this evening. We very much appreciate the way you came to our aid with so little notice to do this installation and to complete it in such a short time is a double bonus."

Geoffrey was more than pleased: Major Percival might visit the barracks on the following week or so and he would be pleased to see the new phone system in place and hopefully working efficiently. He knew that the Major was the one who had ordered it, and pulled strings to get it so quickly. It was part of the Major's plan to bring the systems under his control quickly up to the highest standards possible. Communications and intelligence were his priority and he wanted the most modern equipment available.

Geoffrey invited Joe across to the hotel for a tea break. Both were on duty and it was too early to imbibe in something stronger.

While there Geoffrey thanked Joe again for his introductions the previous evening. Joe said that he would also introduce him to others he had in mind, who could take him on further.

He also mentioned that while the new telephone system was excellent, he would not be too sure of the line connections.

"I know you did not ask when I was installing the system but it would be wise to check out the lines. They've been there for some years and weather conditions in this part of the country play havoc with outside equipment, even iron. You mentioned that the Major might be visiting soon—it might be wise to alert him to this. If that part of the system fails at some stage in the near future you will be able to rely on the fact that you had warned him about the potential for breakdown."

"Very good point Joe. I will definitely mention it. By the way if he instructs me to have it checked out, would you be in a position to do so? I'm not sure we have that type of expertise in Cork to do the job."

Joe had already made up his mind that while that job would require oodles of man hours and manpower, he could possibly manage it. If he could, it would allow him a golden opportunity to control the telephone and telegraph wires in and out of the Barracks. He responded after some feigned hesitation:

"I could do it, although it will take time and require a number of men to check the whole wire system. Anyway, let's wait until you talk to the Major. He may have other ideas. I suspect he is a man who needs to ask questions before you come up with solutions for him. Knowing high ranking brass, like you and I do, they want to believe they, not you, come up with solutions.

"Consequently, if I were in your shoes, I would merely bring up the problem with him. He will no doubt respond asking if you have a solution or someone local who may be able to check out the system. On the other hand, he may have already thought of the problem himself and have something in train to deal with it. Pointing out the problem and simultaneously suggesting a solution may be a bridge too far."

Geoffrey met Jack Lee at the Golf Club later that day.

Jack was waiting for him and offering him a drink at the bar introduced him to some of the members who had just finished a round of golf. The conversation, as it will in golfing circles, first revolved around golf—handicaps and courses and near misses and eagles and almost hole in ones. It drifted on as the evening progressed and others came into the group, tongues became more lubricated, concerns made themselves known and the events of the day were aired.

The group Geoffrey found himself in were of a kind, all Anglo-Irish Protestants and they saw him as a vital cog in the wheel of the establishment they owed not only their adherence but even more so their very existence. 'Had not Carson and Craig and the Unionist leaders in the North of the country warned of the dangers posed by the Home Rule'? 'Had not the rebellion of 1916 showed that one could not trust the Nationalists?'

Geoffrey, who had been in the midst of bonhomie and good-will, was now confronted with questions which could be boiled down to,

'What are you doing about the 'Troubles' we now find ourselves in and when will we return to a situation where the unionist tradition will continue to be in the ascendancy?'

It became clear to Geoffrey that the people he was with at present were fearful of the new disposition in southern Ireland, particularly in this region, where the IRA was very active. They wanted reassurances that the current violent turn of events would be put down and that the Sinn Feiners would be warned in no uncertain terms that their current "Independence" stance would not be tolerated.

Geoffrey had been unprepared for this torrent of anger and outrage, borne, he had since his arrival found out, from years of ascendency and privilege and now fear that not only would they lose those birth rights but they might also lose all they possessed and even too their lives.

He sought to reassure them as much as he could that the authorities would have the intelligence and the manpower in place in a short space of time to deal effectively with the IRA. He was a great deal more reticent about what could be done about Sinn Fein and the politics of the newly formed Dail. That was not a matter for the Army to deal with.

Geoffrey was not unaware of the changes which were happening all around Europe and indeed even in Britain itself. Women were now enfranchised, the lower social classes, having borne the brunt of the deadliest war Europe had ever seen, were demanding their rights and communism, which had emerged in Russia, was surfacing in other parts of Europe as well. Had not the Labour Party threatened to challenge the liberal Whigs? One need not be a prophet to understand that Ireland too would demand change and that the old orders would not endure as before.

For the first time since his arrival in Ireland he thought rather gloomily,

'Good God, what have I got myself into taking this posting?'

'It was bad enough fighting at the Front. At least you knew who your enemy was and moreover you knew you were fighting for the survival of your country and freedom.'

'These people would be better off if they accepted that change was inevitable and try to come to terms with their fellow citizens.'

'Anyway, it is not my role to give advice on political matters and quite obviously it would not be listened to or appreciated by the majority of the people I am listening to here tonight.'

Geoffrey left the club late. He felt he could not leave earlier without causing offence. His head was still reeling from the intensity of the conversation that had been whirling around all night and the abject fear he could perceive in the atmosphere of this group, which he knew represented some of the top end of the economic order in the town and district.

There was one success gained during his visit, although he felt it would be double-edged. He had been invited to join the club.

Chapter 14

Geoffrey had arrived in Ireland in the late spring of 1920. 'The Troubles', which had started in 1919, had been quite localised and sporadic and the attacks were mainly concentrated on the RIC. The IRA campaign had been quite effective in the rural areas, particularly in the south-west where a number of the small RIC barracks were abandoned and subsequently burnt down by the IRA. The towns were in the control of the British security forces, but even there, attacks had taken place against RIC members.

By the end of 1919 and the beginning of 1920 however, there was a noticeable escalation of IRA activity and it became clear that as time moved on that organisation was growing and gaining more acceptance from the population. Retaliations against the IRA, which spilled over to the local population, exacerbated that alienation. The murder in March of 1920 of Tomas McCurtain, the Sinn Fein Lord Mayor of Cork city by a masked gang from the local RIC barracks at his home in front of his wife and children helped to fan the flames.

Having by this time read himself into the local situation and spoken with colleagues at the barracks, Geoffrey understood that if they were to have any success against the IRA it should be achieved quickly, as it appeared to him that as time passed the attrition rate would drive the conflict on further until one side reached exhaustion. Having seen the layout of the territory around farmland, hills, valleys, rivers, mountains, small villages and the demographic of the population and bearing in mind his conversation with the golf group, he was not all confident of an easy victory. It was clear that the IRA would refuse to engage against a trained army in open battle. That would mean they would always have the advantage.

He understood why Percival was so anxious to gain an advantage through intelligence. It would be the only effective way of tackling their deficit in local knowledge, which he agreed would be key to defeating the IRA. After that it would be up to the politicians and from the little, he had seen so far, he was very glad that task would not be his.

That morning he had seen the reports coming in from the outlying districts—more IRA activity, primarily against the RIC barracks and individual security personnel who were unfortunate to be caught on their own in the wrong place. He could see that the IRA's policy was one of attrition. Had they not used the same tactics in a much greater arena during the War, when with the Allies greater manpower and, with America's intervention, far greater resources the longer the war dragged on, without the German side scoring a fatal blow, the more certain the outcome would be a victory for the Allies.

He consequently had an urgency in finding sources that would supply the information and intelligence he needed to put in place, plans to counteract the IRA's current superiority in the operations field. He had now, with little effort, made his way into the local Anglo-Irish community, but that would only give limited knowledge into the areas he wished to explore.

It would be a far greater task to find people from the majority community who not only would have the knowledge he was seeking, but most importantly be willing to share that knowledge with him. In the short time he felt he had, not only in relation to the escalation he could see in IRA's activities, but additionally in what he knew would be demanded of him by the Percival.

Considering this, he thought, *'perhaps I could again ask Joe Ryan, whom I know to be from that side of the community, although on our side. Because of his training he would understand the value of information to the progress of the ending the attacks. I feel I can trust him. Although maybe I am asking a little too much? While he would disagree with the IRA, he may not wish to be seen or indeed even privately actively aiding and abetting its destruction, which after all is the force of the Nationalist Dail (illegal thought that parliament may be).*

I will ask him, however, to point out people, other than those he has introduced me to already, on his side who are known to be either pro-British or at least neutral in relation to the Nationalist/ Unionist divide. I will determine, myself, how I should use those contacts. It is well that at this stage I should keep my cards close to my chest until I am sure of the direction, I wish to go with this.'

He was not looking forward to a visit the next morning by Major Percival, as he knew that he would be expected to show some progress, however little, in the short time he had been en post. He did however, have the telephone system to mention and he was grateful to have something to offer. He hoped the Percival could be content that the new telephone system was now up and running for some time.

He also hoped to be able to expand on this, pointing out that the improvements were very noticeable and that it would greatly improve contacts between the posts. In passing he would also mention the old lines connecting the barracks with the other posts, but would take Joe Ryan's advice to allow the Major to follow up on his take on that and allow him to decide on what if anything should be done to investigate their condition.

Turning to the task of finding useful contacts in the district he recalled that on leaving the Golf Club he was escorted to his vehicle by Jack Lee, the Club Secretary, who had invited him to a small evening cocktail party he was giving at home for a few friends. He had added, rather shamefacedly, that unlike his welcome at the club earlier, it would not be as near heated or voluble.

"I fear I walked you into a storm there Geoffrey. I apologise. I must confess I did not expect the tone of the conversation that occurred just now, of which you were the main target. Gordon Ludlow was the main culprit. I fear he had been drinking heavily earlier. He has a particular chip on his shoulder—his barn was burned down by the IRA as a warning for his treatment of a couple of his Nationalist employees. Others there, while not always agreeing with Ludlow, who is a known hothead, are themselves fearful of what would happen if the IRA are successful."

Geoffrey, outside the club alone with Jack Lee, asked him what his personal feelings were in relation to all that was then occurring.

"Frankly Geoffrey, while I am disturbed by the Troubles, I have to be honest, I am not surprised that they are happening. Far too little has been done by the Government to assuage the long-sought demands of the majority population here. While I come from the other side, I have lived close to them all my life and many of them are my friends.

"I have no animosity towards them. Far from that, I see myself as part of this community and am ashamed sometimes of what happened in the past. I have a business here and my customers are from across both communities. I do not hope to see that change no matter what the outcome. The Gordon Ludlows of this region are living in the past and the future is changing."

Geoffrey was surprised at the frankness of the response, particularly as he had noticed that Jack like himself had had little to drink during the evening. All the more therefore he trusted him and found him someone he could befriend.

At the cocktail party on the outskirts of the town not far from the barracks the gathering was around sixteen people. Large enough to move from one to another but small enough to get around and spend a little time with everyone and longer with the more interesting of the guests. The majority were other business people in the town but also present were a local lawyer and the bank manager and a clergyman. All were accompanied by their wives.

As Jack Lee had advised at the golf club the guests that evening was far more sophisticated than the evening before and while the Troubles came up during conversation there were no recriminations or indeed hysteria and Geoffrey consequently found himself under no pressure.

Talk ranged mainly from business, to agriculture, to the economy, to children going to boarding schools and of course the ubiquitous weather.

"I find supplies still hard to come by and there are still great delays."

"Did you hear any news of the restrictions and rationing being removed? The War is over nearly two years now and they still are enforced."

"At least agriculture is good this year. I hear it will be a good harvest. The export markets are very buoyant and Britain cannot get enough of our produce. Prices however, are accordingly still high."

"But if there are bumper harvests, which we hope for, then there will be an easing of price."

"Still the farmers around are still some of our best customers and so if they do well, we will also benefit."

One of the more outspoken businessmen, Ken Alwright, broaching the question very much in the air but up to then left unsaid, commented, "I had hoped for business to pick up soon after the War ended but it's taking much longer than expected. Unfortunately, the IRA's current campaign of violence is not helping. Captain, not wishing to put you on the spot, but can you offer any hope for an early end to their activities?"

"Well, Mr Alwright, as you know I have only recently taken up duty here and so my knowledge is limited as yet. However, the IRA matter has only recently become one in which the military has had much involvement. Up to now we have only come to the aid of the civilian forces when called upon.

"You will understand that I am unable to discuss the security and logistic plans and operations we have and will be putting in place to counter the violence and the threat. Rest assured however, we are taking the matter seriously and will deal with it. It would however be very helpful if we had the active support of the local population or at least some people in the local population.

"By that I mean information and local knowledge. I do not in any way suggest that locals take the law into their own hands to deal with the situation. I would very much hope that the issue would be dealt with as expeditiously and as calmly as possible."

The lawyer, James Canty, who was in the small group during that discussion, intervened when Geoffrey had stopped speaking,

"Your words are well chosen Captain. It is a matter for the security forces alone and the general public should not interfere, apart from supporting them in going about their duty. Frankly, it is above all a political matter and while we are dependent for now on the security services to deal with the problem, it will only be solved finally when the politicians deal with the underlying issues which are festering here in Ireland."

The discussions moved on from there and everyone was pleased to return to more mundane topics such as the local social activities and of course the weather.

Later in the evening he was talking with the local banker, Alastair Montgomery, asking him about opening an account and the transfer of money from his bank account in England. He was joined after a while by his wife, Julia, a vivacious and bright woman, native of Dublin. She was strikingly feminine and while not flirtatious, every man at that party group, apart perhaps from the clergyman, would be capable of describing her attributes days afterwards.

Moreover, she was obviously intelligent and well informed. She was much younger than her husband. He had married later in life, attracted as he was not only by Julia's beauty and her obvious joie de vivre, but probably even more so because she was his confidant.

Julia, introduced herself and quickly took over the conversation, with no antipathy from either her husband or Geoffrey, to her doing so.

"Geoffrey, it's good to see new faces in this small place. No offence to the town or district, one couldn't be in a more beautiful place nor indeed have such wonderful kind neighbours. But we do like to see new faces and hear new voices from time to time. It shows that we are still part of the outside world. With the War's end we had hoped to enter a new age of more freedom and more happiness.

God knows, we and particularly people like you, who served at the Front, deserve at least that."

"Well for me, at least everything is new and the welcome I received has indeed been warm. I mean in the nicest way and not that kind of warmth which certain people out there would have in store for me if they got their way. The strange thing is that for the first time I am in a place with a Janus face—one bright and beautiful the other dark and foreboding."

Their conversation ran on for about 20 minutes before she gently moved on,

"I fear we have been holding you up from meeting with the others. We must excuse ourselves Alastair, and let Geoffrey get to know as many people as he can."

Before moving on she, holding her husband's arm said, "Alastair and I would like to invite you for dinner one night soon if you are free."

Geoffrey, pleased with the invitation was quick to respond, "I would be delighted to accept."

"I will send you a card to remind you."

Turning to her husband she asked, "Alastair, you are not travelling next week-end, are you?"

Getting an all-clear response she turned to Geoffrey, "Saturday okay for you, Geoffrey."

Agreement reached, Geoffrey continued on his round, with an inward spring in his step.

Before he left the party, Reverend Thomas Foster, the Clergyman came up to him to say in a low voice, so the others would not hear, that he would like to see him alone as he had some information which might be useful.

"This is not the place to discuss matters of a non-social nature, Captain. I would welcome an opportunity to meet soon with you to inform you of certain things which I have picked up and might prove to be of interest to you."

"Of course, Reverend Foster. When would be a suitable time for you?"

"As soon as possible. Tomorrow even."

Geoffrey, knowing that the Major would be around in the morning and, expecting that he would stay for lunch, decided it would be best to wait until the late evening.

"I am having visitors tomorrow until perhaps early afternoon. What about say five pm? And where would you like to meet me?"

Somewhat disappointed with the postponement, Reverend Foster replied, "I suppose five pm will be alright. I do not want to go to your barracks or indeed I do not want you to come to my house. Can I ask you to call to the church office discreetly? Perhaps entering around the back. The office is off Castle Road behind the Church. You take the laneway to the left just after the church as you go out of town. The office is on the left about 100 yards along the laneway."

Geoffrey agreed.

Leaving, he thanked Jack Lee and his wife Louise for their hospitality, saying how pleasant the evening was.

Jack smiling came back, "The least I could do to make up somewhat for the maelstrom I brought you into at the club. Anyway, thank Louise, as you can see, she is a far better host than I. You should do a memo to yourself, 'in future accept invitation from Louise and Jack – ignore invitation from Jack only'."

Geoffrey, laughing with the two Lees, responded, "Not at all. What would life be without a bit of controversy? And truthfully, while it was quite heated at the Club for a time, it would be very foolish of me to ignore what was said. I do need to hear these things if I am to understand the totality of feelings in the communities here."

Geoffrey departing, "If invited, either by Louise and Jack or by Jack alone, be warned I will willingly accept both. Goodnight and thanks."

He was quite satisfied by his evening out. For the first time since leaving England he had felt relaxed and even began to believe he possibly enjoyed his posting in Ireland. He was glad to see that these were a more sophisticated group than the golf club set and while their politics was similar, they showed themselves to be much more open minded and logical about the complexities of the situation.

The long days and nights of inaction during the war had given Geoffrey ample time to think of the senselessness of warfare where no side really wins, no matter what the outcome. He saw that in a more perfect world, anger and emotion would be taken out of the differences between nations and replaced by quiet diplomacy either bilaterally, or through another intermediary, where issues could be solved.

Even where the differences were too complex to find a definite agreed way forward, at least they could be part-resolved by concession and a binding promise to return at a later time when hopefully matters would have cooled down sufficiently to come up with a mutually agreed solution.

He had not realised it before coming to Ireland, but he now feared that he was in such a situation and because of the longevity of the enmity between the sides there was no room for compromise or agreement. His job however, did not permit him to engage in finding political solutions to the impasse. Rather it only allowed him to follow orders and seek a military plan of action that would ensure victory against an enemy that was resourceful and growing.

Geoffrey hoped inwardly however, that the politicians would overtake the implementation of that plan and find a democratic way of ending the current crisis.

He was intrigued by the urgency of the Reverend Foster in seeking a meeting with him the next day. He could only guess. It certainly had nothing to do with his non-attendance at church.

He had not seen the inside of a church for many years—although he had silently prayed on many occasions on the battlefield and in the trenches. He thought, *'there must be something of a very secret nature unrelated to my own personal affairs. I have only been in Ireland a short while and know few people, none of an intimate or compromising nature. I wonder if it has to do with information he wishes to pass on. As a clergyman he would have access to a wide variety of people, even perhaps from the Catholic side. If he has that access perhaps, he could be of some help in introducing me to people of interest. Anyway, the more I think of the possibilities the more I am keen to see the reverend gentleman.'*

Recalling his meeting with Julia Montgomery was something entirely different. Not only was she elegant and attractive but her conversation was exhilarating. Her bubbly personality lingered with him and he was eager to meet her again. The dinner invitation would be most welcome. Only after he had thought about her for some minutes did he realise how attracted to her he had become in such a short meeting. He had not expected to meet someone like her outside London. But then he reflected *'she is a married woman.'*

Chapter 15

Meanwhile Geoffrey worked diligently getting to know the town's people and establishing a good relationship with many of them, although most undoubtedly were from the unionist side of the population.

Joe, true to his word, had introduced him to a number of nationalists but while not unfriendly, they would be unlikely to offer much in the way of intelligence on the IRA.

Percival arrived accompanied by a platoon of troops, (a sign indeed, Geoffrey quietly noted, that they truly were in enemy territory). Percival was not a coward; he just left nothing to chance.

Having had brief words with the barracks commander he met with the assembled officers to brief them on the ongoing situation and outline some new plans he was putting in place.

"You all will probably not be aware that a new bill called 'The Restoration of Order in Ireland Act' is being considered by the government. This effect if enacted will mean that the Government has moved from regarding the IRA activities as breaches of the civil law to declaring them to be military in nature. The IRA would be subject to court-martial rather than being tried in civil criminal courts.

"The primary reason for this proposed change, most likely, is that cases of this nature would not get a fair hearing in a court with local juries and so they have to go to non-jury courts. That may be so, but effectively the Act would bring the military into centre stage and consequently we would be engaged more actively in resolving the problem than, as up to now, merely acting as a back-up for the civil authorities.

"In the circumstance, we must re-organise to take up a more front-line position than the one we have adopted to date. First as this district is one of the centres of IRA activity, it has been decided that the barracks here will be reinforced with additional men and equipment. That has already been set in train.

I myself will operate from Kinsale and here. Bandon will be at the locus of that effort. This change of strategy would require each of you present to take on extra responsibilities, which in consultation with Major Stewart will be outlined to you in due course.

"I will not have to emphasise to you all that the new situation will most likely involve us in more direct contact with the local population. That no doubt will have consequences. Many of them are not good. There may be advantages however, in that some locals may be willing to confide in us, rather than the RIC and indeed their recently arrived back-up the so-called 'Black and Tans' who have not been long in earning themselves a poor reputation for improper behaviour.

"By now you will all be aware that Captain Eastbourne has been acting for me as Intelligence Officer in this post. Any information concerning the enemy you receive, no matter how much you might consider it trivial in nature, should be immediately conveyed to him. I place special emphasis on intelligence. In a location where the enemy is all knowledgeable and consequently, we know this gives them a major advantage, particularly when they use guerrilla tactics. The way to level the playing field and hopefully even gain an advantage, is to know what the IRA are doing before they act. That and how we can roundup their leaders, is our task now.

"Finally, I want to emphasise we are basically in hostile territory and maximum precautions should be taken. Hostility by you to the local population should not be shown unless it is necessary. However, when necessary, force should be used, both physically and psychologically."

Later when he met separately with Geoffrey he got straight to the point as Geoffrey had expected.

"Well Captain how have you settled in? I know there has not been much time since you arrived but can you give me your initial overview on our intelligence security here?"

"Yes Sir. I have had no problems settling in here and Major Stewart and the other officers have been most helpful in helping me to do so. As you say I am still finding my feet in the town and I am attempting to seek, from among the people I meet, those who might be helpful in providing useful information for us. As I have had such little time yet that is at an early stage but I am making progress on getting to know those who support us and whether they can provide useful knowledge."

To show that he was not concentrating alone on the easier Unionist side, Geoffrey decided to gild the lily a little in relation to his work on the Nationalist camp. He had met some Catholics after all, including Joe Ryan, and they could be cast on the Nationalist side, so long as the Major would not ask who they were. Even then he assumed that if he mentioned names the Major would not know them, or even care to find out, if Geoffrey said he met them only in passing.

"On the nationalist side I have met only a few, and then only casually in the company of others. But it is an area I must make inroads into, although you will accept, I believe, I will have to work gingerly in relation to getting information from that source.

"You will understand that in the current mood of the country and particularly in this area most of them would not wish to be seen talking alone with the security forces. I will therefore have to spread my net widely in meeting as many diverse groups as possible in the belief that amongst them I will find those, with useful information, who are willing to impart with it. In the circumstances I hope you will agree, Sir, that I have to go to them rather than expecting them to come to me."

Geoffrey, without waiting for the Major to come back, went on to give his report on the internal security of the barracks and on its communications centre. He said that in conjunction with the camp OC the barracks security was tightened by:

- posting more sentries and changing the guard more frequently and not at specific times,
- those outsiders coming into the barracks were only allowed if they possessed security passes,
- all outsiders were searched coming and leaving the barracks.

He also gave a report on the running of the new phone system after its installation, and, knowing that the Major had had to make several calls to his superiors to get it, praised its superior quality and efficiency and said it was a very important addition to the barracks communications network.

Major Percival thanked Geoffrey for his comprehensive report and was obviously impressed by Geoffrey's work so far.

Good report Captain. I knew you would understand what I want and what you have outlined to me is along the lines I had wished you to go.

In relation to the security of the barracks, I am impressed by what you have said about the increases Major Stewart and you have put in place. That is vital. More and more we receive reports of attacks on RIC barracks in the district and I would not be surprised if we were to be attacked, even if that were only a hit and run situation. We must be on the alert at all times and take nothing for granted.

I am also pleased that you also have upped the security in relation to civilian personnel passing through our gates. One cannot be too careful and the IRA is very resourceful. They have eyes and ears everywhere here and so trust very few. Although there are times when one must risk relying on someone you may not quite know in order to get something you need.

As you know I am very keen on information gleaned through contacts. I am happy that you have obviously set about trying to make those contacts and I want you to devote as much time to it as possible. I agree that it will take time and effort to get to those who can provide the type of information we need on the IRA, but it is very worthwhile and it is a strategy on which I place a lot of emphasis.

If we get the type of intelligence, I am seeking it could make the difference in shortening this conflict. If we go on the way we are, the IRA can only get stronger and the task at that stage will have risen exponentially. So, speed and accuracy in relation to acquiring that information is vital."

"I'm also happy that the new telephone system is up and running and working well. I believe you are mainly responsible for having it installed so quickly. The old system was never any good."

Geoffrey could see immediately the Major's absolute dislike of the old system and his desire to replace it.

"Bloody waste of time and indeed I felt a danger to our security. If you cannot rely on a system, then you are better off not having it in the first place. It can let you down at the most vital time. That's not acceptable."

Eager to please the Major and maybe score some more points with him Geoffrey came back; "I agree Sir. The operators told me that the old system was ever giving trouble and they could never rely on getting through."

Deciding that Joe Ryan's suggestion could be added here Geoffrey added;

"Now that we have a very reliable system at base I wonder if the wires connecting us to Cork and the other posts are in good order."

"Good point Captain, I expect they were put up some years ago. I suppose we should have them inspected. We do not have either the manpower or indeed the skill and equipment to do the job. I will ask the Quartermaster in Cork if he can provide that. I will come back on that again. However, if I don't give you an answer in a week, remind me."

"Very well Sir."

Pleased with himself Geoffrey, when along with the Major to inspect the communication hut and while there he took the opportunity to praise Sergeant Turner and his staff for the way they facilitated the installation of the telephone system and the speed with which they picked up the new instructions that went with the more modern equipment.

Chapter 16

Later on the day of the Major's visit Geoffrey left the barracks in plain clothes and travelled around the town in the least frequented areas to avoid meeting people and to pass by as unnoticed as possible—if that was even remotely possible in a small town in West Cork.

As he crossed the footbridge on the south of the town, he wondered what the Reverend would want to meet him so surreptitiously for. He glanced into the river which although still late summer was reasonably quite high and flowing quite swiftly. Up above the town he could see the lush green fields rolling down to the river on either side with tree cover well-spaced along each moss-covered bank. It was an idyllic, peaceful sight and it quite unexpectedly raised his spirits in a way he had not experienced since the years before the War.

He had from his boyhood loved the serenity of the countryside and growing up an only sibling he had spent long hours alone exploring the woods and fishing in the river near his parents' country home. He knew from his knowledge of the river near his home in England that it would most likely have a plentiful supply of both salmon and trout. He hoped he would be able to find a day or two when he could renew his old passion, tie a few flies and see what the salmon were taking here.

Geoffrey wondered what the Reverend was going to tell him. He did not appear to be someone who would arrange this type of meeting for a frivolous reason. He could see no connection between himself and the clergyman that would necessitate a secret meeting such as that in which they were about to engage. He was nevertheless intrigued by the furtive way in which he had asked him to meet. Geoffrey thought.

'It's rather strange that he did not tell me what the nature of the meeting was and what the subject matter would be. I am certain it is not a church matter—how could it be? I do not even belong to his branch of Protestantism. I wonder

if it's in relation to security matters. But what would a clergyman know or have anything to do with that?'

He wondered how he would approach the meeting. *'Well best to hear first what the Reverend has to say. I expect it will entail some trivial matter or some hearsay. How should I react to that? I want to keep him on my side. No need to belittle what he says. Just listen and say I will look into it. Anyway, if nothing else perhaps my one-on-one conversation with him will give me an opportunity to get a better understanding of the local population and the day-to-day issues that are of primary concern to most people.'*

Geoffrey came the long way around, skirting the town and entered the laneway from the southern end. He arrived at the small building detached from the church and found the side door open as he had been told. The Reverend Thomas Foster was at his desk writing when Geoffrey entered. He rose and came to meet him, gesturing to him to sit on an armchair in the corner of the room while the reverend sat on Queen Anne style couch.

"Thank you for coming, Captain." Rev. Foster did not waste any time in preliminary conversation but went straight to the heart of why he had asked the captain to meet him alone and in secret.

"Forgive me for asking to see you at such short notice. I know you have many things to do and your time is precious but I hope the information I have will be of some use in helping to end the appalling violence of the IRA."

Geoffrey's ears pricked up. He was immediately invigorated by the crispness of the tone and the authority which the voice conveyed.

"On the contrary, I am pleased to hear what you have to say. Indeed, only that I had to be present in the barracks for a visit of a senior officer today I would have met with you earlier."

"What I am about to tell you I must ask beforehand that you treat it as highly confidential. First, I want to keep my informant totally anonymous. That person, you will understand, is from the Nationalist/Catholic side and would be in grave danger if it was found out that he/she was informing on her neighbours.

"Next for reasons of my own standing in the wider community, and of course my personal security, I would not want it to be known that I am an informer for the security services. Lastly, while you may wish to share the information with the RIC. I would also ask that they also should not know of the source of this information. You may be surprised at this last request, but, while I have no proof, it is believed that there are elements within that force that cannot be fully trusted in relation to the current hostilities."

Geoffrey, absorbing what he had just heard, delayed for some seconds before responding. He had to give the clergyman his sought-after guarantee which he would willingly agree to himself. Could he trust his colleagues to uphold his guarantee? He was not convinced and moreover, he was almost certain that Percival would not be bound by Geoffrey's word to the clergyman.

He had seen too much in the Great War to be naive to the whims, vagaries and downright carelessness of the brass in relation to promises made or the safety of others. Furthermore, those promises made by underlings were of as nothing, to be swept aside if need be, in the great scheme of things.

Geoffrey, on the other hand, was not prepared to give his word of honour if he believed that it might not be kept. He made up his mind.

"Reverend Foster, what you ask, I would most willing give. I expect the information you intend to give me is of importance and useful to our cause. If so, it could aid our advances against the IRA and be extremely welcome. However, I must be honest with you, if I were to give all of what you intend to tell me to my superiors, I could not be sure of what they would do with that knowledge, even if I had told them that I gave my word to you."

Rev. Foster was taken aback by Geoffrey's stark but honest admission that they could not guarantee the anonymity of either himself or his informant.

"Good Lord, Captain, what do you expect of me? I simply cannot give you the information I have unless I am sure the source of that information will be secret. That person's life would be in jeopardy if it were discovered that he/she had informed on the IRA. I might find it very difficult to continue here as a clergyman if my name was included. Frankly, as well, I believe I too would be at risk."

"Rev. Foster I am telling you what might happen because you asked me for my word. I cannot give that word without being honest as to its value."

Geoffrey was not going to change his strongly held commitment to his word of honour. He decided however, to offer the clergyman an alternative to avoid the necessity of guarantees.

"Reverend Foster, I fully understand your predicament and fully agree that you have an insurmountable problem in giving me this information. If you agree, I could make a suggestion which would release you from asking for the guarantee and me from giving my word."

The clergyman, still shocked by the dilemma he faced, slowly awakening to the fact that he might be offered a way out responded,

"Yes, I would be very interested in any way you can suggest that might solve my dilemma."

"Could I suggest that instead of you giving me the information personally, you were to convey it to me anonymously? For instance, by a note. You could hide any hint of where the information came from and who the sender was by ensuring there were no tell-tale marks, instances, status of sender, connections with informants, or other indications on the note which could lead the reader to you or the informant. That of course would include some means of hiding your own handwriting. You could send the note to me in the barracks."

Rev Foster thought about this for a little while.

"Yes, I could do that, but you might miss some details in the information that I might be able to convey by speaking directly to you. You might for instance wish to ask questions of the information which might help expand its value."

"You make a good point there, Rev Foster. What I can suggest then is that we speak and you tell me what you can and after questions and answers are complete, we forget we ever met here. Meanwhile you write out the information and send it to me anonymously. In that way, you and your informant will have the security of being unknown."

Reverend Foster agreed: "I admire your integrity and honesty Captain. That shows that I was right in coming to you with my knowledge. I have had it for a little time now but I was reluctant to part with it because of a lack of trust in those I might have revealed my information to.

"Because of your recent arrival here directly from England I knew you to be untainted by the local scene and additionally having met you, even only once at the Lee home I judged you to be a person of trust. In my profession I meet a good many people of all sorts and sizes and I have learned over many years how to judge people.

"What you say makes sense and covers the difficult situation we find ourselves in. As a clergyman let me say that what you propose, even if it offends against the strict rules of military discipline and protocol, is both practically and morally correct. You will get what you need and simultaneously I will be able to convey what I believe to be important information to the security forces."

"Good, I agree, I have seen too much blood needlessly spilt and too many careless instructions given, by people in authority with little regard for those for whom they were responsible.

"Now, can you outline the information you have in summary form first and then we can go over it more minutely to ensure I have the total picture. Can I just say before we begin that you will have to make some allowances for my newness here and my lack of knowledge both in regard to the personalities you might mention and the geography of the areas you might cover?"

"Alright, the information I have come to me by a trusted servant from the Catholic side, whose family I had helped when the bread-winner died. She said she had been in the company of a number of other women from her own background who had talked openly about the activities of the IRA. One in particular is related to one of those they refer to 'the volunteers'. This particular lady was concerned for this young man as he was involved in a number of attacks on RIC barracks in the district and spent nights away on manoeuvres with the so-called "Column".

She heard the woman say that she was particularly worried because he had overheard him mention to one of his friends that the Column leader was planning an attack on a bigger target within the coming weeks. The woman said he had not been informed as to what that target was and would not be told until much near the time.

When training commenced as it always did before such an attack, he would then be told so that he should acquaint himself with the target and its surrounding hinterland to ensure cover and withdrawal. My contact agreed to inform me if she heard more. She is quite often in that group and the conversation amongst them is free and easy as they believe they all are avid supporters of the IRA.

She also said that she overheard this young man saying that the IRA had contacts everywhere, in all public service offices and even in the RIC Barracks in town.

"The name of the young 'volunteer' is Michael Joyce and he lives at 7 Hill Street."

"Thank you for that information, Reverend. Yes, it is very useful. What you say is pretty clear but can I ask a few questions arising from what you have outlined? Did she say where he was active? —what district? Were there any names of the leader of the Column or its officers?

"Did she say where they might be located? or did she say if they had any one location? Were there any mention of safe houses or people who would offer cover or active support for this group? Anything else you can remember?"

"The only concrete thing I can add in that regard is that he appears to be active in this district because he shows he knows the territory they cover very intimately."

Geoffrey thought for some minutes about what he had just heard before responding,

"Was any mention of IRA leaders, names where they lived, jobs they might be doing in ordinary life, family connections, etc.?"

"No, she did not give me anything on that."

"Was there any hint of the type of target the IRA might be considering?"

"No, the only thing she said about that was that it would be a major one—much bigger than usual."

"In relation to contacts the IRA has in the public services, did she mention any specific names of people or even any institution in this regard?"

"Again, the answer I'm afraid is no."

"And in relation to leaks within the RIC?"

"No, again."

Reverend Foster was beginning to feel inadequate now, realising the gaps in his information as Geoffrey asked him the obvious questions, answers to which could have been of prime importance. He therefore added,

"However, my discussion with her was only preliminary and I did not have time to consider what she told me at that time. If you wish, I can enquire again and perhaps she can tell me more, or even find out through the same source."

Geoffrey, understanding how the clergyman felt, thanked him, saying the information as far as it went was very useful.

"Of itself it gives pointers to a large-scale pending attack, which will put us on our guard. It would of course be vital to discover where this attack will take place and other details such as the date and timing, how many men will be involved, arms they have, etc.

"Also, if you can get further information on IRA personnel, locations they are billeted in or frequent, names and institutions where the IRA have contacts, the source of information leakage in the RIC, or anything of this nature."

Reverend Foster, thinking about this, felt he had no option but to try, although he was not a little apprehensive about how much more effective, he could be by going further in the matter. Also, it would mean involving his maid in spying on her neighbours. While he wanted to assist as much as possible to defeat the IRA, he was not happy about seeking his maid's help in doing so.

She was not as committed as him and moreover, he knew he was putting her life at risk. He had no illusions about the ferocity of the IRA and how they would react to a traitor in their midst. But he had committed himself,

"Yes, I will attempt to get further information along the lines you suggest. This may not be easy though. My informant offered the information I gave you by way of conversation and was not aware that I would pass it on to the security forces. I work with a great deal of local people, even outside my own community, in giving advice and comfort where I can. Some of the locals consequently trust me and their conversation around me is quite open. I would not be giving you this information had I not felt a moral duty to do so. I am however, conflicted in that I also want to be fully trusted by the population as a whole and would want to earn that trust."

Geoffrey, understanding the dilemma in which the clergyman found himself, attempted to work around the problem by suggesting that he speak to his informant matter of factly in an informal way and attempt to steer the conversation in a direction where he would get the information he sought.

"I know it will not be easy Rev Foster but it is exceedingly important and could save many lives. I agree you will have to treat the situation very gingerly so as not to scare off your informant. If it would help, I am prepared to find some money to give your informant. I will let you be the judge of how you will approach the problem. Let me know however, if you need assistance or advice."

"I will do what I can. I will make no promises, but I will try."

"Thank you, Rev. Foster. What you are doing is very important and will hopefully help in ending these current attacks. Can I ask one more thing before I leave? In your report, please omit the name of the 'IRA Volunteer'. For obvious reasons I would prefer to have him in the wind for now until we get more information. If he is on file, some idiot might have him arrested and that would prevent us from getting to the detail we most need."

They agreed to meet again at the end of the week in the same place at the same time. If the clergyman had picked up additional useful information before that, he would alert the captain immediately.

Geoffrey walked back to the barracks deep in thought. On the one hand he was most pleased with his meeting. He had received information on the IRA from a most unsuspected source, without his having to seek out an informant to get it. On the other hand, however, it had large gaps and it would not be of real value unless he could fill in at least some of those gaps.

He would as planned wait for the 'anonymous note' before alerting the Major Percival and he hoped he would be allowed to take it on from there himself. He trusted that nothing would happen before the note would arrive. At least that is what the information conveyed.

Foster's warnings about IRA contact in the public services were worrying—mail? telegraph? post office? transport? More concerning still was the news that the RIC had a mole. However, had not the Major alluded to that also.

He has to remember that when he meets them, which has been arranged for the next day.

Chapter 17

Next morning, he learns that the IRA had attacked a fairly well fortified RIC barracks in the western region, killed two policemen and captured a machine gun, a number of rifles, mills bombs and a large quantity of ammunition. The barracks had been burned. There were no known casualties among the IRA.

Geoffrey was deep in thought over his breakfast. While he did not believe that the attack was the one mentioned by the informant, perhaps too small in comparison to the 'spectacular' he was told, additionally it was probably outside the range of the 'Column' the young volunteer was speaking of.

He consequently was anxious to receive the promised note as quickly as promised so that at least he could alert his superiors to the possibility of an upcoming attack.

After breakfast, he went to the communications hut to find out if there was more information. While there he discovered that apart from that attack on the RIC barracks an evening patrol had also been attacked on the borders of Kerry but no casualties were reported as yet.

It was obvious that, as expected, the IRA were getting more organised and consequently it could be expected that these attacks would increase both in regularity and intensity. In those circumstances therefore he firmly believed he needed the additional intelligence quickly and indeed he would have to increase his own efforts to find other sources that might be able to provide it. He wondered if he was up to the task.

Before leaving he told Sergeant Turner to alert him if any new material came in concerning the IRA attacks.

He spent the rest of the morning meeting with Major Stewart reassessing the security of the barracks, although Geoffrey, as he had previously decided, did not tell his superior of the new threat.

He used his time to learn the barracks commander's assessment of the contacts they had with the locals and their use from a logistic viewpoint. While the overview was worthwhile and would make Geoffrey's contact work easier, he did not immediately see any real prospect amongst those mentioned from whom he could perhaps get the information which would be useful for his purpose.

At lunch in the officer's mess with some of his colleagues, he sought further local knowledge and brought himself up to date on events in the area.

After lunch he strolled into the town, casually again taking note of the geography of the place and the names of the streets he passed. He wanted to be able to clearly identify the route he had taken from an ordinance map when he returned to camp. He proposed to himself that he would continue this routine of orientation over the next week at least until such time as he knew the town and all its streets and alleyways intimately.

He wanted to be in a position if needed to move quickly in the dark from A to B in the town, by the shortest possible route, without having to look at the street signs. Additionally, he would endeavour to find out where certain key figures had their businesses and their homes.

He spoke to some of the people he had already met and through them was introduced to other townsfolk, most of them other businesspeople. While these meetings were of little practical benefit, apart from expanding his circle of acquaintances, they did allow him to merge in somewhat with the local scene. He thought,

'The sooner I become part of the comings and goings of the town and am not seen as just a remote soldier in a staff car or Crosley tender, the more I will blend in.'

He noted however, in passing that his contacts were predominantly Unionist and that the Nationalist community were not anxious to meet with him, although Joe Ryan had been helpful in his introductions. While he regretted this, he was not surprised and it only confirmed what he had expected. It became clear that he would have to find a more subtle means of meeting with that side of the community. He decided that he would first have to continue to rely on Joe Ryan to introduce him to other nationalists who were not hesitant to meet him.

He reflected that Joe was unusual in the town, in that while he came from the Catholic/Nationalist side and appeared to be accepted as one of them, he had a good relationship with many Protestant/Unionists also. He put this down to his family background in the town, his good-humoured personality and his business in the town which gave employment mainly to people from his own side (he had one Unionist employee who had a security pass for the barracks). Above all of this he had learned through one of his new contacts that Joe was a very good neighbour and had helped a number of people in the town who had bereavements in the family, or who had fallen on hard times.

Chapter 18

Geoffrey sent a message through Tom Good, the hotel owner that he would like to meet with Joe Ryan if he was available that evening in the hotel bar.

When he walked into the bar later that evening, Joe was already there drinking a medium Murphy. He was smoking a cigarette, a habit he had picked up during the dreadful hours in the trenches. He had, however, changed his brand of cigarette from Woodbines, replacing the cheaper brand with the dearer but larger and better packed Gold Flake. The small transition was not only because he could now afford that luxury, but subconsciously it was another active attempt to remove himself as far as possible from that awful time.

"Hello Joe, good of you to show up at such short notice. Let me buy you a drink."

"No need Geoffrey, I have just got this and I have ordered your drink—you said you liked an Allmans, but change the order if you prefer, Eddie hasn't poured it yet."

"That's great thanks. Eddie, can you give some water on the side with the Allmans please."

"Coming up, Sir."

Geoffrey, feeling that he knew Joe well enough and not wishing to beat about the bush came straight to the point.

"Joe, I need a favour. Can you introduce me to some more people from the Catholic/Nationalist side in the town? As you know I've been attempting to get to know the local scene and while I have met and even been entertained by some people from the Protestant community, I have met very few from your side mainly through you. Of course, frankly it's a bit of a minefield if you don't mind me saying so. How does one, coming into a place like this for the first time, decide which is which? Unless of course when one mentions religion or politics, subjects by the way in which I personally have little interest."

"Well Geoffrey, first, everyone here will not be confused as to where you come from and second, all will presuppose they not only know your politics but also your religion. So, on one hand that is most definitely a plus but on the other it is most definitely not.

"Of course, I will introduce you to some more of the Papes. I suggest that you continue to meet the more moderate ones first. That will give you an opportunity to come to terms with some of their grievances without their voices being raised. You will be aware that some of the security forces have been anything but friendly to the local nationalist population. You could say they're the best Recruiting Sergeant the IRA could have. Beware however, of some of the hotheads; you will appear to them as a red rag to a bull."

"Thanks Joe, I have heard of some of the stories about the behaviour of the Black and Tans and I accept what you say. It does us no good indeed. You know from your own experience that while there are those in the army who act no better than the Black and Tans and indeed that group consists of former army personnel.

"I am totally opposed to any such activity. I do not believe in torture or coercion. In my opinion the information obtained from such treatment is for the most part unreliable or exaggerated. Some people under pressure will tell you anything you want to hear. Others will have stories prepared to give you certain truths but not the whole truth.

"Overall, it only encourages the other side to be as ruthless as you and in the situation we find ourselves here in Ireland, where we appear to be taking on the majority population, it only alienates those who might be on your side, or at best be neutral in the conflict."

"I agree with what you say Geoffrey. Unfortunately, I believe your former colleagues in arms who have recently arrived on the scene to act as a stand-alone Gendarmerie have shown signs of taking the bad behaviour to an even higher level. The very fact that their brief is a 'counter-insurgency' one is telling in itself. I fear it cannot end but in tears."

"I regret, I have to agree. We in the regular military see the development as a recipe for disaster and unless we can get to grips with the situation ourselves before these Auxiliaries can alienate the security forces even further from the public. They will undo some of the work of the more moderate souls in the military, who, I think you will accept would prefer to win hearts and minds rather than coerce people into accepting the status quo."

"I am pleased that you have obviously taken the time to read yourself into the situation here. So many of your colleagues have not. Here's someone over there you should talk to and he also fits into the category that you were seeking to get to know. You will recall you met him a few months backs at the card game and you have seen him since on more than one occasion. However, you probably have had no one to one conversation with him and I believe you would profit from that.

"John, you remember Geoffrey Eastbourne. Like me, he served for some years at the Front and so we have a number of common memories. Geoffrey, this is my good friend and mentor John Walsh. John is a businessman in town and there is nothing about the place or the people here that he doesn't know."

John Walsh, an older man, who had been a staunch supporter of the Irish Parliamentary Party before it was soundly defeated by Sinn Fein in the 1918 General Election, was a moderate Nationalist, who had sought Home Rule away from the Westminster Parliament. He believed strongly in democracy and wanted the 'Irish Question' solved by democratic means only.

He did not support IRA violence. But then again, he would not take the British side against the IRA. While he was utterly against the 1916 Rising in Dublin, as needless, futile and bloody, he was appalled by the brutality of the executions that followed. Now the activities of the security forces, particularly the Black and Tans and lately the Auxiliaries left him and others like him in a dilemma. The recent brutish behaviour of the Essex troops was also causing concern in the town.

He, like many Nationalists, was annoyed by the British Government's dalliance in implementing the 1914 Home Rule Act and their unwillingness to take on what he saw was Unionist intransigence. He firmly believed that their inability to follow through on what was agreed, like their historic carelessness when it came to Ireland, was the precursor to all of what happened subsequently in Ireland.

He was above all an amiable and generous man and would not blame any individual for the mess that he could see unfolding in front of him, even if that man was an English officer in the British security forces. He greeted him as a friend of Joe Ryan's, a young man he had encouraged and in whom he saw much prospect for the future.

"Captain, pleased to meet you again. I hope you are settling in here well. You have come at an awkward time in our history, I fear. Yet from what I have heard you are no stranger to difficult times. It would perhaps have been far easier and I dare say very much deserved if you had been sent to a more peaceful place. Still hopefully the politicians on both sides can resolve the matter outstanding and secure a just peace which we all so badly need, particularly people like you and Joe who have, God knows, already been to hell and back."

"It is good to meet you, Sir. Joe has spoken highly of you. I am glad to have the opportunity of meeting you again. I could not agree more with the sentiments you have just expressed. As soldiers, we are sent into the mouth of the lion without any say in why or when. In that capacity we can only hope that occasion will be far into the future and that when we arrive at the lion's den the lion will not be hungry. Those of us, who have already experienced the traumas of battle and are sane, would far prefer if the powers that be had resolved the dispute with the lion, so that both he and we would accept a truce and avoid any confrontation."

Joe Ryan, pleased with the opening of the meeting, came into the conversation at that stage to send the exchange down a more pleasant path.

"Geoffrey, like the rest of us from that awful Front, would like to spend some time relaxing in a lush countryside enjoying the pleasures of normal living for a time which was denied us for some years. Geoffrey is a keen fisherman, both trout and salmon, and I have told him that the countryside and the river around here would afford him many an hour of pleasure."

John Walsh, having indicated where he stood, was also pleased to move on to more relaxed conversation and took up the sprat, as it were, of the opening Joe offered.

"Indeed, there are few places better for fishing than around here. I spend as many hours on the river as I can. I find it relaxes me and gives me the time to sort out the issues that sometimes arise or even to drift off in absent thought. My preference is fly-fishing and I fish for trout. It is much more relaxing and requires little effort. I leave the salmon to the young fellas. They need to expend their energy. I have to conserve mine at my age."

Geoffrey, warming to both the lighter change in the conversation and subject matter, relaxed, "Most certainly, Sir, it does help to slow one down and contemplate the finer things in life. I spent many happy hours in my childhood and into my late youth fishing along the river that ran through my parents' home. I am equally happy fishing for trout or salmon. I agree however, that trout fishing is much more relaxed and certainly it is the sport to opt for, if one wants time to contemplate. Salmon fishing requires a great deal more concentration and if you hook a big fish it can take up to an hour of play, dragging you through water and bush before you land it. Exhausting but exhilarating. Are there big trout in this river, Sir? What type do you get here?"

"My name is John, Geoffrey. His Majesty has not deemed it opportune to give me my obviously most deserved knighthood and I do not expect it to arrive now. Yes, I've got trout up to three and four pounds from the river and there have been higher weights. The usual is around one pound. Of course, you will get all sorts but we put them back if they are less than a half to three quarters of a pound.

"You will get both brown and rainbow trout in this river, mainly brown. However, if you go down nearer the sea where the rivers are tidal you can fish for white trout. There is one excellent stretch on the Argideen which runs into Timoleague, where I fish often. The trout there are magnificent and they play like salmon."

"Thank you, John. I have never fished for white trout but I have eaten them. They taste delicious. Do you require different tackle for them?"

"Well yes, a stronger rod would be preferable and obviously a line that would have a much higher breaking strength. They are much bigger fish than river trout and can easily reach ten pounds weight. They fight like salmon and the sport in landing one is a joy – after you have landed the fish, of course. As you know when cooked they taste different to river trout and are pink."

Joe, pleased with the way the conversation was going, wanted to help it along,

"I can see the two of you have a passion in common. Me, having been born into a tradesman's cottage instead of a mansion I had to do with catching fish primarily for food. Instead of fly fishing I fished with a worm or a minnow, newly dug out of the ground or caught in a stream. The rod I used was a bamboo, filched out of the local Lord's estate. The line was cheap plain brown cotton, unwaxed and gut. The hook was a single half inch, three for a halfpenny. I could never afford boots. I took my shoes off and rolled up my trousers.

"I fished mainly in private parts of the river where the fishing was better, preserved stretches for the landed gentry, when the bailiffs were not looking and never left the river until I had enough trout to feed the family for the day. If I caught more than we needed, which happened often enough, I would give them to the neighbours who were poorer than we were.

"Occasionally when the river was calm and the light allowed, I would use a three hook and stroke-haul fish from the bridge downstream where I could not be seen. In those days I always justified my actions by my belief that the river was my property anyway, taken from my family by the Anglos years before. I suppose I should add I do not fish like that anymore."

They both looked at him, not knowing immediately how to take this admission of flagrant intrusion into the gentile world. Finally, John Walsh, seeing the glint in Joe's eye said, "Joe you certainly always have a way of bringing us all down to earth. Yours of course was a different type of fishing, and might I say, a much more authentic and practical type, you fished for food rather than sport. But I dare say you enjoyed it as much and possibly more, than those of now who are fully equipped and properly clothed for it."

Joe smiling, "Ah, sure John don't you know what they say: that the apple that drops from the stranger's tree is sweeter than that from your own garden. That's provided that it drops into your lap rather than on your head like Newton."

Geoffrey now understanding the humour as well as the pathos in the conversation, entered into it, "I suppose in that respect I was rather deprived. Everything was handed to me on a plate and I never had the pleasure of expressing the wildness and enthusiasm of youth in going outside the strict bounds of privilege."

"Geoffrey, God knows we did come from two separate worlds, but we were soon enough to find out how dependent on one another we really are during what our friends the Yanks call that 'Goddamn Awful War'."

John intervening; "Let me buy you both another round to drink to that."

And so, the night moved on in light banter and Geoffrey was introduced to others from the Nationalist, mainly business and professional, side.

Chapter 19

Joe Ryan cycled out the country heading towards the sea and his usual hour swim in the ocean he so much enjoyed since his early youth. Cutting short his time at the beach he returned taking a detour to a remote farmhouse off a side road. The evening was still very bright and the countryside was in its best early autumnal colour. He wondered if he should buy a house in the country instead of town.

His mother, whom he lived with still, would of course not change her home for anything no matter how good. Had he not attempted to persuade her to move to a much bigger and finer house in the town when it recently became available? She had admonished him for even suggesting it, as if he had been asking her to move to a hovel.

"In the name of all that is good and holy, why should I move to another house at this stage of my life when I have so many memories here in my own place. Do you think for one moment I would leave your father behind and your brothers Jimmy and Patrick? No son, I will only be moved from my little home when the Lord sends for me and I leave feet first and elevated."

Joe settled for extending the current home by adding a back portion which allowed for the kitchen to be expanded and a downstairs toilet and a proper bathroom upstairs and small studio for himself overlooking the rear garden. He ensured that the house had all modern electrical equipment including heaters. He also added a small workshop at the back of the house where he tinkered in his spare time with radios and electrical equipment. Still, he was thinking of the future and marriage and where would he live then.

Travelling up the long laneway to the farmhouse Joe wondered why Sean Hales had asked to meet outside their normal timing and arrangements. He was conscious of the loneliness of the place and the fact that even halfway up the laneway there was no sign of a building. Additionally, nobody lived nearby, as he could see from the top of the small hill on which he now stood. It would be impossible for anyone to get within a half of a mile without being seen during the daylight. At night one would have to know the layout of the place to sneak up on it and he felt few would have that information, particularly the security forces.

Just over the hill he could see the farmhouse nestling in a small depression and a woman in the yard feeding the hens. As he passed a large field adjacent to the house, he noticed large walls and fences. At the gateway entrance he could see a large bull in the field, which came charging at him as he passed. Luckily there was a strong gate.

The lady had disappeared when he arrived and Sean Hales appeared at the doorway to the house.

"Joe, thanks for coming here at short notice. I would not have called you were it not for the way things are moving. Much has happened in the past month or so and we have to put adjustments in place to try and counteract them.

"You have been of immense help in advising us of some of the developments and particularly on the information that Percival is making greater efforts to find out not only who we are but also to discover our locations and even our plans of action. I fear there are people within our community who either by bribery or coercion would give us away.

"The Brits are considering upping the ante by introducing military court-marshals rather than civilian courts. This is a very clear signal that they are truly at war with us. So be it. There should now be no doubt in anybody's mind that this is a war of independence. We have taken up the challenge and we are not backing down.

"We also appreciate the early warning on the arrival of the Auxiliaries. We had not expected that and having assessed the opposition they could give us we feel they could be a dangerous force. You have told us that while they are officially part of the RIC, they neither take instructions from the RIC hierarchy nor indeed advise them of some of their operations. We have confirmed that through our contacts in the RIC.

"As former army officers from the Great War they obviously will be highly trained and experienced. Our lads are an extremely poor match for them one to one. It would be fair to say they possibly could out-match us in every way of war. They can out-gun us, they can out-shoot us, and they can out think us in matters of manoeuvres. In fact, there are few areas where we can even hope to be superior and we must use those positions to their full potential.

"The most obvious advantages we have are our vastly superior knowledge of the countryside, our support from the majority nationalist community and our ability to strike them when they least expect it. These advantages are not absolute. If they acquire intelligence on us in either of these areas, our chances of success will be greatly diminished. If they can get intelligence on any two of them, we could be badly damaged.

"Already, within a very short time they have set about harassing the neighbourhood near where they are based and the people in our community are very fearful of them. They have as you know already captured a few of our lads and tortured them before killing them. As you have told us their mandate has been extended to defeat us by any means and have no doubt that will include ignoring every aspect of the law.

"The fear felt by our community might extend in time to lack of cooperation with us and in certain cases to a leakage of information about us. We cannot ignore this and must do all in our power as quickly as possible to counteract their terrorist tactics. They must not only be forced to fear us, but the community must be aware of their fear.

"This will mean we will have to act quickly and very forcefully to show them we are a force to be reckoned with. We've got to remove them from the countryside and confine them to their barracks most of the time. This as you know, better than I from your own experiences, will not be easy. We need to hit them hard, preferably when they think they are safe, and inflict a severe reversal on them. They have shown no mercy to our people when they captured them and we will have no compunction in treating them in a similar fashion.

"What we do not have when it comes to the Auxiliaries is even the remotest inside intelligence on them. Because they effectively run their own show and are in their own barracks, unlike the Black and Tans, we cannot get an agent inside. Consequently, we are currently in the dark when it comes to their activities and they are smart enough to vary their routines to render useless, or near useless, any outside surveillance we might have on them.

"As I mentioned briefly already, my fear, shared by Mick Collins is that while we are blind as to their movements, they will no doubt in time, unless we stop them, find a leak in our system and destroy parts of our structure. That would not only reduce our capacity to carry on the struggle, but it would also make us much more cautious and unsure of our own organisation.

"That is the reason I wanted to talk to you about the issue. I know you will have no connection with them and anyway they're based in a different town, but if anyone can see a way to get around our blind spot, I believe it would be you. Can you come up with anything or any strategy that might help us?"

"Hmmm, yes, I can see the predicament you are facing. In fact, when I told you about them some weeks ago, I was already concerned about them. Between them they will have enormous experience and, as I realised at the time and it has since been confirmed, they are ruthless. They will leave nothing between them and their goal. They will be convinced of their own overwhelming superiority in all aspects of war and they will set out to prove it.

"Remember they are all from the officer class and so feel far superior to the rank and file. They will see the Volunteers as a civilian rabble and have no fear of them. They will have already gathered that they are in enemy territory and will not tempt fate. In the towns they will feel confident and attempt to intimidate the populations into fearing them or aiding them. I expect they will not trust anyone, even those from the Unionist population.

"When they venture out, I expect they will use caution and travel in company, or at least platoon, formation in Tenders. It can be expected that they will have a scout car ahead to check out the route before the main group arrives and any unusual activity will be checked out before they commit themselves. Any male they meet en route will be given rough treatment and pumped for information. I believe that, with no witnesses around they will kill anyone they remotely believe to be IRA members unless they feel they can get more out of them by keeping them alive.

"Most of them joined this force as they see it as a means of earning money fast. They will have returned from the War and, having been disbanded, many of them will have been unable to find a job. The British Government is paying them like mercenaries. They earn on average twice as much as they would as officers in the British Army and they get other allowances on top of that. Most will feel that the job will last not more than a year or two and by that time will have put aside enough to give them a start back in England.

"I fear that what I am saying is very gloomy, but I suspect you know most of what I have said already. In order to deal with the situation, however, you must confront the facts and the dangers you face. On the other hand, some of what I have said could prove to be of some use to us if we use it wisely.

"First their superiority in war will make them overconfident and if we are prepared properly, we can use this against them. Second, they are used to facing the enemy directly in front and so it will take them time to find ways around our guerrilla tactics.

"Third, they will be shunned even by the Unionists who will be reluctant to deal with them for fear either they themselves will be mistreated or in some cases that the Nationalists will turn on them in the future if they are seen to be aiding and abetting these thugs.

"Fourth, I do know that the army has little time for them and will not go out of their way to include them in anything they are doing – that includes sharing intelligence. I know they propose to provide them with only the most basic information. Fifth, their reluctance to work with even their own erstwhile colleagues in the RIC and even the Black and Tans can be expected to be reciprocated.

"Finally, I believe their strategy will include variations in movement that is, when they move out of the towns they will do so in bigger numbers and use different routes each time. However, after a short time, when they become more complacent and secure in their position, they will tend to adopt certain stretches of roadway that they feel will lead them past possible targets or/and where they feel they can confidently defend themselves against attack."

"I agree with your assessment that the longer they are allowed to consolidate their position here, the more difficult it will be to confine them to the towns. The IRA has not only to act fast, but wisely."

"Joe, Maith an Fear Thu, I knew I would get a wise readout of the situation from you. Unfortunately, we have very few in our ranks who understand the enemy's tactics as you do and certainly only a small number who could suggest ways of countering these tactics.

"What you say makes sense, and furthermore gives me some hope that we can overcome the threat these guys present. It will take a great deal of planning and the training of our volunteers is vital. We have already begun our training camps and are fortunate to have Tom Barry as the instructor. He is a hard task master but the results are very impressive.

"I can see that we may have to confront them in a more open place than what we would have wished, unless we can get some inside information on their planned movements. Do you see any way that could be obtained?"

"Very difficult. However, let me think about it. I will try to come up with some way to get at their planned activities, if not directly, which would seem most unlikely, then indirectly."

Sean Hales said the IRA was very concerned about the number of informants who were known to be feeding the security forces with information on them. Most of these were from the Unionist community and the information related mainly to suspicion about the activities of their neighbours. However, what they were most concerned about was leakage of information, most inadvertently but some purposely, by Catholics who had much more solid information about IRA members and their activities.

After some discussion on the increase in military heavily armed patrols and the increased search for Volunteer members, particularly its leaders and the possibility of getting additional intelligence on security forces activities, they each went away in separate directions, both on bicycles.

Joe had not been seen by those in the farmhouse and they did not have his name. Sean Hales had made sure of this beforehand in order to protect Joe's security as he had promised. Apropos the informants mentioned earlier by Sean, Joe did not raise the problem he was beginning to have in the town where some of the local IRA sympathisers had already shown their resentment towards him when he came back from the War. A few others were jealous of his success. He was aware that these were attempting to make trouble for him with the local IRA Volunteers from the town.

Cycling home, ensuring that he took a circuitous route, which would bring him back to his normal route from the sea, he thought about the problem of finding information on the Auxiliaries and he wondered could he find a solution. *Perhaps.*

Chapter 20

Geoffrey had given the note, he had just received as agreed from Reverend Foster, to Major Percival. From the paucity of hard detail in the note Percival was sceptical about its content. He discussed it with Geoffrey, who suggested keeping an open mind on the material and hoping either that the anonymous informant would come back with additional intelligence or that they might be able to add value to it themselves.

Major Percival thought about this for a while, before coming back,

"The question is whether this was written by someone who just has a desire to get involved, or someone who has genuine information, or indeed is it the IRA attempting to lead us in a certain direction. Until we know more, we must not place too much trust in it, while at the same time we must bear in mind the information regarding the imminent attack on a large target.

"You should inform the RIC and even the Auxiliaries as quickly as possible about that aspect of the note. They need to be on the alert in case there is any semblance of truth in the message. We here have already bolstered our security and we will further increase our vigilance on our patrols.

"With regard to the information on IRA contacts within the public services we are already aware that such a situation is not only possible but unfortunately most probable. I can tell you that measures have been put in place and traps have been laid to root out these agents.

"The information that the IRA has an agent or agents in the RIC is more disturbing. Unfortunately, this confirms what I suspect already. When we spoke before about your work here, I instructed you to be somewhat circumspect in what you told the RIC. This reinforces that message. I have in mind setting a trap to attempt to weed out any informant in the RIC here. That would involve feeding them information and observing if that is conveyed to the IRA. This will take some time and planning, in that I must do it so that the circle of people in the

RIC receiving the information will be limited and the culprit, if there is one, can be more easily identified.

"The information about the RIC informant is the one element in the note that would appear to suggest that it did not come from the IRA. What would they have to gain from telling us this? Unless of course they have no agent there and they are attempting to sow confusion in our ranks.

"We must remain sceptical but at the same time alert. Hopefully we will get more useful information."

Geoffrey, somewhat taken aback by the Major's scepticism, was momentarily concerned that he had withheld vital information from him. However, as he thought more about it he felt he had done the right thing. Knowing that it was an authentic message would not have changed the situation much. The one addition was the name of the Volunteer and he was certain he had done the right thing by getting the Reverend Foster to drop that from the note.

"I agree with your summation, Sir. I will keep it at the back of my mind and see if we can find other intelligence which may confirm or reject the information. For the moment, as you instructed, I will inform both the RIC and the Auxiliaries of the warning regarding the imminent attack. Will I notify Major Stewart here about the note or will you do that, Sir?"

"Good. Yes, you should inform Major Stewart immediately. Carry on, Captain."

"Yes, Sir."

After Geoffrey spoke to Major Stewart, showing him the note, he advised him of what Percival had said and his instructions both with regard to the increased vigilance and the care which must be taken when dealing with the RIC. The major agreed.

He next went to the Communications Hut and dispatched a memo to the commander of the local Auxiliaries informing him of the anonymous message regarding the imminent IRA attack but excluded the information on the RIC and public services as instructed by Percival.

Afterwards he went to the RIC barracks at the other end of the town where he spoke to Superintendent McClintock. After conveying the message, he took some time over a cup of tea, offered, to get to know the man and to get a readout from him of the local population and any new information he could get from that source. He found him to be an amiable enough man, but he had a deep hatred for the IRA. Geoffrey felt that that hatred was mainly born out of fear of what they could do and the threat they posed.

It became quite obvious after a short time that the Superintendent and, he suspected, most of the policemen in that barracks were alienated from a good proportion of the main Catholic/Nationalist population. Accordingly, his information was skewed in a way which made Geoffrey believe that he was in essence only acting as a neutral policeman for one half of the population.

Geoffrey did gain a good deal from the talk, particularly his understanding of the people who were most important in the town from both sides of the population. The Superintendent gave some good contacts in the Protestant community, refraining of course from giving any of his own informants.

He also mentioned some names whom he called 'fellow-travellers' of the IRA. While he did not trust them, he had no evidence to tie them to IRA activity. Before leaving Geoffrey attempted to extract some more information from the conversation, as well as consolidating his working relationship with Superintendent McCintock.

"I greatly appreciate your overview of the security situation and for your briefing on the local scene. You obviously have a very comprehensive knowledge of locus, as well as the ethos, of the district. So far, I have only been able to meet a handful of townspeople here and so you will understand it is taking me some time and I am only slowly attempting to get to know the area.

"Of course, you will know immediately, I have to be somewhat careful in selecting the people I meet and the friends I might make. My own colleagues in the barracks have been very helpful in that regard, but they would only have a fraction of your knowledge. For that reason, your helpful advice and guidance is greatly appreciated."

The Superintendent, like all policemen, thick-skinned against both flattery as well as abuse, was nonetheless taken by the approach of the captain, whom he knew and admired as a War veteran with honours. While there was always a professional jealousy between the security forces, now in particular as the military were given additional responsibilities, Superintendent McClintock felt that he could have an ally in Geoffrey and decided to be as helpful as possible, without crossing the intra-forces demarcation line that had been unofficially established.

"I fully understand your position and the difficulty you are faced with coming into the current situation here. We, who have been part of the community for years, find ourselves in a quandary at times not knowing which way to turn. Frankly, I fear the security situation is getting worse, not better. And unless we can find the IRA's weak spot soon, I believe it will get a great deal worse. My people, who all have families here, feel particularly vulnerable and between us both I can tell you, I have to reassure them almost daily to ensure their morale is not undermined."

Reinforced by the Superintendent's frankness, Geoffrey decided to dig deeper into the people he had met and to those who might be of official use to him.

"The problems are indeed growing from what I can gather and we do need to get to grips with the IRA threat as quickly as possible. Regarding the people around. I have succeeded in getting a membership in the local Golf Club. Are there people there I should look out for – those who might be useful to me and those others that should be avoided?"

Superintendent McCintock, saying that he too was a member of that club, mentioned a number of names including Jack Lee who would be helpful and accommodating. He mentioned others who should be avoided at all costs and gave reasons in both cases.

From there he went on to say that he might also think of joining the tennis club. Its members were much younger and so he would fit in with little trouble. There was also much more cross over in Protestant/Catholic there and it might prove useful. He mentioned the name of the Club secretary and said if Geoffrey wishes he could set a meeting up with him.

Later they talked about the areas of the town and the demographic divides. He warned against walking out at night alone and even going alone into some areas during the daytime. With Geoffrey's prompting he opened up on some individuals who they suspected were IRA operatives or cooperatives and he hinted that more than one of these, if given sufficient incentive, might be willing to give information on the 'Rebels'.

Before leaving, the Superintendent invited Geoffrey to his home for dinner later that week. The invitation was warmly accepted.

Geoffrey walked back to his barracks very pleased with his call to the RIC barracks. Not only had the meeting gone better than he expected, but it had given him valuable information on the local terrain and inroads into contacts that might eventually prove useful.

Geoffrey noted that one name was absent from the conversation, his friend Joe Ryan. He first wondered why that was so. But on reflection a couple of reasons could be given for that lacuna. Firstly, Joe came from the Catholic background and few names from that side were mentioned apart from those whom the Superintendent suspected were IRA sympathisers.

Secondly, he had been away at the Front or recuperating from his wounds in England for almost five years and he would probably never enter the sphere of influence, official or indeed social. Finally, Joe was a businessman who had relations on both sides.

Geoffrey was beginning to understand that the RIC was not a conventional police service. It was partial and obviously was only supported by one side of the community. Consequently, unless he had to, he could understand Joe not wishing to be seen to befriend the personnel in that force.

Joe's friendly relationship with the army was on the other hand also understandable. He had served his time with honour and the mark of comradeship burnt into him by the awful War, as it had done with Geoffrey and other West-Fronters, would remain with him for a very long time.

Chapter 21

Geoffrey attended a dinner given by the Alastair and Julia Montgomery in their large apartment above the bank on the main street of the town. He had been there a number of times and looked forward to his invitations here more than any other of his social activities. It was not the excellent food he received there although that was superb. Rather he had to admit it was Julia with whom he had fallen very much in love, although this had never been mentioned nor indeed encouraged by Julia. He realised it was hopeless. Julia quite obviously was very much tied to her husband and there would be no question of being disloyal to him.

There was a side entrance attached to the bank, into a narrow hallway that led to a steep staircase climbing up to the floor above over the high-ceilinged bank below. The entrance contrasted enormously with the apartment which burst into the light at the top of the stairs—from the ridiculous to the sublime. The hall above contrasted eloquently with that below and the reception rooms taking up this floor were spacious and elegantly decorated and furnished.

Geoffrey, as before when he visited, was immediately transported back to the grandeur of his parents' house, which he had always felt to be part of what he was. In his early life he had almost total run of the place as both his parents were out of the house during most of the day and sometimes even nights, when Nannie Kate allowed him full reign of the house and gardens.

When they were home, he had plenty of hiding places in which to steal himself away, as his parents were usually too preoccupied with their own interests to bother him too much. Most of all during his War years away he had missed Kate, who played the greater part in his love for the house.

It was thus that he entered into the bosom of a place that, from his first acquaintance with it, he instinctively felt would always hold a special affection for him.

There were ten people at the table, four couples, Elizabeth Caney (a friend of Julia) and Geoffrey.

The only ones he knew there, apart from the Montgomery's, were Jack and Louise Lee. He being the only outsider he was quickly introduced by Julia to each of the guests. She was as always most welcoming and he felt immediately relaxed and carried back to a more tranquil time #and a gentler atmosphere.

Julia was a good hostess, not only did she introduce him, she spent some time with each to give him a brief but good pen picture of his or her personality and occupation. Geoffrey was thus allowed to ease his way into the company, having to make only limited interventions.

George Maybury and wife Lydia were the owners of the local large general merchant/ hardware store in the town. They received him with obvious welcome and interest.

Their son James, an officer in the Munster Fusiliers, had been killed in the war. Even though he had died at Mons some years before they were still grieving over his loss.

John Flaherty and his wife Mary were from a different mould. Still in his early 30s he was the main agent for the newly arrived Fordson Tractor which promised in the fullness of time to revolutionise the agriculture industry in Ireland. Ford Motor Company had set up their first manufacturing base in Europe in Cork city the year before their tractor was already becoming popular with the larger well-off farmers. There were already orders for the Ford Motor car which was to become available in Ireland the following year.

His welcome was circumspect but not unfriendly. Geoffrey understood instinctively that John Flaherty was a Catholic nationalist, though his variety of nationalism was not of the violent type. He was moreover a pragmatist, who wanted to see an end to the current impasse between the British Government and the new political disposition in Dublin.

He had spent some years in America and was convinced that Ireland, released from the machinations of political and colonial turmoil, could take advantage of the new technologies and the industry which was projecting America progressively forward leaving the old orders and antediluvian thinking of the hierarchical and class ridden European societies behind.

Geoffrey understood that, while undoubtedly it would be difficult to number John Flaherty among his potential friends, it would be very worthwhile to establish at least good acquaintanceship relations with him.

Geoffrey used the opportunity to speak with each of the guests before sitting down to dinner and had an initial feel for each of their personalities before the inevitable table discussions took place.

He was particularly keen to learn more about John Flaherty. He found him unusually taciturn for a salesman. Although he recognised there was no untoward malice or indeed lack of goodwill displayed towards him personally.

Julia, winking conspiratorially at him as they approached the final guest, introduced him to Elizabeth Caney.

Elizabeth was a soft spoken slim pretty lady who showed immediate interest in Geoffrey. He realised quickly that Julia had selected one of her friends whom he might fancy. He also realised, particularly from the introduction, that they were being purposely set up for the evening in the hope that something would come of it. Geoffrey was very polite and pleasantly greeted his arranged dinner companion.

He was however, not remotely romantically interested in this demure prosaic lady who obviously showed an immediate desire to impress. Geoffrey had over the past number of years, including those when he had been at the Front, been the subject of his mother's ambition to find him a suitable lady to marry. He had not entertained any of these suitors and had no intention now of any sort of arrangement which would threaten his cherished bachelorhood.

Geoffrey had determined that after the war he wished to live that part of his life which had been sorely neglected during those long horrible years of war. Just because he was now stuck in a far out post seemingly a world away from the emerging glitter and glamour of London and Paris, did not mean he would have to succumb to the meagre half-light of polite Victorianesque society and its mores. As he learned from his rude years of no-tomorrows, life is a crude journey under a thin veneer of respectability and privilege.

And that only for those fortunate to belong to the privileged classes of nobility or family wealth. For the throngs of others, it was for each to find his/her pathway forward, eking out the occasional successes and joys they could find along the way. He was of the former but his experiences had shown him that the joys of the masses, meagre though they be, were much more fulfilling in their essence than those of the privileged. He had between both these worlds and would so remain.

They sat to dinner, Geoffrey politely escorting his companion for the evening to table. Mercifully he as the non-native guest was seated at Julia's left-hand side with Elizabeth diagonally across the table from him.

Julia was an impressive hostess starting conversations and then sitting back to allow the others to participate, ensuring that each who wished to become involved was given that opportunity. Geoffrey was by now settled in as a non-intrusive dinner guest but nonetheless for the others an interesting one, whom each in their turn wished to interrogate to explore the multiplicity of areas of his world, which were so different to their small lives in the quiet backwater of the Irish countryside.

George Maybury directly across the table from him wished to trawl through some of his experiences at the Front, hoping in some small way to be able to capture for a moment the experiences of his dead son. Even though it pained Geoffrey to recall those times he nonetheless understood the needs of George Maybury and attempted to give him a pen picture of life as it was in the trenches dwelling for the most part on the camaraderie of the troops and their ability to appreciate the simplest ordinary things of their harsh daily lives that others in the areas removed from battle could not understand.

Julia seeing the barely hidden tears of one man and the forlornness in the other gently intervened to bring the conversation back to the present and of interest to George Maybury. Geoffrey was both taken by the dexterity of her finesse and of her sensitivity in understanding the depths of despair into which both of the men could sink if that conversation had continued for much longer.

The food was exquisite—the main course Boeuf Wellington, the best beef Geoffrey had ever eaten and certainly the most satisfying meal he had had since way before the war. The wine was a 1916 Lynch-Bages from Bordeaux better than any wine he had tasted from his father's well-regarded wine cellar. Julia had instructed the waiter to liberally keep the glasses filled and it required extraordinary willpower on his part to limit his intake of this amazing vintage.

He spoke amiably to Elizabeth across the table inquiring about her interests and her hobbies. She was eager to expand at length but subtle questions from Julia cut this mercifully short. He also had one to one conversation with Louise Lee to his immediate left. She was, as ever, bubbly and full of good humour.

As there were only ten at table, when it finally came to the dessert stage the conversation was able to include everyone present. The nature of the discussions was varied. They ranged from golf, to weather, to business local and country wide, but finally to politics and the current volatile situation particularly in the local district. All were eager to hear what Geoffrey had to say on the latter subject. Geoffrey noted that it was John Flaherty who first raised this matter, although it became obvious that this topic was the ghost that pervaded the room all evening.

Addressing him formally, while others, led by Julia had called him by his first name all evening, John Flaherty asked,

"Captain, our businesses are still suffering from the economic fallout arising out of war. England, our main market, is still struggling to transfer over from a wartime economy to a peacetime one. Many of its young men returning from war are unable to find work. Women who supported their families through wartime jobs now find themselves without that income. The political landscape there like other parts of the world is changing. We here too are on the verge of change.

"The British Government, now that it has to act in peacetime without its wartime emergency powers, has become very circumspect about the myriad problems it faces. Promises made before the war, and even reinforced by legislation, dealing with Home Rule for Ireland are not being implemented and we hear now are to be watered down.

"Now I understand we are to have a half-baked solution to our problems. I fear the delay in dealing with the legitimate issue has set a course that can only end in disaster if the British Government does not arrive at an acceptable solution to assuage the incredulity of the majority and the downright anger of the growing minority.

"How does the army see the matter on the ground? Do you believe you are at war here or are you acting as a back-up for the police?"

Geoffrey, confronted by John Flaherty, whom he learned afterwards was a master's graduate in engineering from the University of Michigan in Ann

Arbor, felt he had better consider his response well before responding in this mixed audience.

"Mr Flaherty, your knowledge of the current economic situation in Britain goes far beyond my limited understanding of the situation there. You will understand that for some years after I left college, without completing my degree, I was otherwise engaged on the Western Front where the question foremost in the minds of everyone there was supporting our fellow soldiers and staying alive. I am not a political animal, but I know enough about that profession to believe they will only move when they feel the terrain ahead is safest for them. Hence their actions are invariably delayed until they feel here is no other alternative. I regretfully felt that course of action, or indeed inaction, will continue for some time in relation to Ireland and its unfortunate divisions.

"The current action by the IRA is unfortunate and I personally for one deeply regret that it is happening. I cannot forget the bravery and the comradeship, to use a current expression, of my fellow Irish brothers during the months and years of that horrendous experience. I came to Ireland to serve not by choice but by order. I do what I am told. However, I also have a moral code, which nothing or no one will change.

"To answer your direct question, we see the IRA as a danger to the community as a whole and their actions are destructive not only of law and order but of a solvable political solution to the future of Ireland as a whole. We do not see ourselves as a force against the people of Ireland but as a means towards restoring the peace. Unfortunately, the RIC is not fully equipped to deal with the type and intensity of action now being carried out by the IRA. We, the army, consequently have to fill that security void."

Returning John Flaherty asked, "What about the so-called "Black and Tans"? Since their arrival they appear to act beyond the law and 0rdinary people here who have no IRA connections are fearful of their violent behaviour. Whatever little trust there may have been between the nationalist community and the RIC, has certainly evaporated since their arrival."

"The army does not have responsibility for the Black and Tans or indeed for the RIC. I have heard some accounts of the behaviour of this newly created force which certainly bothers me personally."

Julia intervened at this stage: "John, we agree that these Black and Tans should never have been inserted into the situation here. One would have thought that the British Government would have learned after the dreadful executions of the rebel leaders carried out after the 1916 uprising in Dublin that the Irish will not be cowed by coercion. Rather that type of action merely gives oxygen to the IRA who see themselves as patriots not as professional soldiers or indeed policemen.

"There is only one solution and that is a political one and the sooner that arrives the better for everyone on both islands. Geoffrey and his colleagues are in the invidious position of defending a situation which has no immediate prospect of being resolved."

Jack Lee, ever the voice of reason, inserted, "Julia has perceptively struck the nail on the head. We should never have been put in this position. The Irish Parliamentary Party had persuaded the British Parliament to grant Home Rule and the Government should have exercised their lawful power to ensure that the legislation was implemented. The Unionists could have been accommodated by means of a veto on certain legislation which was deemed vital to their community.

"Personally, while I did not vote for that Party, I would have no difficulty in trusting them to govern the country with impartiality. Their effective rejection by the Government ensured that their credibility with the nationalists would also suffer and now we have Sinn Fein and they want total independence. It was and is a recipe for disaster. Geoffrey, I do not envy the position you and your colleagues have been put in."

Alastair Montgomery then intervened to guide the conversation back to more tranquil ground saying that the growth in agriculture since the removal of the restrictions of the war was improving the lot of the country.

The conversation moved on to the happenings in the town and the upcoming harvest time which was always important for the local business community.

As Geoffrey walked across the river bridge to his barracks later, he felt somewhat bruised by the evening's discussions and nevertheless he was grateful that it had been extraordinarily helpful in allowing him a very useful oversight of the thinking by the more informed members of the community from both sides. He could not help but recall in particular the words of his new friend Jack Lee, *"Geoffrey I do not envy the position you and your colleagues have been put in."*

He would have to be wary of John Flaherty, not that he thought him an enemy or indeed a fellow traveller of the IRA, but he did, no doubt, cogently articulate the views of the broad section of the nationalist community. He should if possible, attempt to keep in touch with him. He would be a valuable listening post in his continued need to understand the changing mood in the wider nationalist community.

The one person that shone out for him during the evening was Julia. He was full of admiration for her in the subtle way she maneuverer not only the logistics of the evening but particularly the conversations before and at dinner. Her interventions were masterful. But particularly he was very taken by the ways she had ensured that he was protected both from those who bring him down avenues he would not wish to go and from John Flaherty who could have pushed him into a situation from which he might be unable to extricate himself.

However, he began to realise that his feelings for her went far beyond mere friendship. He would have to curb those feelings. She was after all a married woman and consequently out of bounds as far as emotional affections was concerned.

Still, he was extraordinarily drawn to her.

Chapter 22

Joe Ryan, while visiting his girlfriend, Ellen Griffin, at her home in the county, diverted on his return to keep a rendezvous with Sean Hales at the secret location they had used before. To ensure that he was not being followed he checked the road behind him. First by climbing a hilly field off the road so he could see the road from whence he came for hundreds of yards back. Next, he went down a different road off his route and doubled back after a few hundred yards.

Finally, another few miles on, round a long winding corner, he put his bicycle out of sight and promptly hid behind the ditch, waiting 15 minutes there before completing his journey, secure now in the knowledge that he most definitely was not being followed.

Sean was waiting for him when he arrived. Joe could see, to his satisfaction, no one else was around.

Since the arrival of the Black and Tans the surveillance on the public at large had dramatically increased. The latter cohort were known to use every tool at their disposal to elicit intelligence about IRA activities and even mildly suspicious activities were put under scrutiny by this force. They would use every means possible including subterfuge, financial reward and even torture to get the information they sought. He also knew, through his connections with the British Army, that they too were increasing their antenna to counteract the now known insider intelligence gathering of the IRA.

He was more than aware that he was in an extremely vulnerable position and any slipup on his part could be fatal. There would be no mercy for him if caught. He would automatically be treated as the worse kind of traitor and suffer brutal torture before being killed. It was consequently imperative for him to keep the knowledge of his activities to a bare minimum of contacts.

He recalled again that he had experienced a similar kind of feeling when moving out into the observation signals trenches at the Front—there in No Man's Land, between the trenches on both sides, for hours on end, either on his own or at best with one other signalman, attempting to monitor the activities of the Germans to give his side an advantage in that bloody encounter.

It was no accident that signal men had one of the highest mortality rates in WW1. At that time luck and prayer were your best hope of survival. Your second line of defence was how you went about ensuring that you did not make yourself an unnecessary target. He would have to have both those lines of personal defence in this current encounter.

They wasted little time getting down to business.

Sean gave an overview of the current situation of the IRA on the ground, speaking of their overall strategies and their current targets if they became available. He particularly dwelt on the areas where they lacked intelligence on the ground and where further information was needed if they were to advance their plans.

Joe outlined the information he had obtained since they met previously. It had been decided already that all information coming from Joe for now at least would only be verbal, to ensure secrecy. He then particularly dwelt on the areas that Sean had mentioned as important and said he would bear these areas in mind when he was accessing information in the future.

There followed as usual a toing and froing of information before Sean moved on to the main reason he had called for the meeting.

"Joe, a cara, it's good of you to come at such short notice. Things are moving rapidly and we have got to stay ahead of the security forces if we are to continue our success. As you know by now our attacks and tactics have succeeded in closing all of the rural RIC barracks in this district and consequently, we now basically control the countryside.

"Unfortunately, that success has led to first the reinforcement of the RIC with the Black and Tans. Those former British soldiers from the War who, unlike the majority of Tommies who never wish to see warfare again, on disbandment are still thirsting after blood. They have brought with them a ruthlessness which had not been here before.

"We are concerned about their tactics of fear and intimidation together with their bribery could lead to the arrest and torture of some of our lads. They have already had some success and we are seeking ways of thwarting their inroads into our structures. One of our great advantages, our closeness with the ordinary rank and file members of the Nationalist population, is unfortunately also one of our greatest weaknesses.

"Because we have to depend so much on their good will and local knowledge and our active colleagues come from that part of society, many know us and some have knowledge of our camping areas and other sensitive information about us. We are therefore vulnerable through our strongest asset. It only takes one with even limited information to undermine our most well laid plans.

"Notwithstanding that we now have perhaps an even greater danger looming. We spoke before about the so-called Auxiliaries. As expected, these are turning out to be even better trained and better equipped and hence more dangerous to our cause than the Black and Tans. We fear that many of them have a psychopathic bloodlust nurtured in the War and see us as an easy target.

"As you pointed out last time, we met they are being handsomely paid with blood money by the British Government which is determined to stamp us out by any means, even beyond the normal rules of war. We have to be in position to strike them hard and fast before they settle in and gain a strategic foothold here. Because of their former ranks and the obvious latitude, they have received from the British government they show they will not confine themselves to even the harsh tactics of the RIC to whom they are officially attached.

"Moreover, the RIC will be advising them and will give them all the intelligence they have accumulated on us. Consequently, they will not take long to read themselves into the district and become a very potent enemy. Joe, you have told me already that while the British Army are not tied directly with the RIC, or indeed consequently these new attachments, they, because of their superior communications systems, are probably aware of the plans and logistics of these others. If so, is it possible to tap in to that source to find out some of what these people are doing or planning?"

"Sean I fully understand where you are coming from and I absolutely agree with the analysis of the current situation. I could go further. Since we last spoke, I have attempted to get some information on the Auxiliaries but as I suspected they share little with the army. However, we can surmise the following:

"The Auxiliaries, as former Army officers coming from the Front, will be very aware of the value of intelligence and will no doubt have within their ranks those who are very up to date on the best methods of securing that.

"Additionally, and perhaps even more fundamentally serious from our point of view is the fact that the British Army, since they have been given additional powers are now stepping up their activities and I am aware they are engaged in counter intelligence separate from the RIC or indeed their auxiliary attachments.

I would fear them more than the others because of their discipline and organisational skills not to mind the continuing experience in that field.

"To answer the question, you just posed. I expect that the British Army will have some information. Whether I can get access to it is another matter. I will try. I will have to figure out how best to do so without alerting anyone to what I am doing. Next, once I have a solution, I will set about attempting to get at that information. It may take time as I may have to piece together the bits of information, I collect to come up with something worthwhile.

"I would ask that you would continue the one and one arrangements we have put in place for my security. I must be sure my identity is secure. The other side must trust me for me to get close enough to gather this intelligence. Any hint that I might be other than what they now believe me to be would be doubly risky.

"First from the obvious need for my immediate personal security. But secondly and maybe even more importantly if they did suspect me they might allow me access to information which would lead our flying column or indeed the leaders into an ambush situation."

There was a very short delay before Sean responded. A hesitation Joe, whose instinctive antennae were as well wired as his technological ones, immediately sensed. However, he said nothing, waiting for Sean to speak.

"Joe, your points as usual are very well made. If for no other reason our conversations are extremely important to me because they help me not only think out my own strategy but your additions, I find greatly reinforce and add to that strategy. The pity is I could do with your counsel on a more regular basis but your value to us now as an intelligence gatherer is more important. Yes, the one and one still holds. Any leak, however unlikely, will be immediately relayed to you. Perhaps then I would ask of you a redoubling of your already good work if that were possible."

Joe, not over-inflated by the hyperbole of Sean's praise, came back: "Sean, there is no need to over-emphasise the urgency of the situation. It's obvious that we are in a race to take control of the offensive before the other side out-manoeuvres us. I understand too well that if we lose the initiative, we will see a falling off in our support among the public.

"The nationalists will lose heart and the unionists will demand even more reassurance of their ascendant position. I will do my utmost to find such information as will assist our cause. I will let you know through our usual signal and meet with you here immediately after I discover something which might be of operational use or concern."

Sean agreed and the meeting was at an end.

Joe left, travelling back along the road and diverting to throw anyone off who might wish to guess where he had come from.

He could not help thinking back on the meeting. *Sean Hales, while he was at pains to hide his anxiety, could not totally conceal his concern from Joe's ability to read the inner emotions in the faces and gestures of others. Perhaps Joe's upbringing where he was forced to see (while pretending not to notice) the daily deprivations of his mother and others in the population around who were struggling to live from day to day while putting out a brave face to the world.*

He also wondered about the hesitation when the matter of his security came up. Could it be that somehow others knew of his liaison with Sean? If so, would his position be compromised? He could not dwell on that.

The primary issue now was to get information which might help to counteract the new dangerous situations that were presenting themselves. First, he had to think out ways in which this could be done and then try to carry it out.

He was not at all confident.

Chapter 23

As Geoffrey was preparing to meet Major Percival, who had by now relocated himself for the time being to his barracks, he was more than a little apprehensive. Apart from scraps of low-level intelligence, which he had picked up from petty informers and hearsay, he had little of any real import to offer Percival.

He had his usual weekly meeting with the RIC Superintendent who painted a very bleak picture for him. The Superintendent was quite outspoken about the unorthodox tactics of the Black and Tans who, despite being technically a backup for the regular RIC, were not in reality under his control. Many of his members were very concerned about the methods of the Black and Tans and they maintained that since the arrival of this new force there had been a noticeable cooling in relations with the ordinary public.

While some of this might be related to the success of the IRA, the Superintendent felt it was due primarily to the new tactics, which he as a regular policeman could not condone.

The Superintendent was now even more concerned about the arrival of the Auxiliaries who again in name came under the RIC label, in reality they were a standalone force and openly admitted they would act as if they were at war on enemy territory. He freely admitted that he would lose good regular officers from the RIC, who did not wish to be connected to the new method of policing.

When he met Major Percival in his office that morning, he first gave an analysis of the current situation including the recent IRA attacks on a number of RIC barracks in the district and its fallout both in regard to the morale of the RIC and enhancement of the IRA in the eyes of the local nationalist community.

Next, he attempted to puff up his report with the little intelligence he had received enhanced by some of his own observations and suggestions. He said that he had begun to move into the local community as surreptitiously as possible. He did not wish to be seen to be intrusive or over enthusiastic. People would be wary of that approach. While his method would require some time to bear fruit, he felt it would be more beneficial in the fullness of time.

Finally, he reverted to the Black and Tans and the Auxiliaries and somewhat sticking his neck out he advised that the Army should not associate itself with the tactics that these forces were engaging in. He reminded the Major that while bad things happen during the fog of war, there is always a future accounting for the transgressions of the past.

He believed that the Regiment and the Army, unlike these latter forces, should see itself as standard bearer for correct behaviour into the future. By way of emphasis, he included the murder earlier in the year of the Lord Mayor of Cork city, Tomas MacCurtain, by a hooded gang that the general public understands to be RIC men.

Major Percival listened to the report without comment until Geoffrey had ended.

"Look Captain, I can see where you are coming from and in a normal situation your analysis and methods would be to correct ones to follow. However, we are now faced with a new situation. First the local police force is ill-equipped and inadequate for the task they have had to perform. While we might like to suggest that Ireland is part of Britain, in reality it is and always has been a colony. The Government will never admit this but this is what we have to deal with.

"I might not like the tactics of the new forces and indeed I would not wish for this Regiment to have to account for them in the future. However, to begin with the IRA is not an army in the strict sense since it is a guerrilla force and fighting unequal guerrilla methods. In such a situation an army is always at a disadvantage as it is unable to see what is confronting it. We are not trained to counter this type of warfare. Hence, we must find another way to deal with it.

"There is only one method to deal with such tactics as the IRA is engaged in. That is to outwit these people on the ground. We do that by taking out its leadership and destroying its forces by discovering its weak points. These weak points are its numbers compared to ours, its paltry equipment compared to ours, its leadership compared to ours, and if the latter is true, hopefully its organisations compared to ours.

"The key to all of the above is first hand intelligence. If we do not possess that, we will not defeat the IRA. The Government has taken responsibility to send in the two forces you mentioned. It has obviously given them carte blanche to do whatever is necessary to accomplish their mission that is to eliminate the IRA. This is a political act and we cannot gainsay it. The IRA claim to be an arm of the so-called Dail. That is their belief and consequently we can expect them to fight to the finish.

"Accordingly, while we will not engage in the same brutality as these new forces, we may be able to profit from the results they achieve from these methods. I want you, Captain, to redouble your efforts with the locals. Find out what you can, particularly about the IRA leadership. Also keep in touch with the RIC, more frequently. You appear to have a good relationship with the Superintendent, foster it. Entertain him to dinner; he will be more forthcoming in less official surroundings.

"Use what means we have at our disposal to attempt to lock in to the other security communications systems. Pay particular attention to what the Auxiliaries are doing. I suspect they will be parsimonious with the information they share. I want to say that we now are in a more central position. As you know the Government has just recently, under the Restoration of Order Act, provided for the IRA to be court-martialled rather than appear before Civil Criminal Courts.

"That literally as well as metaphorically puts the matter into our court. We accordingly now have to step up a gear and become more involved. Do I make myself clear, Captain?"

"Yes sir. Perfectly."

Geoffrey left the office feeling like he had been run over by a second row forward in a rugby match. Trying to extract some comfort from the meeting he found only crumbs.

While the Major had not berated him, he most certainly took a more strident line than Geoffrey wished. The only comfort he had was that he had stopped short of cooperating with the Black and Tans and the Auxiliaries in their activities. But Geoffrey, while not present at interrogations under Percival supervision, understood that they violated codes he felt bound by.

He would have to do as asked, however, and set about attempting to find other sources to get pertinent intelligence about the IRA.

First, he would see what could be done to tap into the Auxiliaries communications. He hoped he could get sufficient information from the Superintendent regarding the Black and Tans.

When he arrived back at his office, he immediately sent for Sergeant Turner at the communications office to see what could be done regarding the Auxiliaries.

"Sergeant Turner is it possible to tap into or even break into another telephone or wire communication without the other source knowing you were so?"

"Em—I have not done that before Sir, but it should be possible. When do you need to do this? It may take some time. I have to ask, perhaps from my counterparts in Cork city."

"I would prefer if you could do this without too many people knowing Sergeant."

"I could not be sure that word would not get out if I was to ask Cork Sir."

"Is there no other way?"

"I could ask Joe Ryan Sir. If anyone would know, he would."

"Yes. Do that. You will no doubt have to tell him whose communications you're tapping into. It's the newly arrived Auxiliaries who are stationed in Mallow. However, you are to say it is for his ears and eyes only. I hold you to the same silence. Understood Sergeant? No one besides you and Joe Ryan should be involved in this."

"Understood perfectly Captain."

Chapter 24

Next morning Geoffrey returned to his office. He had spent the night pondering on what he could do to improve his chances of finding additional sources that could give him the kind of information to satisfy the intelligence needs as outlined by the Major that day. Unfortunately, he was at a loss to know where he should begin.

As he was mulling over in his mind how to go about reaching the individual who could give that information, the duty sergeant came to his office with a letter which had been delivered earlier by a source unknown, addressed to him.

On opening the envelope, he discovered it was from the Reverend Foster and he asked that Geoffrey should come alone this evening at 5 pm to the same venue where they had met before.

While he was elated by the call, hoping that its urgency meant that the Reverend had some important information which he had to convey immediately; he tempered his thoughts by reasoning that it might only mean that he had only limited follow-up on his last dispatch and wished merely to stay in touch.

Taking his time and going around the town by a circuitous route he realised that the only real source who had any direct or indeed indirect knowledge of the IRA was the Reverend Foster. He would use this occasion to ask him to put more pressure on his informant to get the names and if possible, the locations of any of the IRA leadership. He intended to ensure that the Reverend was given sufficient funds to encourage his informant and any other inducements which might work.

He would have to work on how else he could find another useful information source. He could inveigle the RIC Superintendent to put him in touch with such a person but he realised that might be difficult. He most likely would not wish to give him a valuable source which would be useful to his organisations. Still he should at least try. Perhaps he may wish to ensure that he had friends in other places if his position got too hot for him in Ireland? He felt uncomfortable even thinking like this about someone whom he began to like. However, if needs be!

Walking now through the countryside at the end of August he could not help but be enchanted by the serenity and charm of such a simple yet magnificent scene. The fields were golden with ripened wheat and barley, the river was running slowly showing the trout rising for the plentiful flies on the water, and the hedgerows were bright with red bell flowered fuchsia (the Irish call "deora De" the tears of God) and filled with the myriad birds, now fully grown, before many of them migrated south in the coming months.

He entered the rear of the church through the laneway at the side. He saw no one around, having taken precautions beforehand to ensure no one saw his movements as he did so.

As previously, Reverend Foster was there before he arrived. The Reverend seemed most anxious to rely on what he had been told and he got straight to that with the minimum of preliminary niceties.

"I am sorry for calling you at such short notice. Captain Eastbourne but I feel what I have to say should be relayed as quickly as possible. My informant tells me that the IRA is planning a major attack in the near future. She said her contact was at that time unsure of the exact location and anyway that would only be known to the leader of the column that would carry out the attack. He would be part of that and was told to be ready to assemble with the others in two days' time to prepare for the attack.

"However, while my informant was listening intently to get more detail, not being part of the group who were discussing the matter, she consequently could not ask questions about it. You will understand she is risking a great deal to relay what she heard and it is important, both for her sake and indeed for her to continue being a fly on wall, so to speak, that she goes on being undetected.

"One point which arose was that this would be a moving target so it would rule out attacks on barracks and posts. Accordingly, it would seem that the likely attack will have a patrol of some kind as its target. I expect that you will be able to pinpoint those likely patrols which may be affected. Lastly, she said she understood that it would take place within a week.

"While she was not close enough to hear all the conversation, she was able to name of one of the IRA leaders mentioned. His name she said was Hurley but she was unsure of this first name, it may have been Charlie or Mickey."

"Thank you for that Reverend. While it would obviously have been of greater benefit if she had heard the time and exact place, it is indeed useful. Hopefully we will be able to ensure that we are prepared for any such attack. It certainly allows us to be at least on our guard. Can I ask a few questions in regard to what you have relayed? First, did the informant hear how many IRA personnel would be involved in this attack?"

"No, she did not say and unfortunately, I did not ask. But she did say that she believed the man she overheard would have been down the ranks and not used very often. I suppose one could speculate that he may be making up numbers which might indicate a larger group of individuals."

"Secondly did he mention who the attack would be against for instance the RIC, Black and Tans, or the Army or indeed the new arrivals the Auxiliaries?"

"Again, I am sorry to say I did not ask that question. So, anything I might offer in that regard would mere speculation."

"Thanks Reverend, just one more question. Did he happen to say where he was meeting the others and/or where the assembly was to take place?"

"She, said the individual in question had said that he would be contacted by someone in two days and he should be ready to move out. She did say however, that the IRA man had mentioned joining the group around the Upton/Innishannon area. Apparently, the leadership is very tight on detail and the rank and file are only told what they need to know and that only at the last minute. This, the IRA leadership says, is for their own as well as the group's security."

"I suppose there was no mention of arms or equipment available for that attack?"

"No. and again I did not ask."

Geoffrey gratefully thanked the Reverend Foster for both his personal involvement in helping the authorities to ensure the return of normality to the district, for the diligence and initiative he had shown. He could be assured that the confidentiality of both himself and his informant would be absolutely protected. To ensure this he got the Reverend to write a note outlining what he had said and had him arrange delivery of it to him at the barracks anonymously.

Before leaving he handed the Reverend Foster twenty pounds to be used in whatever way he thought fit both to reward the informant and to ask him to report any other material on the IRA she could find.

Lastly, he again thanked the Reverend Foster and said he would be available at any hour and at a moment's notice if he wished to convey any more information of this nature.

Geoffrey slipped out of the churchyard into another laneway going the opposite way from which he arrived.

He was deep in thought about what he had just learned and almost ran into Julia Montgomery who was on her own taking her evening walk before dinner. Her husband would continue working after the bank closed to clear the day's balancing of accounts and to finalise and sign the letters to customers. Their cook was preparing the meal and so Julia had time on her hands and strolled out when the day had cooled down to take advantage of the good weather and the open countryside which was only a short distance from that small town.

"Geoffrey, what are you doing on this side of town? Hardly going for a constitutional walk?"

Returning suddenly from his deep thoughts, Geoffrey responded, "I could ask the same of you Julia, although you are, after all, on your side of town. Anyway, I am delighted to see you and you look splendid and you fit in so eloquently with this beautiful natural background in this magnificent late summer Irish weather. Somehow it strikes me you were made for this."

"Well thank you Geoffrey. Your extremely mellifluous words suit the mood just now, though in relation to me they are greatly exaggerated."

"Julia, I do not exaggerate, it is how I see you and more than just that."

"Geoffrey while your words do more than just flatter me, you should have a care about how you play with a fragile emotional lady, who has developed an attachment for you."

"I am not playing Julia. My feelings for you are very real indeed. I have not had the opportunity to tell you this before, but now that I have, I am glad that I have done so."

The veneer of strict society rule was thus removed and two very emotional adults were united in a way which ignored all barriers, as if the moment was all that mattered. Both were joined in the dance of life: perhaps one was free of the strictures of a much-closed community in an artificial setting, the other released for an instant from the commitments of duty in a time of war.

Julia kissing Geoffrey after their intimate interlude, said she had to hurry back home before she was missed. In these days, while she personally felt nothing untoward would happen to her, her husband might start looking for her if she was missing from her very mundane routine.

Before leaving they agreed that their tryst should be kept extremely private and secret.

She mentioned that her husband had been spending some time between Cork city and Dublin of late as he was due to take over the bank's major office in Cork city in the summer of next year when the old manager retired. He would spend at least one overnight in Cork and two in Dublin when he made these trips. She said she would send a coded note to him of the date and time he should come to her house when her husband next travelled. She described the back gateway to the premises which would be left unlocked and he was to be careful to ensure no one saw him.

Chapter 25

Joe Ryan arrived at the Army barracks having had an urgent request for assistance. These days this type of summons, he thought as he made his way there, could lead to, as it were either heaven or hell. Anyway, he was not over-anxious. The request had been made by Sgt Turner and it seemed quite genuine. Perhaps it might help him get him something of use that he could pass on.

"Joe thanks for coming so promptly. Captain Eastbourne agreed that I should contact you to get your help in a rather delicate matter. It will require your total confidentiality both outside as well as inside these walls. What we want isn't exactly a normal piece of work. We are looking to you to guide us in getting intelligence on outside organisations. Can I first swear you to secrecy even beyond what we would normally require in the army? I know it is asking a lot of you as a civilian, but our need is great and you are the only one around who, I feel, may be able to help us in this."

"Tom, yes I'll do whatever I can for you and of course you will not hear it back from me."

"Look to put it as simply as possible we want to know what the new group supporting the RIC is doing. They are rather secretive and it is important for us to know what they are at, particularly as we cannot plan properly if they are doing something which goes counter to what we want. Can you help to get into their systems without their knowing? I know we are asking you as a civilian to go way beyond what we would normally ask, but we have no other way of finding out what we need to know."

"I take it you are referring to the Auxiliaries. I understand they are stationed in Macroom."

"Yes, they are. And we wonder if it is possible to find out what they are up to by tapping into their communications?"

"I will certainly give it some thought. Is it possible for you to find out what methods of communication to the outside they are using and where are the most frequent messages sent? Presumably they are in regular contact with the RIC for instance. Do they come to Cork city? Presumably they go to the HQ there."

"We are at present discreetly looking to see what they have by way of telecommunications. You make a good point re their frequent contact points. Will we look into that? Do you think if we had that information could we tap into them without their knowing?"

"Depending on what they are using, yes. Once you know what they have we can make plans to infiltrate their calls. Let me know as soon as you get that. By the way, it would also be useful if we knew what call signs they have and what codes they are using. I understand they are all ex-army so I presume they will be using our old codes. Can you also find those out for me?"

"Joe, I knew we could rely on you. None of us have a clue how to approach this. So, we are totally in your hands. I will be back to you as soon as I have the information you are looking for. I would ask you to give it priority when we get what you need."

"Tom, I guarantee I will drop everything to see what I can do for you in this regard. Let me know when you have anything."

Sgt Turner invited Joe to stay for a while as he wanted to ask him about a problem, they were having with the radio equipment. He suggested that they both would have a cup of tea and Joe accepted.

While the Sergeant was absent getting the tea Joe quickly looked at some of the correspondence on his desk. Among them was a memo on the possible IRA attack during the week somewhere near Innishannon/Upton. Apparently, a communication had been sent by the Communication section to the regiment in Kinsale and Army H.Q. in Cork city and all the other security agencies in the district advising them of this possibility and advising that all the necessary precautions should be taken to reinforce any patrols that were in the area during that week at least.

Joe had got back to his seat and was reading from his own notebook when the Sergeant returned.

Joe left the barracks almost in a dream. He could not believe that what he was seeking most the army also urgently required. He would now have to put on his thinking cap and decide how best to get this information as quickly as possible.

Most urgently however, was the information he picked up in relation to the possible IRA ambush near Upton that week and the army's alert to the other agencies.

He would have to get that information back to Sean Hales within the hour. It meant he would probably have to take a risk and send word using Ellen to ask her family to arrange for Sean to be at a certain location within the hour. He hoped he could be found in time. Otherwise, he would have to leave a written message for him at that location.

Ellen would have to be warned that under no circumstances could she mention Joe's name in this arrangement. All she should tell her family member was that someone unnamed wanted to see Sean very urgently. He felt he could rely on Ellen to get this done expeditiously. She was both resourceful and determined and knew enough not to ask questions. What you don't know you cannot divulge.

He was sorry that he had not made prior arrangements for such a contingency. It had been his intention but the conversation was so concentrated on the issues at the last meeting it slipped his mind until he was already nearly home. Still a chance had to be taken and he had no option in the circumstances.

Reverting to the meeting he just had in the barracks. It was indeed strange that he could in doing so simultaneously provide vital information to the two enemies. The vagaries of life are indeed strange.

On his way to his business premises as he was thinking about how to go about getting into the Auxiliaries communications systems, he was shouted at by a local layabout who called him a traitor for collaborating with the enemy. Joe ignored the abuse, treating the ignoramus with the contempt he deserved. He was not intimidated by this lout who he knew was not in the IRA and indeed the IRA would have nothing to do with such an indiscreet idiot.

Joe was afraid of no single man and could more than hold his own with anyone foolish enough to challenge him. The verbal attack however, was overheard by others who said nothing. Most of those would have no time for the abuser who was well known to be a local yob. But there were one or two who while saying nothing would not be beyond whispering behind his back.

There were those in the town whom he knew would regard him as outside the fold because he had been in the British Army during the war. His continued perceived connection with the army now would only confirm their mistrust of him. Joe was not unduly concerned about them. They were the same individuals who also despised him because of his business success.

In a small town where everyone knew everyone else the pettiness of some few knew no bounds. He had seen it growing up and indeed when he was a small boy these same individuals sneered at him because of his poverty and looked down on his unfortunate widowed mother who was forced after her husband's death to perform myriad menial ill-paying tasks at that time to ensure the survival of her small family. Now they were saying:

"How could a widow's son achieve so much so fast? He must have had assistance from his friends the Brits? Can you not see they call him to the barracks to even change a light bulb? He must be paying a price for all they have done for him. We should not trust him and indeed he should be boycotted."

Apart from the lout who had abused from afar, who in local parlance "was not the full shilling", none of these others would dare say what they were whispering behind his back.

In normal times he would have totally ignored these cretinous lowlifes, however, he would have to be careful now as some IRA volunteer might take it upon himself to eliminate a perceived British Army collaborator from within the nationalist community's midst. While he realised that this would only occur if a decision was taken at the higher levels of the IRA to issue an execution order on him, it nevertheless was not beyond the bounds of possibility.

He had to continue to have excellent relations with the army to do his work for the IRA, but simultaneously he could not afford to have his IRA membership known to anyone apart from his one contact point. It was a dilemma he would have to do something about. He could not work if he had to protect himself from enemies on both sides of the divide. He was for now anyway it a situation of double jeopardy and it would be extremely stupid of him if he did not attempt to minimise the risks that that posed.

He would have to speak with Sean Hales about this. Perhaps he might do so if he met him today. He would not allow a situation where anyone else knew what he was doing apart from Sean. Strangely if it came to, he would prefer to take his chances with the IRA than be discovered by the army.

For now, he had to concentrate on the job ahead. He hoped that the Auxiliaries would be using the same codes as the army, which would make things easier. The one thing he had going for him was the army was asking him to do this and consequently he could work openly with them without attracting attention. Anything he learned from the surveillance could be easily passed back to Sean Hales. Once he got into the Auxiliaries system, he only had to figure out a way of creating a separate route for himself as once it was up and working, he would have to back off and let the army control the system he would design for them.

He quickened his step and headed straight to where his fiancé was working to attempt to set the meeting with Sean Hales in motion. Afterwards he headed home to change into suitable clothing and collect his bicycle for his journey to the meeting place he selected. He again berated himself for not making contingency arrangements for occasions such as this. He would have to address this lacuna when he met with Sean Hales.

Chapter 26

Earlier that day Geoffrey having received the note agreed with the Reverend Foster he informed the OC and Major Percival. He had been given the task of finding out what patrols would be in the area in the coming days.

As well as instructing Sergeant Turner to alert his own and the other security organisations about the possible ambush Geoffrey took the opportunity to meet with RIC Superintendent McClintock in the town. The Superintendent was grateful for the information and undertook to alert his people, including the Black and Tans and the Auxiliaries. The RIC were reluctant these days to patrol too far away from their main barracks and only did so in the company of the other attachments that had both the numbers and the equipment to be able to confront the IRA who would only attack if they believed they had superior forces.

They agreed to inform one another of the times and places of the patrols on the Bandon/Cork roads around in the coming weeks. They discussed the options of what to do with the information. They could of course halt all patrols in the area during the following days and even weeks.

This was quickly discounted as it would only give the IRA a moral victory, reinforcing the claims they were known to be making at present i.e., the British security forces were now fearful of sending patrols out and that the IRA effectively controlled the countryside. The RIC had abandoned their rural smaller barracks and this had already given the IRA a small victory. They could not afford to compound this by showing little or no presence in the rural areas.

On the other hand, if this was dealt with in a proactive way it might produce a much-needed reversal for the IRA if they were able to turn the tables on the latter by outwitting them. This might be achieved if the IRA was deceived into attacking an advance patrol with a limited force, while a much larger backup force was waiting within easy striking distance. The objective would be to ensure that the larger group was hidden from the eyes of the IRA attackers until they had committed themselves.

It was agreed that this second approach was the much better way of dealing with the situation. It would be a waste of good information, which did not come along often, if they did not take advantage of it. While Geoffrey admitted that while his source, which he kept to himself, was reliable he was getting the information indirectly and to date this is the first time the information from that particular informant will be tested.

Superintendent McClintock said that he would discuss the matter with some of his colleagues, including both the reserve attachments and come back with some ideas. Geoffrey would in the meanwhile also discuss the matter with Major Percival and his colleagues and attempt to see if a suitable operational plan could be constructed which would take advantage of the information they had.

It was understood that they were somewhat limited in that they now did not know the exact location of the ambush which would obviously make the task of drawing up such a plan that much more difficult. However, they should not look a gift horse in the mouth. They were given an advantage and they should make use of it.

Geoffrey returned to his barracks and immediately sought a meeting with his OC and Major Percival (who by now had located himself mainly in Bandon and was later to take over there with Major Turner going to Kinsale in a direct switch) to discuss the issue and decide what measures, if any, the army should take to deal with the matter. Major Stewart together with Percival and Captain Chilcot were at the meeting. Geoffrey, who had alerted Major Percival immediately on receiving the note from the Reverend Foster about the possible ambush in the vicinity of Innishannon/Upton, admitted that the intelligence was indeed sketchy in that it did not have either an exact time or place and that the information was coming from an untested source.

Notwithstanding that he maintained that it was the best lead they had concerning a possible IRA ambush and if it was accurate, it could give the security forces the advantage they were seeking.

He then informed them of his earlier meeting with Superintendent McClintock and the conclusions they had arrived at as a way of taking advantage of the information.

All waited for Major Percival, the Regiment's intelligence/strategic officer, to speak first. He called in the Sergeant Major who was waiting in the outer office. Sergeant Major Gregory Henchcliff, who had obviously been previously briefed by Percival, arrived with maps which he hung on the wall behind the

Major. These maps were ordnance survey maps which showed the territory around Innishannon/Upton in great detail. One which showed an area of 100 square miles around had a scale of 6 inches to the mile.

The other, focusing on a much smaller area of 36 square miles around the area had a far higher scale of 25 inches to the mile and had been produced only in the past 20 years. The first gave an excellent view of all of the roads and laneways in the area. The second clearly outlined not only the roads, laneways, bridges etc. but also showed buildings and more especially the contours of the ground in that vicinity.

Using the maps, the Sergeant Major, at the behest of Major Percival, took the meeting over the ground, first showing the roads leading from Cork city and all the towns around. He then went on to point out the routes which normal patrols would take going through the Innishannon/Upton region.

Percival came in at this stage and referring to Geoffrey's report said that while they should await the promised information from the RIC and its two support forces before making a final assessment, they should view the area to attempt to pinpoint the most likely locations where an ambush would take place.

"I agree with Captain Eastbourne's assessment that we should look at intelligence we have been given as legitimate and act on it. As he said, if legitimate, it is the first real piece of intelligence about a possible major IRA ambush we have got in this area. It might offer us a means of causing a serious setback to the successes that the IRA has been having in the past months. At least if we get it right it would give them a bloody nose and damage their current image with the public.

"Subject to the information that will come to us from the RIC, I can see four immediate locations in the given area, here, here, here and here (pointing out the four locations) where an ambush, if properly organised, could have the most advantage for the IRA. We must presume, going on what we already know, that the IRA is fairly well led and consequently that ambush would be set in the most advantageous situation for the guerrillas.

"We do not know why they have selected the Bandon/Cork roads for an attack but it must be assumed that they either expect patrols to travel along a certain route on a regular basis and/or they already have specific information on a specific patrol on a given day. While the latter situation might seem unlikely, we cannot overlook it.

"We send a patrol of up to 30 troops in two lorries between Bandon and Cork city on a fairly regular basis. This passes through Innishannon but it does not go through Upton. On the other hand, we have only information that the ambush is set for near Innishannon, not specifically Innishannon, so our patrol must consequently be the target, although the Kinsale patrols also go through Innishannon and Upton nearby and cannot be excluded. The problem is that that particular road is the main one between the city and south west Cork and therefore it probably has frequent patrols from many destinations.

"Anyway, until we find out the total amount of patrols going anywhere near Innishannon/Upton this week we cannot tie down the one they may have targeted. So, in the meantime lets us get on with what we can do until we know more. Having examined the area with regard to the roads and the topography I have come to the conclusion that these are the four most likely locations for an ambush."

Marking all four on the more detaned map he went on.

"Each of these locations would be a suitable location for ambush. They cover all the roads leading into the village of Innishannon, to the east there is sufficient cover along those parts of the terrain to give more than adequate cover for the ambushers, and finally retreat from those positions would normally be relatively easy. In the west nearer Bandon there is not much cover and retreat are made more difficult because of the river and its proximity to Bandon.

"Let us assume, they are led by those who have some military experience and even had positions of some leadership in our army during the War. If so, they will have given a great deal of thought to not only the ambush itself but also to the scouting arrangements before the attack and the ability to have a clear exit if things go wrong.

"Consequently, we must plan to take all of this into consideration in the formation of our counter strategy. Seeing that we do not have any idea of where they will be coming from or where they might retreat to after the ambush, we must lull them into a trap if we wish to counter attack.

"The first requirement is to give them a false sense of security. To do this the patrol should be a regular size one in that area. We must assume they have seen our patrols here before and the IRA is counting on a similar grouping for this attack.

"Next, we must have a second or more contingent of troops in close proximity to the ambush to overwhelm the enemy as quickly as possible after they attack. These troops have to be kept back from the site far enough so they cannot be seen before the attack. But not so far as to have them arrive too late to thwart the ambush.

"We must assume that they will have sufficient numbers to overwhelm the original patrol. If that is the case, then they will wish to get out of the area as quickly afterwards as possible. This would not leave much time for our follow-up group to arrive.

"We must use our advantages to the full. First, we must have scouts buried locally if possible, with radio to alert our people to what the IRA are doing. I say buried because the IRA without doubt will also have scouts in the area and they will have the advantage of local knowledge and we must assume local support to tip them off if they see anything suspicious happening. It would be best if our follow-up was spread out sufficiently to outflank the guerrillas and cut off their escape routes."

Finishing up Percival asked for questions, but having received none he ended by proposing they work on a contingency to put the foregoing into operation. However, in the meantime they would await the information expected from the RIC before finalising anything.

Ending, he noted that they were already working on borrowed time.

The C.O. agreed and the meeting ended.

After the meeting Geoffrey walked to the communications office to check on any up-date from the Army in Cork city and from his own regiment in Kinsale.

Word had come back from both to say that troops passed infrequently by Innishannon but regularly through Upton.

From Kinsale patrols quite often were in the vicinity of Upton and they would send notification of upcoming patrols. The first was due in mid-morning two days later. It would travel through Upton from Kinsale via Kilmacsimon Quay. From there it would travel through Crossbarry and on to Riverstick on its return to Kinsale. The information conveyed to them was noted and they would wait to hear back before taking a decision on how they should proceed. Kinsale had also mentioned that the usual patrol contained a company of up to 30 officers and men.

From Cork city supplies were constantly being conveyed to the various barracks in the district. These were always escorted by troops from the city. There were no supplies due this particular week.

However, the train to West Cork which went through Upton travelled at least once each day. It invariably had some troops on board. A bigger contingent accompanied the train if it had army supplies on board. Again, there were no supplies scheduled by train for that particular week.

Geoffrey immediately informed the C.O.

Major Stewart, Major Percival and Geoffrey spent some time thereafter scrutinising the ordinance maps to better pinpoint where an attack might take place along that route. They were almost certain now that the attack, if it took place, would be against this patrol. It was known that IRA operatives were believed to be particularly prevalent all along that road.

Consequently, it would be difficult to conceal a follow-up large force of personnel without scouts and informers conveying that information to the IRA. They would have to take that into consideration before finalising their plan of action.

This indeed would be an audacious move by the IRA. If it was to succeed, it would be a huge morale booster for the IRA and equally a corresponding blow for the security forces and particularly for the Army. On the other hand, if they were able to thwart this ambush it would have the reverse effect. It was accordingly, imperative that they should take advantage of their limited knowledge and attempt to turn it into a victory for the Army.

Major Percival undertook to alert Kinsale and to get the Commanding Officer there to approve of a wider plan of action to deal with a possible attack. In the meantime, they should not alter their patrol arrangement that week. They would liaise again shortly when a suitable plan had been constructed and then decide, in conjunction with Kinsale, how the plan should proceed.

Geoffrey was also dispatched to speak again with Superintendent McClintock to definitively discover what patrols if any his side had arranged for this week around Upton. They need to discount that eventuality as quickly as possible to get on with their plan.

As he emerged from the C.O.'s office Sergeant Turner was waiting to tell him Superintendent McClintock wished to speak with him. He wasted no time making his way to the RIC barracks where he was told that there were no patrols planned by any of the forces on his side.

At least that made the planning a little less complicated. Yet there was the question of which patrol if any was the target? Was it that passing through Upton or the other going directly to Cork city? They would probably have to cover both to be sure.

Geoffrey was at that stage instructed by Major Stewart to devise a plan of action which would be looked at next morning.

He immediately determined that he would have to come up with two separate plans to take account of the two separate patrols which regularly traversed the area. He also decided that in both cases there should be a Plan A and a Plan B because of the lack of specific information which they had.

Chapter 27

Soon after he had begun to work a message arrived from an anonymous source, at least anonymous to all apart from him. It was from Julia who in the coded way they had agreed informed him that the way was open that evening and he would be welcome after dark when he could slip in by the back entrance without being noticed. Luckily, she had also told him where that would be, so he should have little difficulty and be less obvious when accessing it.

Geoffrey's first thoughts were that because of the urgency of the task he was given he would not be able to make the appointment. However, on almost immediate reflection he was determined to be there. Accordingly, he set to work outlining his plans and worked right through the evening meal with no break. By 9 PM he had completed the task and after re-examining it he was satisfied that he had covered the ground to the greatest extent possible.

In addition, because he had drawn up contingencies in both cases, he felt it gave enough scope for the C.O. and the scrutiny party to both choose which course to take or select a combination of all of his proposals. While he was satisfied that he had covered the ground as far as he could, he could not be but apprehensive. Major Percival, he knew from reputation and from his short experience of the man, would not accept anything other than perfection. Still, he firmly believed that even if his plans were not accepted in full, he would at least salvage some aspects of them.

By 9.30pm he dressed in dark mufti to conceal himself in the night and made his way around the back way into town by the narrow footbridge. As it was already dark before he left the barracks, curfew in the town ensured that the streets and alleys were empty.

There was an eerie feel to the evening, not just because of the enforced curfew, as he made his way over the quiet summer river. There was something about it that made him shiver, even in the warm weather. While it was akin to feelings he had experienced during his time at the Front; there was more than that. It was not because he again felt the presence of imminent danger. He had learnt to live with that long ago.

That time he was one of the few survivors of his company during the early days of the Somme and later, when he was past caring about death, when he was involved in the horror that was Passchendaele. No, this time it was different. This time he could not tell himself that he was fighting for a principle or indeed for the rights of man. This was colonialism by another name.

The majority here did not want them. Like in South Africa, the English were no longer welcome as overlords. If the war had proven anything, it was that in the 20th century Empires were no longer acceptable. Woodrow Wilson was right; it was a war for liberty not for colony.

As he pondered on this his only companions were the flies which had emerged for the evening. The midges arising from the semi-dried up river ensured he kept rapidly on the move. Crossing over he made his way down the quay to where he had been instructed by Julia. The quay was a product of an earlier time when the river was the main artery for transport and merchandise. In the past stores and warehouses lined the road along the river. Now they were the storerooms for the merchants in the main shopping street. The town houses had then and still turned its collective back to the river.

As Julia had instructed him, he sought and found quite easily the black painted gate directly across from the third slipway down to the river. As he pushed down the catch the unlocked well-oiled gate opened effortlessly making no noise. He made his way down the narrow passageway between the coach house and the boundary wall of the adjoining building. Passing through the well cared for leisure garden he could see lights in the windows above. There were none showing in the adjacent buildings, which were used only for business and vacant during the night.

The side door to the building was again unlocked and he let himself in. On his way up the narrow staircase, he hesitated momentarily. What if Alasdair was not away for the night on business? What if for some reason or other he decided not to travel? What excuse could he possibly use for this house invasion? No, he decided almost immediately. Julia would have been wise enough to lock the gate and the door if such an event were to happen.

Julia was waiting on him as he arrived on the upper landing. Without saying a word they both embraced avidly, like lovers who had been separated for months by distance and lack of communication. He finally attempted to speak but she cut him off, unwilling to spoil that moment of exquisite passion; that unique time when lovers meet for the first occasion after the initial mutual consent has been given. Leading the way, she took him silently by the hand and escorted him through a place and pleasure he had never before experienced. Gone were the troubles of the day and the war plans, gone was the guilt of trespass in another person's world. Gone even were the ghosts and memories of the past gory times and losses and losses.

They remained together in this embrace for over an hour shielded for the moment from the mores and prurience of the outside world. Little was said or needed to be said. They had entered into a state somewhere between East and West of Eden, from which they wished to remain for as long as the outside world would permit.

Finally, they emerged into the real world, where the realities of time and place had to be dealt with. Julia talked about the town and those matters and people she dealt with both in relation to her role as the wife of the local bank manager and also the friends she had made there. She told Geoffrey that she had a great affection for West Cork and the beauty of the place. But there was a sadness about the place which lay under the surface.

She also talked about the two worlds in the district, not like other places which were divided in the haves and have nots. While that division existed here also, there was the greater divide of two nations or at least the remnants of that partition as well. The present turmoil only reinforced that partition and until and unless that was resolved no real progress could be made in this otherwise unspoiled idyll.

She offered Geoffrey a drink and/or some other refreshment. Geoffrey wanted to accept, anything to linger on in her presence. Now he began to think of all the questions he should ask, but decided against that, not wishing to spoil the occasion with any intrusion from the real world outside, which was already beginning to rattle the windows and doors of his exterior reason.

"I had better get going. I don't wish to raise any suspicion, for you in particular. It has just gone midnight and I can slip into the night and get back to barracks without anyone being the wiser. I cannot explain in mere words how much that evening meant to me. I have no former yardstick by which to gauge it. All I can hope is that you too feel as I do."

"Of course, my darling, I do. Since we first met, you have been on my mind. I tried at first to put this aside but that feeling just got stronger each time we met since."

"Julia, I do not wish to spoil the moment. Just tell me that we can meet like this again?"

"Of course, my darling, I must see you, I will arrange another occasion as soon the time permits."

She came with him to the back gate. Pausing only for a last goodnight embrace Geoffrey slipped away into the shadows. Julia locked the gate and also remembered to lock the back door of the building on returning.

Chapter 28

When Geoffrey returned to his billet, he reviewed his proposals for a plan of action which he would present to the OC, Percival and the others in the morning. He was determined that he would cover the ground as far as possible, taking into consideration the likely ambush areas that the IRA might use and having particular regard for those locations marked out by Percival. As least if he was to get lambasted by the rejection of his plan, he would at least not get it totally wrong.

His thoughts however, were never far from his rendezvous with Julia. His spirits were higher now than they had been for many years, even surpassing that which he had felt at 11AM on the 11th day of the 11 month in 1918 when the War ended and an armistice was agreed.

Because of war and his particular relations with his parents Geoffrey had been deprived of many of the normal intimacies that human beings experienced at various stages of their lives. Geoffrey's only real intimate relationship before Julia was with his Nannie Kate, who, even now, was never far from his thoughts. She had been the one person he felt he could totally rely on, who would understand him and his needs. She was his rock. Not only did she give the love he needed as a child. Because of this he had understood from an early age not only the vital necessity of receiving love, but in many ways the ability to be able to return that love.

Now he believed he found someone else with whom he could share that intimacy of trust and love. He was not unaware of the minefield he was traversing. He was after all used to the physicality of war. Those of the mind however, could be just as dangerous and indeed less obvious. For now, he would not dwell on this. Rather he would allow himself to be absorbed in the moment, in the realms of the ascendant rapture. He was in Arcadia.

Next morning, he appeared before the Barracks OC, Major Percival and the other senior officers to discuss the plans.

He was asked to outline his proposals taking in all of the information they had already gathered.

Geoffrey first took the meeting through the information they had received from Army H.Q. in Cork city and their District Regimental H.Q. in Kinsale and also of course that which they had received from the RIC and its associates. He then went on to his proposals.

"Taking what we know into account, I have assumed that the IRA has planned to attack one of our patrols which move through the area frequently. They would not gather in the numbers required for such an operation unless they were somewhat confident that a patrol was likely to pass by their selected ambush site. Additionally, I have assumed that they will decide well beforehand where that attack site will be. An ambush is only really effective if the target is moving rather than the attacker.

"There are two main patrols that pass near Upton almost once each week. One from here to Cork city and return on the main road and the other from Kinsale, through Kilmacsimon, Upton, Crossbarry, Riverstick and back to Kinsale. Accordingly, knowing the routes our troops will traverse one can select ambush sites around Upton. As Major Percival pointed out at our last meeting a number of locations would appear to be possible attack sites. I agree from the standpoint of the cover these locations give the attackers and the ease of quick withdrawal in a number of directions if the ambush was not successful.

"If we take these considerations into account, then we must provide for a plan to lure the IRA into a false sense of superiority. This will require the patrols to take place as normal. In doing so we must ensure that we have sufficient backup troops to both overwhelm the attackers and get there quickly after the initial attack has started.

"We should be in a position to minimise the damage inflicted on our troops if we are able to get quickly to that site. However, if we fail to do so our casualties could be high and the enemy could make their escape. The issue therefore is how far away can we afford to keep the follow-up force to ensure that the IRA scouts will not observe them early before the attack commences.

"Because we do not yet know the exact location of the ambush, any prior positioning we might place our troops in would have to be difficult. There is an alternative. I propose that we should place scouts, well hidden, along several of the roads leading to these attack areas more than 24 hours before our patrols are due to arrive.

"Additionally, if possible, we should be able to close in from several directions to trap the IRA in the ambush position. This would inevitably require a large number of troops and obviously a good deal of coordination which at this stage we may not have time to do.

"In order to do all or even part of what I have outlined we need to make decisions quickly; particularly in relation to the scouts who should be dropped into position by at least in the very early hours tomorrow morning, as the first patrol form Kinsale is due to pass Upton at about noon tomorrow."

Geoffrey waited for reactions from the assembled group, particularly from Major Perceval.

As expected, Major Perceval, who was the Regiment's chief local strategist and intelligence officer, was the first to comment.

"The proposals you make, Captain, are reasonable and appear to cover the ground as well as can be expected in the given circumstances. There are a few points I wish to make however.

"First, we do not have much time before the first of the two patrols you mentioned will take place, which is tomorrow. It gives us less than 30 hours from now. To operationalise the plan, you outline would take much more time which we do not have. In order to carry it out properly we would have to coordinate with the Regiment in Kinsale, brief the officers who would be leading the patrol and also the follow-up troops and then prepare the troops for dispatch.

"Secondly the Kinsale force will be moving through territory which we know contains quite a number of IRA volunteers and many supporters. It would therefore be difficult to move a second contingent close behind the patrol without there being seen early on. That would possibly give time for the attackers to disperse before we arrived. We arrested one of those we believe to have a leading role in the IRA last month.

"He is from that area and we believe his family is deeply involved. While we have failed to get any information from after interrogation, we know he comes from a hotbed of republicanism. Finally, because we do not know for certain where the attack will be we are at a great disadvantage.

"That having been said however, we have committed ourselves to using the limited knowledge we have to defeat the IRA. If we can do this, we will have inflicted on them a decisive blow in this area. If we decide not to send the patrol, then we are conceding that we are unable to control the district.

"Accordingly, I propose to accept part of your plan, particularly the idea of scouts under deep cover to be there even earlier than you suggested. We have, I believe, some radio equipment between here and Kinsale. While it is cumbersome if we can use it, it would give us a great advantage. We should be able to know well in advance where the IRA is congregating. While I suspect it might not be the ambush area immediately, as they might wait behind until nearer the time to take up the ambush positions, it will be sufficiently close to give us a good idea where the ambush will be.

"We should therefore insert our scouts late this evening after dark. Next, we should send the patrol as usual from Kinsale with additional troops well-armed for immediate engagement. Hopefully we will be able to alert them before they arrive at the ambush area. So that they can dismount their vehicles and approach quickly and stealthily by foot taking the would-be ambushers by surprise.

"In the meanwhile, the follow-up contingent should come from here moving quickly by the road until they get near the target area. Hopefully our radio signals will be effective so that both sets of troops will be in communication with what the scouts are saying. If we are not able to use our radios, then we need some runners with bicycles to report back if the need arises. The movement of both patrol and follow-up contingents has to be extremely well timed so that each will know where the other is at a certain time. With your permission Major (speaking to the OC of the Barracks) can I ask, are there any questions or has anyone any other suggestions?"

Major Stewart, responding, agreed with the plan of action just outlined by Percival and he said if no one else had anything further to offer he would ask Major Percival to speak with Kinsale and set the business in motion.

No one else spoke.

Geoffrey left the meeting with some feeling of satisfaction. He knew that his plan would not be accepted by Percival in total. However, neither was it totally rejected and indeed a great deal of it was retained. Percival would always want his imprimatur on any plan which was devised. Geoffrey had allowed for that and was more than happy that Percival took the responsibility for its final design and also of course for any outcome which would arise from it.

Percival had himself undertaken to coordinate the plan with the Regiment in Kinsale and with the company commanders. Geoffrey, as well as being asked to inform Superintendent McClintock that they were dealing with the matter, was instructed to make contact with any of his informants who might have more information on the expected ambush.

Other than that Geoffrey was given no other role in the plan. He was quite pleased about that as a meeting with Julia again that evening was still a possibility. She had told him before he had departed the night before that Alastair was to phone her in the early afternoon to let her know whether he was staying in the city for another night or not. She would know before the 5pm train left Cork which he would have to get if he was coming home. He never failed to let her know so that she could have a meal for him when he returned. Either way if he was to arrive, he would be home just after 6pm.

Chapter 29

Geoffrey called immediately after the morning's briefing at the RIC barracks to inform Superintendent McClintock that the Army were dealing with the possible IRA ambush. He did not make known the full detail of the countermeasures the Army was taking but nevertheless he let it be known that they would attempt to thwart the attack if it took place. He was particularly advising the Superintendent to ensure that the RIC and its cohorts would not interfere or go anywhere near the area during late morning to early evening the next day.

McClintock thanked him for letting them know and he reassured him that nothing from their side would move in that area all next day unless the Army called on them to help. Though nothing anyway had been scheduled to move in that area the next day even before Geoffrey spoke initially to the Superintendent, the latter had used his initiative and stood down all activities in the district for the following day. He had told no one why he had made that order. While he had no one of his staff under suspicion of leaking information to the IRA he was nevertheless mindful of that possibility.

Geoffrey was pleased with the manner in which McClintock dealt with him on the issue. He had not asked about any of the details of the Army's plan and he had quietly ensured that his people would not interfere with that plan. Geoffrey was impressed and felt he could in the future take him further into his confidence.

Afterwards he went by a circuitous route to the Church entering around the back way to see if the Reverend Foster was in his office. If he was not there, Geoffrey had intended to leave a message to meet later in the same place. He was lucky however, in that he almost bumped into the Reverend gentleman as the latter was leaving to attend a meeting elsewhere. Their meeting did not take long however, as the Reverend had little else to add to what had previously been relayed. All he could say is that he understood that his source mentioned that she had heard no word on any change to the arrangements.

Geoffrey went another route through the town and called in to see John Flaherty on the way. He had been intrigued by the man when he met him and while he could not say that they had formed any type of bond, he felt he should know more about him. At the very least he felt he should listen to what he said as he probably spoke for a good deal of nationalists who, even though they wanted some type of independence from Britain, would not condone the IRA violence.

Geoffrey found him in his office and, offering some excuse for his unexpected call, asked to see the new Fordson. He understood that his father had purchased one for his own property in England at the behest of his land agent: although Geoffrey who spent little time at home never actually saw it. Flaherty took him round his showroom and showed him the few he had there.

Apparently, they did not stay long in the showroom before being purchased by eager major landowners. Flaherty pointed out the multitasks it could perform from pulling trailers, to ploughing, to cutting corn, to driving threshing machines and even small flour mills when the rivers were very dry. The day of the working horse was gone.

Geoffrey well understood that. He had first-hand experience of that change occurring during the war. Although God knows the animals made an enormous contribution and indeed like their human companions paid an enormous price.

They also spoke about the Ford car which was fast coming into production for Europe and would be assembled in Cork. Then of course, the ford family came originally from near Bandon before moving to Cork city and then to Detroit. Geoffrey was very keen on having his own motor car as it would give the freedom to move that he had craved for some years. *God, he reflected, why then am I here where in my very role I restrict my own movements. I could not arrive here at this business premise without taking evasive action to do so. I am a wayfarer's soul in a settler's body.*

John Flaherty, showing his American influence, invited him to have coffee with him in his office, prepared by an efficient secretary. Geoffrey gratefully accepted and admired the elegant, but very practical layout of his office. The relationship between them improved considerably to the point where they both referred to one another by first name.

This came about both because John Flaherty had adopted the American informal customs and after their conversation about the new Ford machinery where Geoffrey impressed him by showing a knowledge far above what John

Flaherty would have encountered amongst even the more sophisticated of the local population.

After some minutes of banter, while enjoying the coffee which John had imported from America, Geoffrey eased his way into asking about the current local political situation by way of the economic one.

"John has the local economy shown much recovery since the end of the war?"

"It has been very slow in recovery. As you know the British Treasury has been depleted and is currently running an extraordinary huge deficit and an enormous national debt. This feeds back into the total economy through cuts in services, money flows and infrastructure. In addition, taxes have increased. This situation is expected to go on for some time and I would be surprised if that situation together with the aftermath of the war would not exponentially change politics in Britain as it already has done in many parts of Europe. We are and cannot but continue to be affected here by those events."

"How will it affect your business?"

"Yes, it is bound to hold it back from its natural trajectory. However, it will not totally restrain it. Our technology is the future and if we are to recover, we must take advantage of that new technology. It will change everything as it has already in America. Like the winds and the tides, their energies cannot be ignored."

"You make some very good points. I saw first-hand how mechanisms changed the face of the war in such a short time. I do not believe we will ever see a war fought like that one again because of the advances man has made in machines and technology. Next time it will be machine against machine, more death, and more destruction and more widespread. Nowhere will be safe. There will be no hiding place.

"On the other hand, I understand the very positive side of technology and machinery. Your machines can do in a day what would take a man a week. It certainly would help an economy like Ireland's which is based as I can see on agriculture. But can most of the farmers here afford a tractor?"

"Of course not. Unfortunately, the majority of farms in Ireland are very small and barely support a family. There is no marginal income from these places. I spoke to the banks here and they tell me that most of them do not even have bank accounts. It's a hand to mouth existence for them. Added to that there has been a falling off of demand for agriculture products since the war.

"Britain is not taking as much food and there are scarce funds. Additionally, the population of Europe has declined significantly with a large proportion of the young and most vital part of that population gone because of the war and the subsequent Spanish Flu."

"What then?"

"Well, that's a good question. In the short term, stagnation. In the longer term this can change. The populations of Europe are growing rapidly. Most households have large families. That can of course have good and bad outcomes. Depending on the policies of the countries concerned, it can lead to expansion and development or indeed abject poverty. The differences will be the availability of funds and technology and the willingness of governments to foster growth.

"That's where America is ahead and is likely to go even further ahead in the years to come. The problem for Europe is that like a magnet attracts steel America will continue to attract the most energetic young manpower from Europe unless Europe can refocus its energies away from internal conflict and toward using its vast resources, including its manpower."

"Where does that leave Ireland?"

"Backward unfortunately. We have been sending people to America since Columbus. What was a stream is now a river and that is set to continue as siblings and kin attract more of their own. There is no real industry in Ireland to provide jobs. Ford is the only major company to set up here for some time and that because of sentimental reasons. There is Guinness in Dublin. A thriving business in Ireland. Alcohol is of course the Scylla and Charybdis of the Irish, through this is not the fault of Guinness.

"If that industry did not exist, another similar product would appear to lead us down the same passage. The main industrial centre, if one can call it that, is in Belfast where the steel and shipbuilding give a certain amount of employment, but unfortunately this has been very divisive as it favours only one community there."

Geoffrey seeing his opening went on to the topic he had been seeking: "That unfortunately has been the problem for Ireland—the Unionists also blocked the implementation of Home Rule. It obviously led to the rebellion in Dublin in 1916. And now how do you see the current Troubles here?"

"Quite a question indeed! Frankly I firmly believe we have now arrived at a junction in this country where the old remedies, if you would call them that, will no longer be enough. Neither defeat of the IRA, nor a proroguing of the Dail, nor the substitution of Home Rule by the proposed twin devolution parliaments in Dublin and Belfast will no longer suffice. The die is cast.

"The nationalists have now overwhelmingly gone over to the "Young Turks" of Irish politics. Gone are the days of Parnell, where the Irish would have been satisfied with Home Rule and a parliament with filial ties to Westminster. What is demanded now is total independence and anything short of that will require total subjugation by Britain.

"I do not believe that is feasible in the 20th century. For one, the Irish would continue to rebel and it would require a standing army to keep the country under control. Secondly, I do not believe the Americans would stand for it and as has been proved in the War, Britain needs America.

"There is only one way out of this and that is a negotiated settlement with autonomy for Ireland. The sooner that happens the better for both islands. Geoffrey, confidentially, I hope I can be frank with you and I take it that is the object of this conversation and why you came to visit. You may defeat the IRA and annihilate the volunteers as they stand but the British Forces will not annihilate the existence of that force. Others in time will replace them. You are not fighting just men. You are fighting their raison d'être."

"Thank you for being so candid with me John. Our conversation will remain here and I am very grateful for your views. As you know I have only arrived in Ireland these past number of months and my knowledge of the place is very poor indeed. You are the first person locally to have spoken to me so frankly and I have to admit so cogently.

"Most soldiers will admit that they do not wish to be burdened with the reasons they are sent out to perform their duties. It only gets in the way. It is for the politicians to say why and what outcome they require before the task you are sent to perform ends. Good commanders like good civil servants are guided by the instructions they receive from on high rather than foolishly obeying them without reasonable grounds for doing so. We weren't always so lucky during the war."

Deciding to change to a more non-contentious matters Geoffrey asked: "It intrigues me John, why you, obviously very qualified to take on leading roles in industry, should waste your time here is this beautiful but low-paced backwater? You obviously have already done well in America. Why return?"

"Many reasons Geoffrey. I had been offered an opportunity by Ford, as a local, to help set up their company here. I did so and I am still on the board of the Company in Cork. However, I also wished to return to my roots, even for a short time. My mother still lives here and I wished to spend some time near her having been away so long.

"In addition to my duties at Ford I decided to take an agency for this area which would allow me to run my own business. So far, I am enjoying the area and a much-needed rest. I will reconsider what I will do after a year or two. Once I have got something up and running, I like to move on and let someone else bring the business on further."

"In many ways I envy you John. I wish I could go home."

They parted soon after that, both establishing a better understanding of one another: easy acquaintances, though never as real friends.

Chapter 30

Joe Ryan noticed the flurry of activity in the barracks when he visited that day. He purposely did not enter any lengthy conversations with Sergeant Turner, merely advising him that he had made progress on the task he was given to tap into the communications of the Auxiliaries in particular. The Sergeant gave him the Auxiliaries and the RIC call codes and informed him that they apparently were using the old codes in their communications.

Turner seemed preoccupied when he spoke with Joe and obviously wished to end their meeting as quickly as possible to get on to more urgent matters. Joe took the hint and left soon after. He believed that the scene he had observed was related to the information he had previously picked up and conveyed to Sean Hales. He had overheard the words scouting party and that was sufficient to warn him not to be seen to be overly ambitious to find out what was going on.

On his way back to his business premises he diverted to write a coded note to Sean Hales, updating him on the situation, particularly mentioning the scouting party. He would use the drop box location in the town, they had both agreed on, which was visited many times in the day in case there was a message. This again was at the behest of Joe who understood the heightened levels of suspicion introduced since Major Percival had taken up semi-permanent residence in the barracks.

He was also conscious that Sean's brother Tom had been captured some weeks before with another IRA leader and he fully understood what pressures were more than likely brought to bear on them to extract information about the IRA. When he had met Sean two days before, he was very concerned for his brother but he did not show any signs that his brother was aware of Joe's involvement. Joe had not asked him directly about this, as to have done so he felt would show a lack of confidence in Sean that he did not have.

He was satisfied that Sean would get the message quickly and be able to act on it.

As he was making his way through the town to get to his business after his drop he bumped into John Flaherty. In a small town everyone knew everyone else particularly in the business community. John had had dealings with Joe and had found him efficient and flexible. He admired the way he had come from a poor background and had educated himself the hard way to achieve what he had in such a short space of time.

Again, he saw him as a modern businessman, who understood and saw the exponential possibilities with advanced technologies. While he saw Joe playing a big role in the business life of the town in the future, he wondered why, with his abilities, he had not moved to a more populous and progressive place when his talents and ingenuity could be put to much more productive and lucrative use. He had on a number of occasions hinted that Joe would do very well in America.

"Hello Joe. How is the business going? I would be keen to know sometime we can have a quiet chat, how far the electrification of houses has got in the town. Likewise, those other than business premises who have or are seeking to install the telephone. It would give a fair indication how much progress we are making."

And Joe thought also showed who could afford to pay for those installations for personal use, luxuries for most people. If they could afford those, can tractors and even motor cars be far behind?

"Delighted to do so anytime John. It is interesting to see how once one gets into modern equipment it leads on to other labour-saving devices new to the market. In addition, neighbours, particularly those who see themselves as on a par with the upper end of the population, will not allow their equals to get too far ahead of them in acquiring new machines that they feel will either enhance their profit or, given human pride, their prestige. No one, with any aspirations, wants to be left behind. Good for me and I dare say you. By the way, I would be interested in a commercial vehicle in the near future. I would of course be expecting a trade discount in addition to a luck penny."

"I'm sure we can come to terms on that Joe. Let me know when you want to go ahead. Hi, by the way I met that acquaintance of yours, Captain Eastbourne, today. Called into my place unexpectedly. Had only met him once before at dinner and then had only fleeting exchanges with him. He strikes me as a cut above the average army officer. He has an inquisitive mind and an ability to unobtrusively chivvy out of your things you might not say if you were being cautious. His very pleasant personality lends itself admirably to that."

With that he said he was in a hurry to meet a client at the bank to complete a deal and they parted, agreeing to meet for tea next morning in his office.

Joe thought about what he had just heard. John Flaherty was not only an astute businessman with a masters in engineering from a prestigious American university, he was also a very shrewd judge of character and an extraordinarily insightful individual. While many were wary of him and did not understand his American-way-learned, extremely direct approach to business, and even in day-to-day matters, Joe was very taken by this approach.

He trusted John and saw him as no nonsense type of man who did not suffer fools gladly. He wished more could be like him here, but still understood the culture of denial that people here had lived with for centuries. The war had educated him in ways he did not fully understand until his return. There was no pettiness there, no time for niceties and finesse, no in-between, only the quick and the dead.

Accordingly, he understood the message that had been sent. *I don't know what you might know about things and people who are important to the British security forces, but whatever you might know, be aware of what you say in his company.*

Joe was momentarily stunned by this. Did John Flaherty know about his involvement? One could not put anything beyond him. He had the most widespread connections at every level of society. Businessmen relied on him for his advice and judgment. People who were employed by him, and he took them from the humblest backgrounds to the highest, were totally loyal to him and would absolutely confide in him.

No, he decided. He was merely warning him that information picked up in the nationalist community, which might seem every day to Joe, might be used by the security forces in the jigsaw of the greater picture in their fight against the IRA.

He had not shown any reaction at the time to the message given by John Flaherty, but it showed that he must be very aware of the dangers of giving his position away. His reaction afterwards also again displayed his renewed sense of walking down that dangerous pathway he thought he had felt when in Passchendaele's muddy and bloody No Man's Land.

Later before lunch he wondered if his earlier message had been passed on to Sean Hales. He was tempted to return to the drop box site to check but quickly decided against it on two grounds. First it would be unwise to be seen twice in the same location within hours of each other if someone was observing him. Secondly if the message had not been picked up by now, he could do nothing more at this stage, without declaring his involvement, and anyway even if he could it would be too late now to act on it. Anyway, he had told Sean Hales two days before about the matter and he expected that countermeasures were already in place.

He had worked on a solution for tapping into the Auxiliaries communications for the British Army. He had also found a way to ensure that he would also get that information separate from the Army tap. He should return to the barracks to set it in motion but he decided against it as it would be more advisable to stay clear of that place today as tensions were high there because of the ongoing operation against the IRA.

He could see that as time went on the activities of both the IRA and consequently also the security forces would be ratcheted up. That would more than likely involve him more in the collection of intelligence. Accordingly, his position would become more and more vulnerable. He must therefore ensure that he is doubly careful about protecting his cover. He has learned enough about Major Percival to know that he in time will suspect everyone that has even the slightest connection with what is happening inside the barracks.

Everyone entering it, particularly the civilians, will be under automatic suspicion. His previous role in Army intelligence during the war will stand him in good stead for a time but that cover can be quickly blown with the slightest mistake. His good relations with Captain Eastbourne, while now a major plus, could in time turn against him. Geoffrey, as John Flaherty pointed out, is no fool and he will pick up on any lazy misstep on his part.

He was mindful of his intimate relations with his fiancé, the daughter of a former senior figure in the Land League, and the Irish Republican Brotherhood (Fenians), who had spent a good deal of time incarcerated at both Her and His majesty's pleasure. On the last such occasion he had been sent to prison in Frongoch with the others after the Rising in 1916. It was surprising that so far, the connection had not apparently been made.

If it had, he would have expected that some question would have been asked about it. It could only be a matter of time before that was discovered. He would then be questioned at length, either to discover his affiliation with his prospective father-in-law's views or indeed to ask of him to spy for them on the associates of that man. Perhaps they already suspected him and were watching to see what he was at and who he was talking to. On the other hand, would they have asked him to undertake the tap into the Auxiliaries communications if they mistrusted him? He judged not.

However, he decided that he nevertheless was working on borrowed time and he hoped that he would be able to get out in time before they discovered his affiliations with the IRA.

Chapter 31

After his return to the barracks Geoffrey informed Major Percival that there was no additional information forthcoming. He also informed him that the RIC and its cohorts would remain in barracks for the day and not move out anywhere near the Upton region.

There had been no information from the scouts, who were for some hours now well hidden in the countryside back from the approaches to around the expected ambush sites, apart from the initial contacts to say they were in position and all was quiet. They had been instructed of course to keep their communications silent until such time as there was some activity in the area which might be IRA related.

The contingent from Bandon was ready to move out at a certain point so as to be within striking distance of the Kinsale patrol when it reached the ambush areas. To ensure no hint of security countermeasure was seen by the IRA the backup contingent would be delayed until the last moment.

All they could do now was wait until they heard from the scouts who would be able to tell them when the IRA was gathering and getting the attackers into position. Percival presumed this would be at least an hour before the ambush. One of the army scouts had earlier in the day reconnoitred the whole area and reported nothing could be seen that would in any way suggest a formation of an ambushing group.

Geoffrey, after he had gone to the communications hut to ensure that no recent messages concerning the operation at hand had arrived, went back to his other duties in the barracks. At this stage he was no longer involved in the operation.

Sitting at his desk he could help reflecting on his meeting that morning with John Flaherty. He had been most useful. Flaherty's analysis of the current situation was both very incisive as well as frank. The Army in Geoffrey told him to reject what had been said and even to consider it virtual treason. However, his logic differed saying that Flaherty was absolutely correct in his assessment. Had he not seen this before? The world had gone to war on the basis of past outdated feelings of Imperial superiority and outrageous rights and did not end despite the annihilation of millions and the destruction of the countries and empires of all the participants.

There were no real winners in that contest. Early or late disputes involving peoples and territories must be resolved by discussion and compromise rather than by force of arms. That, he saw first-hand, is today more obvious than at any time in the past. John Flaherty was right: machines and technology used for economic progress will determine our future rather than military conquest.

Later in the afternoon, there had been no word from the scouts and the Kinsale patrol was on route. At the last minute the OC decided to send out the support contingence from the barracks just in case the scouts had unwittingly not seen the IRA group. They had taken the side road through Kilbeg and were to arrive within striking distance, through the fields, if necessary, if the patrol were to be attacked.

By 3.30pm the patrol was passing Riverstick and well away from the probable ambush sites and too near Kinsale for the attack. The contingent was recalled, as were the scouts who joined them stealthily so as to go unnoticed by any onlookers.

Back at the barracks in Bandon there was a brief meeting of the planning group. The C.O. asked Major Percival for his comments, who, while attempting to hide his disappointment, was noticeably irritated by the no show.

"I regret the operation did not go as planned. We can assume four scenarios. The first, that the information we received was poor or the second, that the IRA at some stage discovered we had been informed and consequently abandoned their attack, or the third, their plans were disrupted by extraneous circumstances unrelated to the fact that we were waiting for them.

"If it is the first, then we should seek to find out why? Captain Eastbourne we will leave that matter up to you. While we should encourage individuals from the public to come forward with information, we should simultaneously try to ascertain whether or not we can trust those reports.

"If it is the second, then we must diligently seek out the source of the leak from our side if indeed there was one. It is possible that somehow our activities in the past 24 hours were noticed by the public. We are surrounded by potential IRA informers and it is difficult to know who to trust or not trust in the general public. One way or another we should ensure we are watertight and redouble our efforts to prevent any leaks emanating from our side.

"It could however, be the third scenario and some hitch prevented the IRA from carrying the attack: which frankly I am inclined to believe. In that case we should be aware that what had been planned for today will possibly be carried out a later time. I believe that if an ambush was planned for the Upton region, the IRA will quite likely wish to stick to whatever plan they had today.

"If that be so, then we have to consider what we are to do to beef up our patrols to prevent a surprise attack. In that case we should follow today's plan for the next few weeks at least.

"The fourth scenario could be that it is the patrol to Cork city from this barracks which usually is carried every week is the target. If so, then the ambush could be in two days' time. Like the situation in scenario three, we should continue with the same plan for that patrol, only this time the contingency back-up should come from Kinsale.

"Accordingly, in cases three and four we go ahead with today's plan adjusted according to which barracks the original patrol comes from. Even in the case of scenario two there is a good possibility that the IRA will return to their plan and so we should also cover that eventuality. In the meantime, Captain Eastbourne should take all of the scenarios into consideration when confronting attempting to seek information from his contacts.

"There is at least one positive element about today's action. It was a very useful exercise which showed that we could at short notice put an effective operation in the field quickly. No doubt we will have similar occasions in the future and we must be prepared. The type of warfare, and have no doubt that is what we have here now, we are facing is very different to that which most of us have previously experienced or indeed been trained for. The IRA has already shown that it can be a formidable force, which appears out of nowhere and disappears back into the countryside just as quickly. We must learn how to cope with that type of warfare.

"Intelligence is the key to our eventual success. The IRA has the advantage on us at present, as we must assume they are cosseted by a large section of the nationalist community. We must attempt to infiltrate that community, whatever way we can, to tap into their network. I expect all of you to bear this in mind when you are dealing with the public and to take every opportunity to gather even the minutest piece of information about the IRA and its leadership.

Remember no matter how trivial it may appear it can be pieced together with other information we have gathered to give us a better picture than what we have at present."

The OC of the barracks responding agreed with the assessment made by Major Percival.

"Thank you Major. I agree with your assessment of the situation but I would place a more positive view of the operation we have just carried out. The operation is still ongoing in that we do not know which patrol was the target. The patrol from this barracks could be it and therefore we must act accordingly. On this occasion, as we have more time, we should use it to put out scouts in place earlier and during darkness to ensure they are not observed.

"Even if the IRA does not appear we have shown that we can respond promptly and fully to control the situation. Perhaps we should introduce a proactive policy in regard to our patrols, taking into consideration that they may likely, rather than just may, be attacked. The operation has given us an opportunity to use all of the forces at our disposal effectively. I have spoken earlier to the Regimental C.O. in Kinsale and conveyed that. He agrees and wants it to continue.

"I want to commend Captain Eastbourne for his initiative in gathering this information. While we do not know the source, we can assume it came from one of his many sources as it was addressed to him. Even if it does not prove entirely accurate on this occasion it may eventually. In that regard I will reiterate what our Intelligence Officer has said, we must all be vigilant and gather as much information about the IRA as is possible even in our ordinary social engagements.

"I also commend Captain Eastbourne's work with the RIC, which is operating separately; we must liaise with them to ensure we are not at cross purposes. The next step is to prepare for our patrol in two days' time. As Major Percival has said we have already coordinated with Kinsale to ensure they are prepared to send their support contingent and also to provide scouts."

After the meeting Geoffrey sat in his office attempting to access the outcome of the operation and decided that Percival would take no prisoners in the event of any failure. He would undoubtedly use him as a scapegoat if there was any fallout from the operation. On the other hand, his assessment of the OC, from even his first encounter with him, had been proved right. He was both a straightforward and solid commander who stood behind his men. He would, however, have to be careful of Percival, who was his immediate superior and was known to be very well regarded in Regimental H.Q. back in England.

However, as his French colleagues used to say, *we have to return to our sheep.* He must again make contact with the Reverend Foster and impress on him the need for further information from his source. Any information might be useful, such as; did she hear if the IRA volunteer had left to join his unit or indeed if the attack was called off, why?

On his way to drop off the note for the Reverend Foster he would pass by the rear of the entrance to Julia's residence to see if the signal they had agreed to was present.

Chapter 32

Later that evening after curfew Geoffrey made his way in mufti along the side streets away from the main residences, crossing the footbridge to the back quay. He met no one but still he travelled stealthily along by the walled rear entrances stopping occasionally for some minutes to ensure no one was following him. He was certain no one could see him where he was unless they were very close. When he was satisfied that he was not followed or observed, he made his way to Julia's gate which he was pleased to find again unlocked.

His reception on arrival in Julia's stairway was met with unconstrained affection: the secrecy of the affair and their capricious nocturnal reunions adding to the excitement of the moment. Again, as before by mutual unspoken understanding nothing was said until the love-making was complete and the mind again took over from the emotion.

Having spoken in lovers-speak for some minutes they retired to the sitting room where Julia offered, and Geoffrey accepted, some refreshment. Mindful of the need to retain his full alertness in the circumstance of his return to the barracks, Geoffrey asked for and received coffee.

After discussing the more mundane aspects of life in the town, which especially coming from Julia who conveyed a different and more analytical view then he normally heard, they moved on to the topic they had both avoided up to then.

"When do you expect Alastair to return home?"

"Oh, he said he would arrive in the morning train. He has been very busy lately; between his works here in the town and the preparations he is making for his transition to take over the bank operation in the city."

"Are you happy about the forthcoming move to the city?"

"Geoffrey I must be honest with you. However much I would wish things were different and the past weeks with you have shown me a happiness I never had before, I am not unhappy about the transfer, because it is what Alastair has longed and worked for, for some time. He thrives on his work and is never happier when times are busy.

"I love Alastair dearly. We are very content in our particular relationship. He is, and has always been since we met in Dublin when I first started to work, a central figure in my life. Geoffrey, I am going to trust you with information I have never imparted to another living soul.

"It is very personal and could harm Alastair and me if it were known. However, before I share this matter with you, I want you to assure me that you will never divulge it to anyone for whatever reason." Julia waited for Geoffrey's response before continuing.

"Julia, I give my word of honour that I will keep whatever secret is shared between us and never divulge it to another person. You know I would never do anything that might put you or indeed Alastair in harm's way."

"Alastair and I are bound together differently from other married couples. Our love is not a physical one. Alastair is not made that way. I knew this well before I married him, but nevertheless I went ahead because we both realised, we needed each other. I still feel that way about him."

Geoffrey responded attempting to comprehend what Julia had just said, "Yet you are very much a woman and quite obviously, unlike Alastair, your physical feelings towards the opposite sex are very normal."

"Yes, you know I am. However, that does not mean that I eagerly seek out men to compensate for my lack of close physical heterosexual contact. Before you, there has been just one since I married Alastair and he died in the war."

"Julia, you know I am in love with you. And no, I am not just saying that. It is not just my physical attraction to you. Our paths converge in many ways. I know for certain that for me I have met no one your equal to whom I felt so close so soon in our relationship."

"Geoffrey, I feel an equal attraction for you and in a different world there would be no barrier between us to declare this feeling to the world. However, even though this is so, my loyalty to Alastair is total. He understands my needs and is prepared to turn a blind eye to that side of me and any intermittent liaison I have from time to time. He does not wish to know and the subject is never discussed between us, but it is nevertheless understood.

"The expectation is that any such liaison should be secret and unknown to the outside world. I will never let any harm or public opprobrium befall him. It is not so long since the world turned its back on one of our greatest playwrights, just because he was different. I can see and indeed feel that our relationship is moving rapidly and heatedly to a point where our emotions might not be swayed by logic. I want to warn you before that time where I stand. If it is to continue, there must be no showing of our affection for one another in public.

"We should meet publicly only in normal social circumstances where it would be quite usual for both of us to be in the same company. Even then we should be extremely careful not to show any sign of over-familiarity with one another."

Geoffrey was stunned by the revelation. Not because of Alastair or indeed his way of life. He had known and indeed been friends with many men during his college and army years who were of a similar nature. In fact, he liked Alastair and found him a very pleasant and erudite companion. He was pleased that he had not exactly cuckolded him.

His relationship with Julia was only just beginning and while he would have been overjoyed to have met her when she was single, he had to accept the situation as it was. He had always accepted that life did not travel in straight lines and so he would take what it had to give either way and be satisfied. He would prefer a thousand times to accept the current situation knowing its limitations, rather than having no connection with Julia.

"Julia, I want to continue our friendship and all that goes with it no matter what limitations are imposed on that relationship. I have lived through a continuous hell for years. I have had a lonely existence for a long time. I am again in a battle that I feel cannot be won and I am not sure where I will end up. What I have with you I have never had before. I would dearly desire it to go on – a day, a week, a month – whatever you can allow. I will keep my word. I will honour your vow. I will stay or I will go. I will do what you wish."

Julia, by this time in tears, "Geoffrey it is hard for me to speak as I have, without feeling the same emotion you have so eloquently expressed. I am torn as it were between two worlds. Each of which is forbidden to us. I have lived one for years without regret and I would now live the other simultaneously likewise. If you are prepared to accept the limitations of our relationship, then I would wish it to go on. But I must ask that if at some time you are even in doubt, regarding these limitations, you must be prepared to end that relationship and walk away— and walk away."

"Julia, I have lived all my life with limitations. I grew up in pecuniary privilege and emotional poverty. I am an only child whose parents left my emotional needs to others. I learned early in life not to take friendship and affection for granted. In doing so I understood a kindness given deserved at least an equal return.

"In boarding school, together with others likewise skewed souls, we learned early to take the meagre comforts, which came our way, where we could. In the war I found friendships that rapidly came and as swiftly went away at each mad foray into the maws of death. Yet I have not forgotten, now, nor never will. I take life as it comes. True affection is not limited by perfection.

"Whatever you give me, I will return. Whatever your needs will also be mine. No claims, no demands, no expectations, and no doubts—I too wish for our liaison to go on with no conditions other than those needs which are of crucial concern to you."

No more was said, as they embraced, sealing their unique pledge to an open liaison in a strange and secret world.

Before parting Julia informed Geoffrey that Alastair would probably be absent during the same days the following week and she would again show if that were so on the day by displaying a red bandana on the hook which could be viewed through the opening in the rear iron side gate as before in the early afternoon after the train would have arrived from the city.

Escorting him silently through the garden, Julia locked the outer gate after Geoffrey's exit.

Chapter 33

When Joe Ryan called back to the army barracks the next morning as he had been asked, he found the place a hive of activity. Taking no obvious notice of this unusual sight he told Sergeant Turner that he had found a way of connecting with all of the communications systems used by the Auxiliaries and the RIC if needed. The Sergeant was very pleased to hear this as he mentioned in passing to Joe that the brass was all over them, and him in particular, to ensure that everything was secure and airtight.

Joe said he would prefer to explain and even show Sergeant Turner how to go about the work rather than do it himself. He explained his reluctance to do so that, being a civilian, he might be shot without question if found out by the other security services. In doing so Joe was not only protecting himself from the Auxiliaries and the others, he was also showing clearly that he personally wished for some distance between himself and any question of illegal activity.

Sergeant Turner, wanting to get all that was possible from this operation to satisfy the "brass", he pleaded with Joe to at least assist him while he was carrying out the work needed. Joe showed a great reluctance before he finally said he would agree provided he was given authority and that all important cover to shield him personally. This would have to come directly from at least the relevant officer responsible for the operation. Sergeant Turner agreed and said he would contact him again after they had spoken to the OC's office.

Joe made a big show of his reluctance, saying that he was only agreeing because of his relationship with the army and because he trusted Sergeant Turner.

On his way back down the town to his business premises Joe was happy with the way things had turned out. Despite his protests he was very pleased to be involved directly in the actual operation, as this would give him additional cover to enable him to create his own spurs into the Auxiliaries systems. He had already worked out how he would achieve this.

In addition, he also picked up that there was something major happening regarding the movement of troops. He presumed this had something to do with the previous day's manoeuvres. He would mention this later when he would be meeting with Sean Hales.

Sean Hales had signalled earlier that he would like him to meet him at the usual location in the early evening, to which Joe had agreed.

As he walked through the town, he again got some hostile looks from a few of the local layabouts but otherwise no one said anything. He could sense the steady rise in the anger of some of the nationalists during the recent past. He put this down to a number of incidents in the past months. First there was the murder of Nationalist Mayor of Cork city, Tomas McCurtain at his residence in front of his family by, people who were discovered afterwards to be, masked RIC members.

Next was the arrival of the Black and Tans and their brutal treatment of prisoners. Later came the Auxiliaries and their equally bad reputation. Then recently, was the arrest of the new Mayor of Cork city Terence McSwiney, who was now on hunger strike. In addition, some leaders of the IRA had been arrested in late July and were so badly treated by the Essex, under the explicit direction of Percival, that one was now in military hospital in Cork city and the other transferred from there to a psychiatric hospital with brain injuries.

Thought of the arrests again worried him. Did any one of those arrested know of his involvement with the IRA? While he felt reasonably confident, he could never be absolutely sure. Until he knew otherwise, he would have to go on trusting that Sean Hales had not told anyone about him. Meanwhile he would literally have to continue to walk into the lion's den to secure the information he needed to be effective.

He was not paranoid and did not wish to show any signs of paranoia, but he did need reassurance. He had learned in a previous perilous position it does pay to be alert. He would ask this in the context of what Sean had done to ensure that none of the hotheads in the IRA would take upon themselves to shoot him as a traitor conspiring with the British Army.

Joe thought about the recent arrests and the heightened activities of the Essex regiment in the district. First, they were very strategically located, between their headquarters in Kinsale and their post in Bandon. The British always had a penchant for locating in Kinsale. It had historic significance for them since the Battle of Kinsale in 1601 when the English finally defeated the Irish and completed their conquest of Ireland. It was also on the coast, which ensured both protection and supplies by the British navy.

That location was also significant in that a number of the IRA volunteers came from locations nearby and consequently a good deal of the fighting in West Cork would inevitably take place in and around the region.

He realised that the Essex were proving to be a formidable force and they were instrumental in the recent capture of the IRA leaders. He knew that his erstwhile fellow war brother, Geoffrey, was an intelligence officer in the regiment and consequently he posed a serious threat to him and his cause. Try as he might he could not find it within himself to dislike him, enemy now though he be. He cursed all war and the need to engage in it.

With tensions building up between the security forces and the IRA the nationalist community, whether it now liked it or not, was being dragged into the conflict. The intensification of the attacks was forcing people to engage with the unfolding situation. The atrocious behaviour of the security forces particularly the Black and Tans and now the new RIC adjunct, the Auxiliaries, against the nationalist community in general was ensuring more and more tacit and even some active support for the IRA.

The Essex too was seen as anti-nationalist and not just anti-IRA. Their troopers' treatment of ordinary folk from the nationalist community was seen as a step back to the old ways of Anglo-protestant denomination. This resentment was palatable and in 20th century post-war Europe where the world had changed forever there could be no return to the old ways of Empire and colony within a free Europe. The rescue of the world by the USA had assured this.

Joe was convinced that the principal actor behind the aggressive activities of the Essex was Major Percival, their Intelligence Commander. He had emerged from the war with an elevated reputation for authority of command and brilliance in tactics. He obviously saw himself as a total career officer with sights on the highest office. He was determined to increase his reputation here by defeating the IRA utterly. He had already indicated that nothing would come between him and his final goal.

Because of his reputation and standing with Army superiors back in England no one here, even the Regimental C.O. in Kinsale, would stand in his way. The fight in Ireland however, was not a normal war against nations as such, as was WW1. It was a war by a nation which had for hundreds of years claimed its right of self-determination. This war unlike the others previously was being fought by people who, understanding their inferiority against a well-trained and extremely well-armed force, were using their superior knowledge of the area and their acceptance or at least non-interference by the majority of the local population to attack the alien forces when they had advantage. The cruel indiscriminate retaliations of the British Forces, rather than acting as a deterrent against the IRA, were day by day adding support for the IRA cause.

Since Percival was spending more and more time in the Bandon barracks reinforced Joe's belief that his time as an effective spy for the IRA was limited. It was inevitable, especially if he was successfully getting relevant information that the spotlight would fall on him. Percival would turn every conceivable stone to find out if there were potential spies in his ranks and particularly those who had access to the barracks. If he came under investigation, it would be a matter of days if not hours before he would be arrested. He did not wish to ponder that, but nonetheless he realised his effective time as spy for his organisation was short.

Early in the afternoon he cycled out the country travelling his usual route to his fiancé's home. After a few miles, where he as usual ensured that no one was following him, or indeed at this stage no one was around, he turned off the road using laneways and even fields to avoid houses to get to the rendezvous. As usual Sean Hales was waiting for him. There was no else.

Sean took him over the events of the previous day: "The information you supplied was invaluable. I also received your follow-up message yesterday morning. On that note your drop box idea is excellent and working well.

"Having been informed the leadership stood down the column. Instead, the column leader designated selected volunteers to watch from a safe distance where they could not be observed as the Essex plan had unfolded. They had been in place early enough to even identify the army scouts being put in place earlier before the patrol for Kinsale was due. In addition, they observed the contingency coming from Bandon.

"The information not only ensured that our ambush plan would not be turned against us but it also allowed us to see at first hand the tactics of the army in the operation. This would be very useful for future planning. It showed how important not only prior information is but in addition how important it is to have our scouts not only place near the sites of any future ambushes but, in my opinion, placed also well back from those sites."

Joe agreed with the assessment and warned that the army was potentially more dangerous than the combined forces of the RIC and its two cohorts.

"Looking at it strategically: the Essex Regiment and the regular army are located in strategic barracks. What I mean by this is they can operate in many directions from where they're located. However, if you look at the map of the area, we are operating from you can see a great deal of it lies in a triangle between Kinsale, Bandon and Cork city. This gives the army a great advantage.

"With any knowledge of our ambush plans in this particular area they can rapidly deploy troops because of their transport facilities to the centre, or off-centre of the triangle a pincer movement in a relatively short space of time. To guard against that one needs not only scouts but their ability to communicate rapidly.

"In the scenario I am outlining our scouts would have to be spread far out, well beyond the ambush location to guard against that. However, if they are too far apart from the main column, I believe communication will prove difficult if not impossible. We do not have the same equipment as the Essex and the army in Cork.

"I have been thinking and assuming that I am right, the army, having seen the benefit of the plan of action they just thought up, will continue to use it and indeed expand on it. We need to adjust our strategies to take account of that."

"Joe, I understand what you are saying and logic would suggest you are right. In addition, you understand the British Army much more than I and most of our colleagues. However, while you are most likely to be correct, we are in the invidious position of lacking even the most basic equipment and consequently must operate the best we can with what we have. We will have to take our chances if we are to go ahead with our attack plans. We need to keep pressure on the British Government to come to terms with us politically.

"I can tell you and you alone, I spoke recently with Mick Collins who ordered that we advance all our plans for attack and use every opportunity to show our force. He believes some of the measures taken by the British recently, such as the introduction of the Auxiliaries and the passing of the Restoration of Order in Ireland Act providing for the IRA to be court-martialled rather than to appear before civilian Courts, smacks of desperation by them. Mick believes that if we increase our attacks and they are successful we might force them to consider negotiation. This is undoubtedly a tall order against such overwhelming force.

"You know we have a tiny force of volunteers and very few arms. God knows we do not have enough rifles to equip even the small numbers we are able to put in the field and we only have enough ammunition to last for short durations on engagements. All of our earlier engagements against the RIC were primarily focused on the arms and ammunition we could collect on those raids. We still reequip ourselves from what we can retrieve from the enemy after our attacks. We have failed so far to manufacture our own bombs, which we badly need to attack barracks and to halt the leading and rear vehicles in the case of ambushes, because of the lack of experience in bomb making in our organisation.

"As for the little bombing equipment we do possess, that like the rifles was purloined from the RIC and the army. In addition, so far most of what we stole from them has proved to be dud. If this is an example of what you and your comrades had to use at the Front, then one wonders how any of you came back alive. I expect were it not for the arrival of the Americans not only with their numbers but particularly with their better technologies and equipment the bloody war would still be going on.

"Joe we are virtually near the precipice, depending on bluff and bluster. God I sometimes feel like we are like the Spartans at the Pass of Thermopylae. Like them we are as much fighting for the soul of the country as we are for its freedom.

"Anyway, I am telling you because I know you most likely have reached the same conclusion yourself. Also, I hope it impresses you enough to go even beyond the great and dangerous work you are doing for the cause. I know damn well that having come out of that goddamn awful war, at times way out beyond the front-line trenches, you, more than anyone I know, are aware of the dangers and yet you volunteered to go again into the lion's mouth."

Joe was not shocked by what Sean had just told him. Indeed, he was quite pleased that the IRA leadership understood the risks they were all running and at least Mick Collins had an end game in mind rather than that of the blood sacrifice a previous generation had adopted. He did not mind putting his life at risk if he believed a positive outcome could result from doing so and that the leaders were of a similar mind. He would mind however, if he believed it was for no achievable purpose in the short term.

"I had understood as much, Sean and I quite logically expected the probability of the lack of our arms since the failure of the Casement expedition and of course the handing over of a great deal of the Childers weapons to the British Army after the surrender in 1916. I am extremely pleased however, to learn that Mick Collins sees the fight as a means to put us in a strong position to negotiate a form of independence with the British. That, because of the numbers we have in the field together with their shortage of weapons, even of the most basic kind, indicates we need a short but sharp and effective series of successes."

Joe then went on to give Sean an update on the situation in the Bandon army barracks when he visited there this morning.

"Sean there was an unusual amount of activity in the barracks this morning and while I did not enquire about the reason as it would have attracted attention to myself at such a sensitive time, I know enough about military manoeuvres that they were preparing for another sortie and not just a mere regular patrol. I assume they believe that there potentially might be another ambush and they are planning countermeasures against it. Anyway, you should be on the alert and warn the column.

"Again, I would emphasise the importance of on-the-ground watchers who can observe from a safe distance what the security forces are doing. On that point Sean, I would again warn you that now the Army is more directly involved in the fight against us since the recent Restoration of Order Act they will become much more active. In addition, I must mention one of our most formidable enemies, Percival.

"He is nothing if not persistent and he will stop at nothing to defeat us. As you know he was behind the capture and ill treatment of your brother Tom and Pat Harte. He is known to be wildly ambitious and he will see his success here as a major stepping stone to his rise in the British Army. He now spends a great deal of time in the barracks in Bandon.

"I will get what I can but I expect as time moves on it will be more difficult to extract the type of relevant information, we need without giving my cover away. You and I know that they are most definitely getting information about the volunteers from a source or even maybe sources with connections to the IRA. Their activities recently have quite clearly shown that. Therefore, we too should keep our eyes and ears open for any slippage within our own ranks."

"Thank you for the update on the movements, I will pass it on. There is a regular army patrol which travels from Bandon towards Cork city and back. It should probably be due most likely tomorrow. Presumably that is what they are planning for. If so, they will be sending out scouts and a contingent will follow the patrol either from Bandon or even more likely from Kinsale. I will advise the column immediately.

"Your point about the leak from an IRA source or indeed sources is valid and we have to look to ourselves to see where that could be. If it exists, it is highly dangerous to our operations and if not stopped could easily lead to the British scoring a decisive victory against us where we are currently very strong. It would be devastating. Your information, which we just acted on probably saved us from such a disaster.

"The Flying Column is our greatest weapon. Tom Barry has done a wonderful job of training and preparing the Column for more adventurous ambushes. With it we can virtually control our rural region and make it a no-go area for the security forces unless they are present in very large numbers. Without it we are just a rabble which can easily be dealt with.

"I agree with all you say about the army and we are very much aware of the dangers Percival poses for us. As you point out I have a personal score to settle with him but that will not overrule the need to approach each operation on its merits and where we know we have the upper hand. What about his man, Captain Eastbourne? We understand he works directly to him. He has been very active in the town and even though he is of the English ascendancy, he has a winning way with people, or so we are told."

Joe was rather taken aback by Sean's question. Did Sean know of his acquaintance with Geoffrey? If he did, was there an element of mistrust in his question? Who has been telling him about Geoffrey? Is it someone in the barracks? Have they been checking up on him? No, he decided this was coming from a source he knew well placed in the town.

He answered matter of factly.

"Yes he is all of what you have been told. He is in charge of communications etc. in the barracks and as such reports directly to Percival. And yes, he has a very pleasant personality and has been making his way steadily through the more established people in the town. I know him quite well and of course have had direct dealings with him because he is the officer in charge of communications.

He is bright and would pick up on information easily if it was forthcoming and I have no doubt he has put himself in the way of receiving such information. I would not, however, put him in the same category as Percival. He is not as ambitious and I believe neither is he vicious. I have a good relationship with him and it is important to maintain that relationship for as long as possible. While it obviously has dangers attached to it, it, at the very least, gives me cover."

Sean, picking up the slight hint that Joe was not gruntled by his question, came back immediately.

"Sorry Joe that was not in any way meant as a slight. I assumed that you would know him and I am very pleased that you have been able to establish a relationship with him. I should have expected as much. The question was asked more because of Percival and his tentacles to the community. I have no intention of suggesting how you go about your work for us on intelligence."

"No offence taken Sean. I suppose I am actually glad that you have other sources in the community. It is most useful even if to compare with the information I receive and hopefully to add value to it. As far as Captain Eastbourne is concerned, I see him as a valuable asset for me in the barracks and whatever about Percival I hope the lads have no evil intent toward him. It might undermine my work."

"Point noted and I will ensure he is not a target Joe."

"For God's sake be careful when you are doing so, make sure my name is not mentioned. Regarding that, I hope you were able to get across to the leaders that action should not be taken against any perceived enemies without first referring it back to you. I am of course taking about myself. I do not wish to be shot both in the front and the back simultaneously."

"Yes, I have personally talked to the other commanders locally and informed them that no action should be taken against anyone without it passing through me. I will reiterate that when I again meet them next."

"On other business the army has unwittingly made it easier and at the same time gave me cover to get through to the Auxiliaries communications. As it happens, they do not trust the Auxiliaries to tell them what they are doing and wanted to listen in to what they are planning to ensure there are no cock-ups—one side not knowing what the other is doing etc. Anyway, I have found solutions to hopefully get that information for the army. Consequently, I will be able to run my own tap-in in the course of providing one for the army. I will let you know if I get anything useful from the operation."

"Excellent. Sometimes we do get lucky. But then that is the benefit of you being their expert and our agent. Anything you get will be more than welcome. Since they arrived in Macroom they have been a major thorn in our side. They have a viciousness even greater than the Black and Tans and appear to have carte balance when it comes to the treatment of even the ordinary civilians.

"We have to do something about them before they settle in too long and become too familiar with the territory. As former military officers from the War they are both well trained and pose a very great danger to us. As you know we have limited resources in men and arms and we have just seen how vulnerable we can be with the triangle you outlined. Coming from the west they could cut off our safe areas and expose our weakest positions."

"I understand. I'll see what the taps will do initially and come back. Okay. Was there anything else?"

"Just to say for your information it was a businessman in the town that passed on the info regarding Captain Eastbourne. Your name was not mentioned."

"Good. I am glad you told me that Sean. I do not want to be blindsided."

Their meeting ended shortly after and Joe, to cover his tracks, made his way again ensuring he was not being followed first to his fiancé's home only some miles away. There he had an evening meal and discussed the general affairs with his father-in-law to be. The old man was fully engaged in the events of the district having strong connections in the republican movement. Joe had not informed him of his involvement because he knew it was wiser not to do so for the old man's sake and not because he had any fears of him telling anyone if he knew. As usual he had a great in-depth knowledge of everything happening around which Joe found valuable.

On his way home that evening Joe again went over what had been said by Sean. He thought it had been worthwhile and he was pleased to know that the leadership was not engaging in a mad do or die blood lust. He hoped that his advice would be taken on board and form part of their strategy. He was concerned about their future ability to gather good intelligence on the army in particular as he believed that Percival would personally ensure that all chances of leaks would be prevented.

His thoughts however finally were of the "businessman" in the town who had informed Geoffrey. Joe knew straight away that this could only be John Flaherty. His instincts again, as in the past, proved correct. He had met John yesterday for morning tea as agreed and they had an interesting conversation. While it mainly concerned the business in the town and those who might be useful as clients for both of them, Flaherty did stray into the current political situation with references to the IRA and its activities. Neither had given any hint that they had any involvement other than to have a reasonable interest in what was unfolding.

Chapter 34

Geoffrey wondered what the day would bring. He had not got word from Reverend Foster and the operation had already commenced with the scouts already in place strategically located in the approach roads to the target area around Upton. The patrol would not leave his barracks until early afternoon to ensure that if the IRA was gathering forces their final position would be clearly identified and relayed back to both Bandon and Kinsale to ensure that the patrol and contingent back-up were simultaneously moving to that location. So far they had heard no word back from the scouts apart from an earlier call that they were in their positions. Radio silence was ordered until there was something of relevance to the operation to report.

As he was not involved in the operation directly, he set about ensuring that he had covered all eventualities. He would again cross the town to the RIC barracks to confer with Superintendent McClintock and ensure that his people were not anywhere near the Upton region that day and he would also make his way to the Reverend Foster's church to see had there been any last-minute news from him.

Crossing over the main bridge into town his thoughts drifted as they did very often now to Julia. He thought about walking up the quayside to see if their agreed signal was inside Julia's gate but then immediately decided against it, knowing that it would not be there. *God, how juvenile and illogical emotion makes of us. Still, it was a pleasant thought and certainly helps in this murky world of war.*

He buoyed himself up by thinking of her and their next encounter. He thought again, as he had on numerous occasions since there tryst two nights before, about what Julia had told him and the conditions of their liaison. If that was the price, then he was more than willing to pay. For him it was as if he had discovered a series of oases as he crossed a Sahara-like desert. The anticipation was almost as sweet as the reunion itself.

He spoke with Superintendent McClintock who reassured him that there would be patrols or personnel in the Upton area that day. Geoffrey, having to take the Superintendent into his confidence, told him that there had been no show by the IRA the day before. He further added that they had been working on fairly slender information and therefore could not be certain why the expected ambush had not taken place.

McClintock, feeling there was a need to reassure Geoffrey that no leak had come from his side, said that no one other than himself had been told of the possible IRA attack and the army's plan to counter it. He added that while he had no reasonable doubts about any of his staff, he could not be entirely certain in the current political situation. He said that he had never before experienced the same depth of feeling in the nationalist community as obtained now.

He also admitted that even his usual informers from the nationalist side were now very reluctant to say very much, if anything at all about IRA activity or even to mention the names of those involved. Part of this he said was due to the fear of reprisal if the IRA found out and partly because they were not prepared to challenge the new political order in Ireland.

He added that the Black and Tans were no help in this regard and the Auxiliaries were proving to be even worse. He argued that captured IRA suspects would give no information about their organisation away without being tortured and then one should not rely on the information obtained in this way.

He was by now trusting Geoffrey and he let him know that things had moved on a pace in the past year and the vehemence against the RIC was palpable. Apart from the attacks on rural RIC barracks and their being unable to keep them open in West Cork because of IRA activity there, they were also finding themselves under siege in the larger towns particularly after dark.

Threats to their personnel were ever present and only weeks before a detective sergeant had been murdered on his way to attend a church service. In his opinion the conflict went way beyond police work and to be effective the RIC should not be used for political reasons. All of this was said in confidence which Geoffrey would keep.

Before he left, McClintock warned Geoffrey that he should be very vigilant even in the town as he had learned that the IRA were prepared to target individual army personnel at any opportune time.

Coming away, Geoffrey was even more convinced that in the long term this particular war would not be won on the battlefield.

Geoffrey went for a long walk around the outskirts of the town and entered the church grounds out of sight away from houses and passers-by. He again found the Reverend Foster in his office writing as he entered.

"I'm sorry if I have intruded on you in this unexpected way but I have been anxious to find out if you have any further information to offer me."

"Did anyone see you as you entered the church grounds? I'm sorry but I have become even more nervous about my involvement in this not only for my sake but more so for the source providing the information. I am told by another member of the nationalist community that the IRA is asking questions about informants in the community. Apparently, they have become very determined to root out people whom they feel might betray them, particularly after the recent arrests of some of their leaders."

Geoffrey, seeing the fear in Reverend Foster's face, tried to reassure him that he did not have anything to fear on his account.

"Don't worry Reverend about your anonymity in all of this. I came by way of the back entrance and I took great care to ensure that nobody either followed me or saw me. In addition, I have made sure that no one except me is aware that you are the one giving the information. In addition, I have also taken the precaution to keep the name of the IRA member from our internal files in case any trail would lead back to your source. Again, let me reassure you on my honour that I will not divulge your name, even to my superiors, without your permission."

"I am sorry to doubt you Captain and I appreciate and thank you for your assurances. They are important and I am glad to hear them reiterated. I suppose instinctively I am over-reacting due to your unexpected entrance.

"Regarding the matter we already discussed I do not at this time have much further to add. My source tells me that she has not seen the IRA man since. However, this does not mean much as he is quite often away from his home. She did say however, that he has not been home for the past number of days. Whether one can read anything into that is a matter for conjecture.

"Another source however, as I have already mentioned told me about the increased IRA activity regarding the search for informants within the nationalist community. She also said that she had heard that there were now IRA men operating in the town after dark and they were prepared to shoot any security personnel they came across. Apparently, the message the IRA wants to give to the town's people is that curfew imposed on the population will also apply to the British security forces."

"Thank you, Reverend, for that information. We are aware of the threat the IRA poses and indeed its desire to control the public by its threats and its propaganda. Rest assured we will not be intimidated by this. However, I am very thankful that you were able to get this information and willing to convey it to me. Everything you give me is useful, even if it's only to help us construct a fuller picture of the activities of the IRA. As they are a shadowy force it is difficult to pin them down and consequently, we need all the information we can get to rid the community of that threat."

"I am happy to be of some service in that respect. The IRA poses a great threat to us all and many of us are frightened of how we would be treated if we lost the protection of the security forces."

"On that Reverend I would be grateful if you could give me even a general picture of how your community feels about current affairs and the IRA?"

"Well as you probably are very well aware my people have been very apprehensive since the introduction in 1912 of the proposed Home Rule Bill in Westminster by the British Government of the time. Despite great opposition to its passing by the loyal Unionists in Ireland the government forced the bill through parliament and it became law. The start of the war delayed its introduction and owing to the rightful concerns of the unionist population here, reinforced by the rebellion of the nationalists in 1916 during the height of Britain's danger, it has, as of yet, not been brought into force.

"Now that the nationalists have gone ahead unilaterally and formed their own breakaway parliament in Dublin and set these IRA men loose, we are fearful of what will happen next.

"While the unionists in the north of the country hold a majority there, they presumably will be in a better position than we down here where we are but a tiny minority. In this town in particular Protestants have always been in the ascendancy. It has always been a protestant town since 1600 because it was founded and settled by English Protestants who down through the ages have asserted their rights to be the premier citizens here.

"We had been living peaceably here until the home rule matter was raised. Since then, tensions have noticeably risen between both protestant and catholic communities. As the Catholics now greatly outnumber us we are fearful for the future."

Geoffrey hesitated before replying to this. *God, what a mess he thought. Is there any immediate solution? Surely it would be best, no matter what happens for the Protestant community to find some modus vivandi with their catholic neighbours. No wonder the problem has escalated. It is not just about the British/Irish question it's much more. It's as much an Irish/Irish question as it is a British/ Irish question.*

However, I must deal first with the military end. Politics and religion are not my forte and frankly those people who claim to be experts in those areas have not fared too well in pursuit of Aristotelian and Christian virtues.

"As a military man I could say that in a war of attrition, if the current situation were to go on, the army would most certainly win. We are already increasing our forces and reinforcing even former RIC barracks such as in Ballineen to ensure we not only control these areas but also to put our forces within easy reach of each other to engage the enemy rapidly. The IRA's active numbers are obviously small and so if we were to meet them face to face, we would quickly end the conflict. They of course understand this and only attack when they have a much greater advantage of both surprise and numbers.

"We need to counter their advantage by knowing more about the enemy we face. This of course could be achieved much more quickly and, if I might say so, with less bloodshed and disruption of ordinary life here. What I mean is that our victory would be far easier if we knew who our enemies were and we were able to locate them. Because we are strangers here, we have to rely on local information for that.

"That is why we are grateful for your contribution to our efforts. I only hope that other concerned citizens would also come forward to help. As in your case all this could be done anonymously."

"I feel it is my duty to come forward. We must preserve our old way of life. Did we not fight a vicious world war and lose so many of the best young men to achieve that end? Is there to be no rest for us? When will it all end? We have to know whether we can sleep easy in our beds at night. I agree many more of our kind should come forward and tell you what they know. Most will not. Some are confused, some are frightened, some have already given up hope and then again, to my sorrow, I have to say there are a number who would support independence for Ireland.

"There are a number of us who want to help and I will go back and tell them what you have said. I believe a number of them will do what has to be done and provide any information they feel might help in ridding us of this nightmare."

"I very much appreciate your commitment Reverend Foster. It is mainly people like you from the community that we rely on to put us in a position where we can be most effective. It is after all for your protection and your place in Ireland that we are here."

He left shortly after with the Reverend Foster telling him that he would be in touch again as soon as he had further information.

Geoffrey, on his way back to the barracks, again by a circuitous route, could not help but reflect on the irony of that encounter. He wondered what Nannie Kate would make of it. *It was as far from her views on ethics and happiness as is the distance from the earth to the stars in faraway galaxies.*

Chapter 35

The second operation too passed off with an IRA no-show again.

The OC however, felt it was a very useful exercise that enabled them to have a strategy in place to deal with ambushes should they occur and also to see how fast they could prepare for a quick response. It was decided that they would not call off the usual patrol but their timings would be varied to take place earlier or later than regularly carried out in the past. In addition, they would be reinforced and much more cautious with scouts etc dispatched in areas where there was a chance of ambush.

In the following days his conversation with the Reverend Foster paid off and they received a number of contacts, most by anonymous letter, from the unionist community about the IRA. In particular names and addresses of suspected IRA members were given. While some of those were either based on vague suspicion or, worse, revenge, some others were useful and led to the arrest of a number of IRA volunteers.

The treatment of these prisoners was in many cases abominable, particularly by the Auxiliaries, the Black and Tans, and much to Geoffrey's shame by the Essex Regiment. The instigator of this treatment by the regiment was Percival and while most of the officers including the C.O. felt uneasy about the methods, he used in an effort to extract information from the prisoners, none protested primarily because it was known that Percival had the backing for his actions from higher up the command chain.

One anonymous note dropped into the barracks was of particular interest. It said that it had been noted that a number of individuals not from the immediate area had been seen examining the area around the Brinny river on the road from Bandon to Innishannon.

This was immediately picked up as a possible ambush linked to the information already received.

When Geoffrey asked, he was informed that from time to time recently the army had begun to patrol that particular road which was only a few miles from Bandon. It had not been considered before as it was believed the IRA would not risk a full-blown ambush against heavily armed troops so near their base during daylight. However, it was something that should be fed into the system they now had been put in place.

A patrol was scheduled to go down that roadway next day but that being Sunday it was unlikely an attack would take place. Nevertheless, using some of the tactics now in place, they sent a scout out before the patrol and delayed the timing of the patrol. In the afternoon he reported back that he had observed men gathering near the area of interest. The reinforced patrol travelled to a point about a mile from that location and approached through the fields from the north catching the IRA unawares waiting in ambush on both sides of the road.

Wasting the element of surprise, the army fired on the ambush group to the north of the road too early and the IRA were able to hold the patrol at bay until the main group had escaped southwards across the river which in late summer was extremely low. The army succeeded in killing one IRA man. The rest escaped.

While the army were satisfied that they had successfully thwarted an IRA ambush and had inflicted a casualty on that group there was a great deal of annoyance that they had missed an excellent opportunity to deal a very severe blow to the IRA in the area. Percival in particular was peeved that he had not been informed. He had been back in Kinsale at the time and so not available.

The OC of the barracks however, took a more balanced view of the matter and said that in the circumstances, with only vague information to go on and little time to plan a major operation, the action had been reasonable and the outcome had been a victory.

"Yes, it would have been excellent if we could have destroyed and captured the IRA ambush party. And I regret that we were unable to do so. But let us not forget that we used the little information we had received to good effect and we totally surprised them. They lost one that we know of and perhaps more are injured. We had no casualties.

"We might have done much better if we had used our advantage fully. However, valuable lessons would be learned from the operation and we have an important victory however small over the IRA. They will be very concerned about that and it will no doubt make them think before they attack us again.

"I want a report on the operation and its outcome as quickly as possible to send to Kinsale and we should meet again to look again at our strategies in the light of what we now have learned. I would also like to know if it is possible to identify any of the IRA operatives, particularly its leaders."

Geoffrey reflected on the event later and felt he had scored a small success in tapping additional sources of information from the unionist community. He would have to meet with the Reverend Foster in the morning to thank him for the new spate of information, which Geoffrey believed resulted from the Reverend's exhortations to his community.

He would further encourage him to redouble his efforts in that regard. Perhaps this was the key to securing the intelligence which was proving to be vital to any chance of defeating the IRA.

Geoffrey decided to take up an offer of dinner in the town hosted by one of the business communities. He did so despite the word of caution, which was issued by Major Stewart that great care should be taken by staff when venturing outside the barracks at night, especially now after the IRA had been rebuffed and had a loss and even losses. They might retaliate quickly against lone security personnel to regain some ground after their loss.

He had convinced himself that it was important to socialise with those people who not only supported the security forces but also could provide the vital intelligence which he sought. He also hoped of course that Julia would be present even though he would not be able to spend much time with her and indeed, as they had agreed, he would ensure that no sign of their close relationship should be seen.

As it turned out Julia and her husband Alastair were present among the 12 at table. Regretfully, but simultaneously fortuitously, they were at opposite ends of the table, so Geoffrey did not have to endure the strain of the pretence that Julia was just the wife of a passing acquaintance. As it turned out he was placed by his hosts next to Julia's friend Elizabeth and engaged her in pleasant if tactful conversation during the evening.

He was asked about the earlier attempted ambush and was pleased to note that all present appeared to express their satisfaction at the outcome. He used the occasion to indicate that part of the success of the operation was due to information forthcoming from the community. He went on to emphasise how important this was in the fight against the IRA and he left the dinner group in no doubt that if they wished for an early end to the violence the cooperation and assistance of the community would play a large part.

He was pleased that his appeal was taken with a certain degree of support and even he felt mild enthusiasm. If for that alone, he was quite pleased with the evening.

When they were all standing around at the end of dinner, Julia having discreetly alerted him by eye contact from across the room, when no one was looking passed by his side and slipped a note into his hand. Geoffrey, nonchalantly engaging someone near, put the note unseen into his pocket.
Having said goodbye to Elizabeth and having a few words with each of the other guests including Alastair and Julia, Geoffrey thanked his hosts and walked back alone to his barracks quarters.

He did not read the note until he was on his own in his rooms. It was hastily scribbled.

"Monday, Tuesday and maybe even Wednesday. Sign out."
The end of an almost perfect day, Geoffrey thought.

Chapter 36

After the part success it was decided by the army to become far more active, particularly in the search and capture of IRA members. In addition, the Auxiliaries were also involved in similar tactics and it soon became difficult for the IRA to move around as freely as they had formerly. Part of the reason the security forces were now successful in doing so was the information they were receiving from the community through coercion, bribery and through some elements of the unionist population.

The IRA continued their attacks and it became obvious that the conflict was moving much more rapidly than before. An ambush on the Ballineen/Dunmanway Road in the early autumn was being stood down and part of the IRA column had left when the army happened on the remaining force which was retreating at the time. Despite that fact that they were outnumbered and in poor positions the IRA still managed to keep the army at bay until they all withdrew safely. The IRA was proving to be a formidable force that could hold its own even against a greater number of seasoned troops with superior weaponry.

In early October there was a much more significant engagement. Early in the evening after dark when near Newcestown IRA volunteers, who had been billeted nearby, informed by a scout, engaged the Essex troops who they were on their way back from raiding the village looking for IRA suspects. Even though they were up against two lorry loads of troops and were both outnumbered and outgunned, most carrying only shotguns, the IRA held its ground. After about thirty minutes engagement the soldiers, led by Major Percival, fled eventually in the lorries towards Bandon.

Two soldiers, apparently officers, were killed. The IRA had no casualties. Percival in his report admitted the casualties on his side but claimed that the IRA had fled with ten of their number killed. However, there were no bodies and no indication that the IRA had suffered any casualties. (Percival subsequently succeeded in getting honoured for his action being awarded both the MBE and the C.S.M.)

Geoffrey, however, knew something of the detail of the attack from Sergeant Turner who had been informed by one of his colleagues present. This man had ensured that the body of one of the officers, who had died in an attempt to outflank the IRA, had been brought back to the lorries. Percival, who had not taken part in the counterattack against the ambushers, had ordered the retreat when it became increasingly obvious that the IRA would not be dislodged and that he would have to receive many more casualties if he was to have any hope of defeating them.

While his colleague understood the reason for the retreat, he was contemptuous of the account the Major was known to have given of the encounter. The sergeant, who had been a war veteran, said that it would have been better if he had admitted that they had come up against people who stood their ground and were now no amateurs. He had seen the results of officers at the Front who had failed to train and warn their troops against an enemy who at times were led better than they had been. They would have to understand that as time went on, the IRA force was improving both in tactics and accuracy and they would not flinch, even under heavy fire, fighting as they were on their own ground.

Geoffrey was appalled at the unprovoked retaliations by the Essex troops taken that evening indiscriminately against the nationalist community in the town. No attempt was made to control these activities. His protests against this were ignored and a blind eye was turned to the outrage. Percival was in control and his strategy determined that a softening up of the community would warn nationalists against giving aid and comfort to the IRA.

Geoffrey's hands were tied and yet again, as he had learned at the Front, as a junior officer in the British army you are just cannon fodder and your views and honour will be sacrificed on the altar of expediency by a careless cadre of the great and so called noble to enhance their ambitions and reputations. He was sickened by what he saw, but powerless to change its happening.

In the meanwhile, he was fortunately allowed to shift his mind to other things where the powers that be were unable to intrude, nor could control. Geoffrey, thus free in this other dimension where for a time neither war, nor politics, nor convention would intrude, floated away from the concerns of his barracks to a place apart inhabited only by Julia and himself.

Those three special evenings spent with Julia that week in the quiet and solitude of their secret affair were an escape from the exigencies of duty and a balm to his self-belief. During those happy hours of caress and affection, nothing was spoken of the outside world of callous careless talk, of unspoken suspicion of neighbour, of misunderstanding, of broken promise, of privilege unearned, of have and have not, of contrived conquest through division—of hate and of fear. Nothing during that time would be allowed to enter their world of that garden before the advent of the serpent of the delusionary mores of human orthodoxy.

Chapter 37

It was decided by Percival that the IRA had probably seen the concentration of effort by the army in the triangle between Bandon, Kinsale and Cork city and consequently his strategic effort moved more to the west. This was accordingly given more attention by the army and there had been a perceived lull in IRA activity in the Bandon region for a couple of weeks. Percival even started to believe his own concocted narrative that a good number of the IRA had been wounded or killed during the encounter at Newcestown, especially when there had been no immediate counter to the army's continued search and round-up of suspected IRA members.

In effect the IRA, because of its limited forces, had to constantly keep on the move and locate in out-of-way places or else disband until they were called together for training or action. It also strategically moved its concentration of effort to different locations to throw the security forces off-guard and to ensure surprise. What the security forces misunderstood was that the IRA volunteers, learning from their past mistakes, particularly the set-back at Brinny, now went into ambush position a short time before they expected a patrol by the security forces to pass by.

If that patrol did not arrive within a short space of time after it was expected, the ambush would be abandoned. Consequently, some arranged ambushes were placed and abandoned without the security forces' knowledge, leading to a false sense of security through mistaken IRA inactivity.

During the summer Tom Barry, a former sergeant in the British Army, had been specially selected to lead the main force of IRA attack. This was the so-called "Flying Column". He had decided on strict training before combat for all the volunteers taking part in the ambushes and so there was a very high degree of coordination of effort and shooting accuracy among those chosen for the Column.

After each training session he attempted to end up by an ambush attack when he deemed his volunteers would be at the height of their enthusiasm and efficiency.

Joe Ryan was beginning to feel more concerned about his own position as time passed. Sean Hales had told him that the army was receiving letters informing on individual IRA suspects. While they were mainly from the unionist population it was suspected that some nationalists were also providing information. He had learned this from his source in the Post Office who had intercepted some of these letters. Joe was aware of this from what he could glean from his visits to the barracks in Bandon.

He felt like the walls were closing in on him. He was surprised that nothing had been mentioned about his associations with the daughter of a man who had been in jail many times for his Fenian, Land League and even 1916 activities. He realised that this could only last for a short time. He was particularly concerned about a retired Army Colonel who lived in the big estate house near where his soon to-be father-in law lived. There always had been an unhappy and indeed malign relationship between both men.

He had not personally met the Colonel but he could not help feeling that his name would somehow arise, perhaps in conversation with one of his many employees from the locality. The knowledge of the informer letters disquieted him.

Joe had through his tap-ins to the Auxiliaries discovered that they were making regular sorties from their barracks in Macroom to the districts around patrolling but mainly to harass and capture IRA members. As time went on they were regarded as a vicious and formidable enemy by the IRA and presented a grave danger in that part of the county. Their presence also negatived the efforts of the IRA to rid the rural area of the RIC and they made IRA activities and safe passage more difficult.

That information was passed on to Sean Hales. He was pleased to have it as the IRA command had decided that the Auxiliaries should be attacked. However, they were regarded as a daunting and ruthless force and great care would have to be exercised in going up against them.

Joe had also seen a change in the manoeuvres of the army with more emphasis being placed on the western side of the district. This too he passed to Sean Hales.

Some of the leading IRA fighters had been captured by the security forces in the past weeks and it was felt that there should be another attempt to shore up morale with another significant ambush. The place chosen for this was Toureen on a road east of Innishannon. This road was frequently used by the British Army for patrols and equipment transport between Bandon and Cork city.

Towards the end of October Tom Barry and Flying Column set up an ambush at Toureen only a short time before a patrol was expected. He had taken this decision after previous experiences of enemy counteractions, to minimise the chances that word would get back to the army that they were lying in wait. He had also ensured that scouts would warn of any dangers before engaging with the patrol and the retreat directions were already marked out.

The patrol came shortly after they had positioned themselves. There were two lorries filled with Essex troops. The bomb placed on the roadway to stop the first vehicle failed to explode. This was a recurring problem for the IRA and they never quite got that problem solved. That lorry sped off, not stopping and leaving their companions in the lorry following up at some distance to fight it out with the IRA.

The action was short lived with the army troops surrendering. The army had been left with two dead and four wounded. Their arms and ammunition was captured and their vehicle set on fire after the wounded were removed and laid at the side of the road. The uninjured were released to tend to their injured colleagues.

Because one of the vehicles had escaped and after its occupants had raised the alarm it would not be long before reinforced troops would probably converge on the area from a number of sides, the Column changed its decision on its retreat plans and headed for the tidal river as this would be the least obvious place that would be considered a quick retreat option.

One man was dispatched by bicycle however, to secure a boat that would be waiting for the Column when it arrived at the river. Despite the unplanned last minute arrangement, it worked perfectly and the boat was present for their arrival so no delay was experienced and the entire Column number was conveyed over to the other side in a few crossings. Within hours they were many miles away in a safe location and the army arriving from different directions saw no sign of their escape.

There was a deal of shock and anger in the barracks in Bandon after the encounter. Some troops took this anger out on the town's people that evening.

Geoffrey too was shocked, particularly as he lost one of his officer friends in the ambush. However, he approached the C.O. and protested at the actions of a minority of the barracks troops who had engaged in the retaliation. He argued that apart from the lack of discipline and injustice of this unofficial action, it would give the army a very bad name among the town's people, including those who otherwise supported them and were totally against IRA violence.

He was able to tell the OC that on previous bouts of this type of retaliation his friends on the unionist side said that they were appalled by this and nothing could justify it. The OC, who himself had reservations about what was happening in the Regiment's name, told Geoffrey that it was understood that the government had unofficially sanctioned reprisals and that their own superiors were ambivalent about them. However, he accepted Geoffrey's argument and the following evening the troops were confined to barracks.

Chapter 38

On October 25 Terence McSwiney, Lord Mayor of Cork, died in Brixton Prison in England. He had been on hunger strike for 74 days after he was arrested and charged with the possession of a police cipher code by the British authorities in August. His ordeal had been well published not only in Ireland and England but internationally, particularly in America where there were already strong voices even in Congress against the treatment of Ireland by Britain.

He had refused to cooperate with the British and demanded his release as a democratically elected representative of the Irish people who had overwhelmingly declared their independence from Britain. Despite numerous pleas for his release, even from the British monarch, George V, the coalition government under Lloyd George refused. The coalition which came to power after the war in 1918 was made up of both Liberals and Tories.

Included in the Tory party, at the highest level of government, were those who had supported the unionists in their fight against Home Rule for Ireland. These individuals had agreed with the Northern Unionists setting up their own armed force to fight against Home Rule and had supported the British army officers who mutinied against the Government and refused to accept the Home Rule Act which was passed by parliament and signed into law by the king before the Great War.

The IRA now had another martyr, which gave its members even more impetus to press on until it had achieved its goal. The war would take on an even greater intensity in all spheres of the conflict in the weeks and months ahead. The British Prime Minister Lloyd George and his Cabinet had again, by their decision to let the Lord Mayor die in their prison where he had been held after a British court-martial found him guilty of a minor offence, shown their callous determination to destroy by any means not only the IRA but the whole concept of Irish freedom.

More than any other event since the 1916 rebellion and subsequent execution of its leaders by the British, the perceived martyrdom of MacSwiney had a profound effect on Irish Nationalists, even among those who up to then had grave misgivings about IRA violence. The mystical potency of a hunger strike finds a profound resonance in the Irish psyche. That event coupled with the ruthlessness and lawlessness of the British security forces left few of the Nationalist community on the side of Britain in the ensuing conflict.

Even moderate unionists particularly in the southern part of the country were now demanding a reasoned political solution from the British Government. Moreover, the English public was now taking notice of the events in Ireland and many were not at all pleased by what was happening there in their name. The time for a return to the past so-called Union of Britain and Ireland was gone. Like the borders of Europe all had changed and in W. B. Yeats words *"all changed, changed utterly: / a terrible beauty is born."*

The reason behind the greatly increased numbers of arrests of IRA leaders being made, it was believed, for the greater part was due to the intelligence gathered from the unionist community and even from the nationalists. Michael Collins who was, among other things, Director of Intelligence for the IRA ordered that people who were proved to be spies for the British Government in Ireland should be eliminated as they posed a grave threat to the IRA's existence.

In Dublin he had identified, through his own agents in Dublin Castle, a group of British undercover agents, known as the Cairo Gang possibly from their espionage exploits in Egypt. Towards the end of November, in a synchronised operation the IRA shot and killed fourteen agents on an early Sunday morning raid on their individual places of abode. Later that same day that action was met by the ruthless retaliation of the Auxiliaries, who invaded and opened fire on innocent spectators at a major Gaelic football game being held in Croke Park, the main sports ground owned by the Gaelic Athletic Association. Thirteen people were killed.

In West Cork meanwhile one of the defining engagements of the War of Independence was about to happen.

The Auxiliaries who were billeted in Macroom about 20 miles from Bandon and 26 miles from Dunmanway, had since their arrival in the summer caused a great deal of concern for the IRA. Lately they had spread themselves further out into the countryside and had not only captured IRA members in doing so but also made it more difficult for the IRA to move themselves and their equipment around the area. The rivers in the area, particularly at that time of year when they were invariably swollen, meant that by controlling the bridges the security forces could effectively shut down the area relatively easily.

There was also their recent savage attack on the innocent spectators in Croke Park.

Going on the knowledge they had gleaned through Joe Ryan and from observations, Tom Barry decided to ambush a patrol of Auxiliaries about half way between Macroom and Dunmanway. The place selected for the ambush by Barry was Kilmichael. An IRA volunteer present could not help reflecting on the name: *in English it's a bloody name, but in Irish merely an ancient landmark name for the Church of Michael.*

Learning from the past and being extra cautious now, particularly as this was their first major encounter with the Auxiliaries whom the IRA respected as an intelligent enemy who would neither give nor expect any quarter, Barry posted scouts hours before moving into the ambush site in locations at intervals well away from that site.

As they were awaiting the patrol's arrival a pony and trap with four occupants came galloping past and nearly upset the whole operation. They were hastily pushed off the road just before the first of the two Crossley tenders entered the ambush site. Shots were fired when the tender reached a selected point on the road. The first shot killed the driver and the lorry came to a sudden halt. Before the soldiers could alight, a hand grenade was thrown into the tender. It killed all its occupants. The second tender stopped and the paramilitaries took whatever cover they could find and engaged the IRA volunteers in merciless gunfire.

The fighting lasted less than half an hour and at the end 17 Auxiliaries and 3 IRA members were dead. In addition, 2 IRA volunteers were injured.

The Volunteers arranged for the transport of their dead and wounded and having collected the Auxiliaries arms and ammunition, which were so vital to their continued operations, moved off to safety. Their scouts had ensured that the route they took was free from enemy patrols and they crossed the river, out of the area, without incident.

Having marched for some hours they arrived at a safe remote location before resting and eating their first real meal for days.

Joe Ryan received a note from Sean Hales via the drop box that day to keep his head down as trouble was expected. Joe had experienced a great deal of personal animosity in the past month particularly after the death of Terence MacSwiney and the other IRA hunger strikers in Cork Gaol who had not even appeared before a court. There was also great public outrage still being voiced over the execution by hanging of the young 18-year-old medical student Kevin Barry, in Dublin for his IRA activities. His pleas to be shot like a soldier rather than hanged were ignored by the British who were still attempting to suggest that the ongoing war was some kind of police action against criminals.

Joe was identified by the locals as pro-British Army and therefore not only anti-IRA but as time went on now as even anti-nationalist. While he had reassurances from Sean Hales that the IRA would take no action against him or indeed anyone else without approval from the leadership, he could not be absolutely certain that someone would ignore that order or indeed when Sean was absent that an order would be given to shoot him. He was now aware that the very recent elimination of the Cairo Gang in Dublin by the IRA meant that others suspected of helping the security forces might also be in jeopardy.

When he heard late evening of the encounter at Kilmichael against the Auxiliaries, he became even more anxious. So far only preliminary accounts of the ambush were known but it was becoming obvious that there had been an extensive encounter. The Army in the town was out in numbers and the majority of the population had locked themselves into their homes.

He now had to consider if he could be identified in the same way as having something to do with the ambush. On this occasion the Army would be able to immediately connect him with the Auxiliaries and knowledge of their communications. They surely would be attempting to find out if they had had a security leak—what now with Kilmichael and before that Tureen and also Newcestown. He was at a loss to understand that so far, he had not been questioned in any way about a possible leak. He wondered why. Percival surely would follow up any suspicious activity and a civilian, no matter if he was a former army veteran, who had access to the barracks would have come under scrutiny.

Merde: as the French would say. Where is all this going to end?

Joe headed home and even though it was late told his mother that he was going to see his fiancé in the country. He hoped by doing so he would be out of the way in case anyone came looking for him, particularly the security forces. If they had, it would perhaps give him a small window of time to go "on the run". Despite the curfew he cycled to his destination by the side roads, to avoid any patrols and to allow him space to think about what he should do next. He suspected that Sean Hales would be elsewhere but he knew he would hear a fuller account of what had transpired that morning in Kilmichael.

He could feel in his bones that a critical juncture had been reached in the fighting. He sensed this previously in Flanders. Then there had been great bloodshed before it was over. He hoped that would not be the case now.

Chapter 39

Early next morning in the Bandon army barracks OC, Major Stewart, called a meeting together of senior officers to discuss the current situation and to decide what additional measures should be taken in view of the escalating situation locally.

Percival, because it had become the centre of the conflict in West Cork, was by now was spending much more time in Bandon than the district H.Q. in Kinsale. He was asked by the OC to outline the recent situation and to give his views on the current strategies of the British security forces response to the IRA and what further could be done by the regiment to enhance their own contribution. The OC, no great admirer of Percival, referred to recent successes of the IRA, namely Toureen and now even more deadly Kilmichael. He obliquely mentioned Newcestown and questioned why if the IRA suffered so much damage there, they were able so quickly and numerously to regroup and attack again so vigorously?

Ignoring the barb about Newcestown, Percival began by giving a full briefing of the events at Kilmichael the day before. This had been provided by Geoffrey, who had spent a good deal of time with Superintendent McClintock the evening before. The RIC commander had visited the area and spoken to the officer now in charge of the Auxiliaries in Macroom, as their Colonel had been killed in the fighting.

Percival did not mince his words. He described the battle, as the most devastating event to befall the British security forces in Ireland since the beginning of these troubles. There was no way around it. Despite the Auxiliaries putting up a fierce resistance it was a fight to the death on both sides. Up to now it was expected that the IRA would hit and run, if they could not get their opponents to immediately surrender because of the vast superiority. But in this case the RIC determined, from the great amount of blood spilled on the IRA side that they were not prepared to leave the scene until they had won. It was obvious therefore that the security forces were no longer dealing with an amateur and unprofessional enemy.

They now faced enemies who are skilled in guerrilla warfare, to an extent that the security forces were currently playing catch-up. This radical situation would have to be dealt with by a radical solution.

There would have to be a much more aggressive approach taken to capturing the enemy, especially their leaders. Those captured would be interrogated until they revealed details about their activities and gave names and locations for their fellow IRA men. Percival left no one at that meeting in any doubt that he was determined to use any means to extract, by force, if necessary, this information from his prisoners.

He also said, looking at Geoffrey in particular, that he would ensure that further efforts would be made by them to get their informants to provide additional intelligence about the IRA. He said that all officers should make it their business to seek this out even during their social dealings with the civilians.

Finally, he said that they would have to admit that they were caught offside by the Toureen ambush. Previous plans they had made to scout out the terrain before regular patrols were made were on that occasion neglected because they had misread the IRA and their tactics. Here again it showed that the IRA leadership was very astute and read not only the terrain but the movements of the security forces exceedingly well.

Here Percival digressed to say that he had grave suspicions that the IRA had access to information about their movements. He insisted that locations chosen and their preparations for these recent ambushes showed that the IRA had intelligence about security forces schedules. He believed there could be no other explanation as these attacks were so well planned. Accordingly, they would look again at their own security and advise the other forces to do likewise.

He finally said the regiment should revert to the plan they had already agreed on and this time ensure that they both re-arranged their schedules, even changing them at the last minute in addition to reinforcing these patrols. Referring back to informants and the extraction of intelligence from prisoners he said that the ultimate goal would be to capture or kill the main force of the IRA at one of their ambushes.

He believed that if they were successful in achieving this it would deal a massive body blow to the IRA, weakening its potency in this area both with regard to its military strength and also its morale. In addition, it would greatly reduce the regard that the Nationalist population has currently for the IRA.

Major Stewart, obviously already aware of what Percival was going to outline, accepted the strategy regarding the plan of action and increased vigilance. He said that all patrols would again be looked at to see how they could enhance their security. He also agreed with the need for further efforts to be made regarding the provision of information about the IRA.

He stopped short of endorsing Percival's policy of aggressive interrogation but nevertheless did not oppose it, knowing that it had approval from the top brass. Finally, he agreed that they should look again at their own security and ask the other forces to do likewise.

Geoffrey, who had already the evening before met with Percival, had instructions to go over minutely their security at the barracks and also to talk to the RIC Superintendent to persuade his side, including both his other paramilitary forces, to also look at their security. They also instructed him to return to his contacts to pressurise them to seek further intelligence about the IRA.

Geoffrey, went first to speak to Superintendent McClintock. On his way he reflected on all that had occurred since his arrival. He felt he had reached the nadir of his belief in what he was doing in Ireland. Never before, even in the most awful times when fellow junior officers and ordinary squaddies that he respected as brothers were falling around him like chaff from a winnowing wind, did he feel so dispirited.

No, he told himself it was neither fear nor concern for his own safety: neither was its war exhaustion, nor the reconsideration of his military career. Rather unlike the holocaust he had endured for unremitting savage years, this contest is not for kin or kind. There are no real honours to be won here on his side. It was merely a war to defend past injustices. It was not his.

Each time he had spoken to his unionist friends in the town in recent days, particularly after the death of the Lord Mayor of Cork in Brixton Prison, all apart from one or two of them had spoken about the need for the British Government to enter into negotiations with the Irish Nationalist representatives in the new formed Dail to find a solution for the current situation.

Joe Ryan and John Flaherty, the only people now on the Catholic side that would speak with him socially went further saying that as time moved on the British authorities were losing, more and more, their authority in the southern part of Ireland and the harsh events which had been introduced had only exacerbated the situation and attracted even greater numbers of young people to the IRA. British civilian courts were no longer functioning outside the major cities and Sinn Fein had set up their own courts to which nationalists were giving their allegiance.

The RIC was unwelcomed in the countryside by an overwhelming majority of people in the greater part of the country. The Coercion Act and the Restoration of Order Act introduced by the British Parliament for Ireland only highlighted the loss of control here of British acceptance by the majority.

While in the town he skirted around to see Reverend Foster in his out of the way office at the rear of his church. The Reverend as before was writing one of his sermons at his desk as he knocked and entered. Not surprised to see Geoffrey he said that he had been quite active in encouraging those in his community to transmit any information they could find on the IRA.

Asked about the unionist community in the town the Reverend Foster said that the majority of his flock were appalled by the turn of events in Ireland and felt very threatened by what was happening. He admitted that most of them wanted a solution and would now easily accept Home Rule. Some even blamed their compatriots in the north of the country, who were in the majority there, for preventing it from coming into force. By setting up the Ulster Volunteer Force they argued that Carson and the others precipitated the events of both 1916 and now the IRA violence.

Many were fearful that if the IRA wins, they will be the target and revenge would be taken for perceived past injustices done to the Catholic side. Some he said were contemplating leaving the country if first they could dispose of their assets here. Others who felt immediately threatened had already left.

The Reverend Foster himself clung to the belief that the IRA could be defeated. He further believes that the actual active membership of that force was quite small and that while they have a good deal of support among Catholics this is only tacit and would evaporate if the IRA was seen to fail.

The Reverend said he accordingly would be doing everything in his power to assist the security forces. He understood this to be his civic duty. Bandon had always been a Protestant island in a Catholic sea and he was not prepared to abandon it to Papist ideology. He had already succeeded in getting others to provide intelligence on the IRA, which he knew had been given to both the army and the RIC. He would continue to advocate this and also contribute whatever came his way.

Returning to his barracks, avoiding the centre of the town, he felt less secure than he had previously when taking the same route. While he met few on his way, he could not help feeling unkind eyes were watching.

He consoled himself by thinking of Julia. He very much looked forward to meeting with her again tonight. She had opened for him a new dimension into a life unknown before, where war and want and injury and hurt were unknown and untold. He would lodge there in this nirvana for as long as his soul mate would or could stay within the boundaries of that exquisite place.

Chapter 40

Joe Ryan stayed overnight at his fiancé's home and he got a full report of what had happened at Kilmichael. While it had been a complete victory for the IRA there were some misgivings about numbers that were killed in the operation. It had previously been the policy of the IRA to force a surrender and having disarmed the prisoners and destroyed their means of transport, they were immediately released. In this particular case there were no prisoners.

While they were not virtuous it had been understood that despite provocation, they would not be vicious. The Auxiliaries had a bad reputation among the nationalist public and were feared. However, some sympathy was expressed for their Colonel who was also killed. Unusually among the Auxiliaries he had earned a reputation as a fair and just man.

The victory however, came at a cost. Among the three IRA volunteers killed was a local lad, a friend of the family. Joe knew his brother, who was one of the IRA leaders and also present at the ambush. There were no celebrations in that house that night. Joe talked well into the night with the old man. Both knew that the sad news in reaching that young man's home would be shared by other families in the coming time. *How many would all depend on how long,* Joe reflected on previous occasions not long ago when many families in Ireland had to endure a similar Calvary.

Joe cycled back home early the next day. No one had been looking for him. He left after having tea with his mother and discussing the events of the previous day which had reached the newspapers. Joe listened and made no comment. He had no wish to involve his mother in what he was engaged in. His mind was elsewhere.

In town he busied himself in his work. During the morning he went out of his way to meet with John Flaherty whom he knew would be having a morning coffee break in the hotel nearby. He wanted to find out without asking what the business side of the town was saying. He instinctively felt that if there were any vibes of suspicion about him among those who were close to the security forces in the town John might know and if he did Joe felt he would warn him.

The subject of Kilmichael naturally came up and John told him that there was a great deal of apprehension in the security forces because of the extent of the 'massacre', as they were calling it. He said there is an amount of foreboding too amongst the unionists who see the whole thing as getting to the stage where everyone might be forced to publicly take sides. He believed, as did Joe, that the great majority of the unionists in the town just wanted to live normal lives and get on with their businesses or jobs.

They would accept any democratic decision including self-determination by the Irish if that was what it would take to bring stability and allow them and their families a full role as citizens. They feared that a prolonging of the war, particularly now as its intensity has grown exponentially, might put them and their families at risk.

On the nationalist side too, John added, there were certain fears. Lately the security forces on all sides were much more aggressive and even quite innocent locals were being questioned and harassed. Even he, for the first time, had experienced that recently when stopped by a Black and Tan. He only relented when signalled to quit by a local RIC sergeant.

John, finally, as was his wont, bluntly asked Joe how the whole issue affected him. In doing so he added that he would have thought that as a nationalist with an army background, he might be at the receiving end from both nationalist purists and security hotheads. Joe, by this time trusting John, was more open than he would be with others. He admitted that there were elements in his own community, even those he grew up with, who even on his return from the war had shunned him. Now that he was known to have done some work for the army, this animosity increased further. However, the majority still regarded him as one of them and had no misgivings. On the other hand, so far, he had not experienced any problems with the security forces. Then pointedly hesitating for some seconds Joe added,

"But then that could change at any time soon."

John looking at Joe for some sign and getting none promptly came back to say, "Joe if you find yourself in difficulty and you have nowhere else to turn for help, I will be available." Pausing he added, "I would of course expect the same assistance from you."

No further words were needed. They both left on a handshake.

Joe returned to work, confirmed in his opinion about John Flaherty.

Chapter 41

Geoffrey also began the re-examination of security of communications in the barracks as instructed by Major Percival. On this occasion he was ordered to inquire into the movements of those in the barracks who would have access to information on patrol scheduling and who might have contacts with people outside the barracks. In particular he was to thoroughly investigate any compromising relationships any of the soldiers, including officers, had with outsiders.

He was also instructed to carry out an in-depth search into the background of each civilian who had access to the barracks. Percival told him he had the full backing of the OC for any searches or interrogations he had to make. However, if something came to light which might indicate a leak and the individual suspected was known, Percival himself would conduct the interrogation.

Geoffrey enlisted a junior officer to assist him in this and set about the task immediately as Percival wanted a report back within a day on the initial results of this enquiry. Geoffrey did not relish this particular task, although he fully understood the need for it. It would most certainly require him to place everyone, both in barracks and those who in any way visited it, under suspicion. He was grateful though that he would not be conducting any interrogations of suspected individuals.

He guessed that there would be some soldiers in the barracks who might have romantic relations with local women and these would fall under the suspicion umbrella. Indeed, he thought, *and where do I fit in there: although I can immediately exclude myself as Julia and I never spoke about my job or what I am engaged in. No, at the very beginning of the relationship Julia informed me that she was ambivalent with regard to whether Ireland was independent or attached to Britain. She just wished that a consensus agreement on the way forward could be reached without bloodshed.*

Geoffrey set about the task at hand dealing with the groups, both inside and outside the barracks, simultaneously. He instructed the Lieutenant to begin dealing with the military side; he would deal with the civilians.

"Hopefully," he told his colleague, "You will be able to quickly eliminate most of the soldiers from the enquiry fairly rapidly. If there are questions to be asked of specific squaddies or indeed members of staff, tell me beforehand. I would ask you to begin with the sergeants, particularly Sergeant Turner. I expect they will be easily eliminated from the enquiry. Once they are clear we can use their assistance to look at the others. I want Sergeant Turner to assist me as quickly as possible so please deal with him first."

While the Lieutenant went about inquiring into the movements of the Sergeants and their connections outside the barracks Geoffrey asked the duty office to produce a list of all the civilians who came into the barracks, especially those who were regular visitors.

Later in the day, having got that list and finding that all but one of the Sergeants were cleared, he met with Sergeant Turner and instructed him to minutely go over the activities of the communications office to ensure that no leaks were possible from that quarter.

He got the other Sergeants to look at their own areas of responsibility where they might be in contact with civilians delivering goods to, or servicing equipment in, the barracks.

Meanwhile he began the delicate task of interviewing his officer colleagues excluding the OC and Percival. He did not labour the matter however, and confined himself mainly to asking if it was possible that they in some inadvertent way had said something that might have got back to the IRA. The task was completed rapidly and as far as he was concerned thankfully with a negative response in each case.

Toward the end of the day, when he was looking at some anonymous notes the barracks had received concerning information on possible IRA connections, he came across one note which gave a list of what was described as "rebel families" in the Kilmacsimon/ Ballinadee area. Recognising only two of them, where the sons were well known to be IRA members and they were "on the run", he left the note down and began looking at the others.

He was leaving that evening to keep an appointment with Jack Lee and some others at the hotel when it struck him that one of the names on the note, he had seen earlier was familiar. Before going he dropped off at the office to examine the name. Yes, he thought *it was Griffin. If I remember correctly, someone told me Joe Ryan is engaged to a lady named Griffin and she is from that neighbourhood. Could it be? God what a mess!*

Geoffrey said nothing but headed off to keep his appointment. While there he discreetly asked if others were around and Joe Ryan's name came up. After casually talking around the issue, he got to the question of Joe's fiancé who was a noted beauty in the town. While the others, some of whom would have known of her father's rebel reputation as he had spent many years in and out of British jails for "agitation" and other rebel causes, keep quiet, Robin Jefferson who was in the periphery of the group around the bar was only too eager to inform Geoffrey. The conversation passed on quickly and Geoffrey went on from there to keep his rendezvous with Julia.

On his way back to the barracks that night he made up his mind that Joe Ryan was probably the source of the leaks from the barracks. At the very least he would have to be investigated. He knew that Percival would want to handle that and the thought concerned him. He did not sleep that night.

Next morning, he carried on with his investigation, which at this stage had all but been complete. He spoke with Sergeant Turner and asked if Joe Ryan could have had access to any communications through his office. The Sergeant was greatly surprised that Joe would be in any way suspected and at first said no. However, pressed by Geoffrey to give further consideration to the question he admitted that Ryan had from time to time, while he was in the office, the ability to see some communications without being observed. On reflection, he also mentioned that Ryan had helped them tap into the communication systems of the Auxiliaries in Macroom.

Geoffrey submitting his initial report in writing said that they had cleared all but a few names and he was continuing to examine this before making his final report. In the meantime, he was calling on the RIC Superintendent to follow up on a few names that had just come through anonymous notes.

He left the barracks early to walk to the RIC barracks at the other end of town. He timed his walk so that he might meet with Joe Ryan on his way to his usual morning tea break where he met other businessmen. Joe had at times mentioned this venue as a possible opportunity for Geoffrey to meet some of the locals. He crossed the main bridge over the river and took a turn for the railway station so that he could come to town and delay his approach until he saw Joe

Ryan on the way. Fortunately, Joe was alone. Geoffrey walked by gesturing to him not to stop or speak. Passing by he said,

"Get the hell away from town and don't go back to your business or home. We're on to you."

Joe did not hesitate passing by, without a word and keeping the same pace but not entering the hotel, went on.

Geoffrey was satisfied that no one saw the encounter. He moved quickly to meet with Superintendent McClintock. There he asked about the names on the note he had received and McClintock immediately knew most of those mentioned. When asked, he was able to give a full briefing on the Griffins and particularly Michael Griffin who was a notorious offender of the King's peace and tranquillity. He had in fact been sent to Frongoch prison in Wales with the other leaders from around here. Geoffrey asked about Joe Ryan, but McClintock said he knew of him as a businessman in the town who had been in the army during the war.

Geoffrey returned to the barracks and having spoken to his colleagues assisting him in the investigation, made his final report to Percival in person. He first said that one of their Sergeant's had been approached regarding the possibility of an IRA attack on the barracks. Percival said he would talk to the Sergeant immediately about the matter.

Geoffrey then told Percival that there was one suspect Joe Ryan, in relation to the possible leakage of information. While he could at this stage say that it was only a possibility, he felt that he should bring his suspicions to Percival's attention.

They spoke about Ryan for a short time Geoffrey outlining why he had his suspicions. Percival agreed and instructed that an immediate arrest should be made and the RIC alerted to ensure Ryan did not abscond before they had a chance to interrogate him.

In the meantime, Joe Ryan had unhesitatingly decided to act immediately on Geoffrey's warning.

He could not go home or to his business and as he made his way out of town, he spotted an RIC patrol and did not take a chance that they might have been alerted and turned back to find another exit. Unfortunately, that meant walking back into town and the dangers that posed for him. Just as he was about to head for the railway as his only out, he almost bumped into John Flaherty. Without hesitation he asked John for help and it was immediately offered. It was agreed that Joe would continue out of town by the railway line and he would meet him at a location just outside the town on the main road.

By the time he had crept down by the railway embankment and reached his preordained spot the military and the RIC were everywhere looking for him. From his hiding place at the roadside, he even saw a military patrol pass by and return obviously looking for him. He presumed all the roads around would be patrolled and he was concerned that John Flaherty seemed to be running late.

Finally, after nearly an hour waiting John pulled up in his very new Ford and beckoned him to get into the back where the seat was pulled over him so that if stopped a cursory glance would not observe him John told him that everything was being held in the town while they obviously looked for him. He himself had his vehicle searched and asked where he was going. Luckily an RIC sergeant vouched for him and he was allowed to proceed.

Nearing Innishannon they were stopped again by an RIC patrol but allowed to go by an RIC man who knew John because his father-in-law had just purchased a Fordson tractor which was the talk of the neighbourhood and because he much admired John's new Ford car.

Before they crossed the bridge over the river near Innishannon John turned into the side road for Ballylangley. After about a mile on that road Joe asked him to stop and he got out. Before thanking him, Joe said he was being sought by the army but by mutual consent he said no more. John needed to be able to deny knowing anything about Joe on the off chance he was questioned by the security forces.

John stopped at a farm on the way back to town to speak to a farmer who had been inquisitive about the tractor. There was no chance whatsoever that the farmer could afford the tractor but it would certainly give him a good reason for being on that road in case he was stopped on his way back.

Joe headed off toward the south, keeping well away from dwellings and roadways. He travelled by lanes and fields, high enough up to keep following the smell of the sea which he knew would bring him close to his destination where he could pick up his true bearings again.

It took him some hours but he finally arrived at the house where he had met Sean Hales. Going down the small corridor in the cottage he found a bedroom where he lay down and for the first time in hours felt relaxed. In the quiet of that lonely place, he realised he felt neither fear nor indeed apprehension. All that had been blown away long since in the trenches of Flanders. The only concern he had was for his mother and his fiancé. They would surely search for him where they lived. He could only hope they would not be mistreated.

His next thought after that was John Flaherty and his total willingness to help him despite putting himself at risk. He wanted to ask why but for John's own security he decided against that. Hopefully he would have the opportunity to do that at leisure sometime in the future when they could put all this behind them.

His deepest thoughts though were on Geoffrey. *Why?*

Chapter 42

Within days after Kilmichael, a convoy of two lorries coming from Cork towards Bandon were fired on, but then the firing stopped when the IRA saw that there were civilians in the vehicles. Two RIC officers and a civilian were wounded in the attack. The IRA had no casualties. Apparently, the civilians were witnesses for the crown attending a Court in the city, where British Assize courts were now only taking place. The Sinn Fein government had by this time set up their own courts and other administrations in a great deal of the south outside the main centres of population.

After the ambush the security forces were confounded by the audacity of the IRA as it took place near Brinny where the IRA had previously been surprised by a flanking exercise by the Essex and as it was a good distance to the east from Kilmichael. The security forces knew enough to understand that the IRA columns moved only by foot primarily by side roads and through fields.

When the security forces had travelled into Cork in the morning they had an additional escort, which they decided to drop on their return as it was felt the enemy would be most unlikely to be there in late afternoon during winter. They were now left with an understanding that the IRA had more than one major attacking column and that they could shift their attacks wherever suited them in the district.

Meanwhile that same evening the army had lured three senior IRA volunteers into an ambush near Bandon. They were to meet with an army sergeant who said he would give them information about the barracks; however, the latter had reported his deception to Percival when he was interviewed during the leak inquiry. When the IRA volunteers showed up at the appointed rendezvous, they were surrounded by the army and shot dead. The bodies appeared to have been mistreated before they were shot. A much more malign shift in the conflict had taken place.

Later in December 1920, the Auxiliaries, in reprisal for an IRA ambush earlier that day in the city, burned almost 5 acres of the centre of Cork city including City Hall. It was taken as a belated attack on the Nationalist community in retaliation for the ambush at Kilmichael and a clear signal that they would stop at nothing and were not accountable. It was quite clear now that not alone was the British Government not furious with this outrageous brutality against the nationalist population but on the contrary condoned it.

The year closed with further attacks on their main target, the RIC barracks in the district and a very open challenge from the IRA to the security forces.

This had begun as a resumption of hostilities by a very small group of breakaway Irish Volunteers, known as the Irish Republican Brotherhood, in early 1919, which at that time did not have the approval of the new Dail, and indeed it could be said that very few in the nationalist community would at that time have supported it, by late 1920 had the tacit if not the active support of much of the nationalist population. What started out as attacks on the RIC, which at that stage were made up of individual officers from both communities, was exacerbated by the introduction first of the imported Black and Tans and then of the Auxiliaries.

This widening of this locally recruited paramilitary force, which had been targeted by the IRB as the local yeomen of an alien state, and particularly their extremely coercive tactics and retaliations as time went on, pushed many nationalists into either a reluctant tolerance or supportive role for the IRA. The IRA came about in August 1919 when the Dail sanctioned the action against the British security forces which they declared to be agents of a foreign colonial power.

Meanwhile Geoffrey, instructed by Percival, continued to seek informants among the local community. While this was very limited, they were receiving much more information than they had and some of the information from the countryside about the presence of the IRA in particular locations was, and would prove to be, very useful. Many unionists, particularly in the southern part of Ireland, where they were a small minority of the population, were very frightened by the IRA and were fearful of what would happen to them and their families if the IRA were to succeed.

This applied primarily to those in the countryside where they tended to be the folks in the big houses with larger farms who were surrounded by nationalist small holders. In some cases, there had been tensions between both and consequently in the current situation these individual families felt themselves very isolated.

Geoffrey as a staff officer rather than a line officer confined himself now to operations in the barracks and did not venture outside the towns limits as there was no role for him there. He felt that the army had now been dragged into that war situation which the Government had refused to call it, which in his estimation was a great mistake. Armies do not make the peace; their role is solely to win wars. To a professional soldier that is what one accepts when one signs up. However, the expectation is that if a soldier is called upon to meet his country's enemy, that enemy would invariably be a foreigner.

He found it hard then to reconcile what he was asked to do in Ireland, which the British Government claimed to be part of Britain. Furthermore, he was further reinforced in the belief that some of the methods and actions taken by the security forces and even his own regiment were reprehensible. He found it impossible to reconcile his code of ethics with what was happening now.

It did not make it right that some of these actions had the tacit approval of the government. He explicitly declined to take part in the interrogation methods which were being applied in relation to some IRA prisoners and he was suspicious of some of the shootings of IRA suspects in recent times.

He was more and more furious with his posting here in Ireland. The conflict for him had turned sour and he realised that like the last months of the Great War it would not be a case of who would win but rather who would survive. He looked elsewhere for a haven from this wearing williwaw.

More and more he turned to the one place he felt could offer him that solace of the mind that soothes our inner core. He thought of the friends he had from the war years and even those he had made here, regardless of all that was happening around him and all the madness of the times. Most of all Geoffrey looked forward to his meetings with Julia on those evenings when Alastair was out of town. He realised how important these interludes were for him. Though he would never share those times with anyone but Julia, it did not make them any less precious, rather like a mystery, its profundity and its uncertain span making it all the more sublime.

Before Christmas the British Parliament passed the Government of Ireland Act 1920. This provided for two parliaments in Ireland North and South which would be subject to Westminster. The act thus overturned the unimplemented Home Rule Act of 1914 and gave the Unionists in the north of Ireland a majority in the northern parliament. It was seen as a defeat for the nationalist and a win for the unionists.

For the nationalists it merely confirmed that the British could not be relied upon and the reneging on the law passed before the Great War and the British commitment at the time to introducing it immediately after the war was over, only reinforced the nationalist view of Perfidious Albion. This new Act now stiffened their resolve and gave more impetus to their increasing desire to be rid of Britain for once and for all.

Chapter 43

1921 began where the latter part of the previous year ended, with renewed energy on both sides of the conflict. The security forces by now were travelling in greater numbers and taking more precautions outside the towns. In the locality the IRA were continuing their attacks on RIC barracks and even entering the towns at night to challenge curfew patrols.

It became obvious that the security forces had received information on many of the IRA volunteers and villages and houses were sacked searching for them at this stage many of them were 'on the run'. As of course was Joe Ryan.

He was particularly sought after as he was regarded as a traitor by the army who duped them into believing he was one of theirs. After he escaped, they ransacked his home and business attempting to find evidence of his espionage and they hoped information on the local IRA and its leadership. Joe, who had realised for some time that an event such as this was probably inevitable, had meticulously ensured that nothing, which could in any way implicate him or lead the security forces to others in the IRA, would be found among any of his possessions or in the premises of his abode or business.

He wanted to ensure that neither he nor the IRA would be incriminated by anything that was found. In addition, he wanted to be sure that neither his mother nor his staff would find themselves having any questions to answer about material that was found. He knew that any perceived suspicious documentation or equipment would allow the security forces to suspect and interrogate the people who were found anywhere near them.

Since early in the New Year all of the security forces were concentrating their efforts on capturing known individuals with IRA connections. Some of the information coming to them from informants in the community was providing not only names but also where they might be located. All of the security forces were mobilised to seek out and search not only individual homes but also whole villages and even parts of towns in these operations. These search parties would have upwards of between 100 to even 200 police, paramilitaries and soldiers. The searches were carried out meticulously in the areas designated. Houses where the IRA volunteers, or evidence of their presence, were found were ransacked and in some cases even burned down.

These raids were quite often successful with both men and arms being found. This caused a great deal of anxiety in the leadership of the IRA who could ill afford to lose either the men or the arms, both of which were vital to the continuation of the success of the columns. Additionally, the IRA was also apprehensive about the information the security forces would extract from some of their prisoners, who might succumb to the inevitable torture meted out to them.

The IRA was aware, from the manner and precision in which the searches were carried out by the security forces, that they were being guided by information received locally. Responding to that and acting on instructions coming from IRA H.Q. in Dublin these informants were vigorously sought out and where they could prove them guilty in their courts, which the IRA had set up specially to try these cases, those convicted were more often than not shot or else in the case of women and children told to leave the country immediately with their families.

These actions included the burning by the IRA of some houses owned by well-known established loyalist Unionist families in retaliation for the burning of nationalist houses. These measures taken by the IRA not only concerned those in the unionist community who were giving information to the security forces but also to even many of the ordinary innocent unionists who feared for their own and their families safety.

On the IRA side the massive searches by the security forces and their reinforced patrols made it much more difficult for IRA members to travel and to feel secure in the locations where previously they had felt they would be beyond reach. With the arrests of so many of their people it could not be guaranteed that the enemy would not find them or indeed their arms dumps and equipment.

This meant that nowhere was absolutely safe and to avoid detection and capture they had to change locations much more frequently than before. As a consequence, Joe and the others were constantly on the move. He did however return at times to Bandon, where he had friends, he could trust and even from his knowledge of the town and the activities of the security forces there he could continue to still be of some value. While he was very much on the wanted list he could still move around there cautiously as the security forces would not suspect that he would make an appearance in the town. He also wanted to ensure that while he could not be present his business could tick over without him to keep it alive and to secure his employees jobs.

Notwithstanding this the Flying Column under Tom Barry continued to manoeuvre around the area and to emphasise that the IRA were still a force to be reckoned with. They surrounded the town of Bandon at the end of January during curfew time and waited for the security forces to show themselves. However, none of the three forces there, army, RIC and Black and Tans moved out of their barracks even when the column opened fire on them. After waiting some time, they departed but days later were still active attacking an RIC barracks in a village nearby.

Joe's time as an inside spy for the IRA was over but he kept very much in touch with Sean Hales and was aware of what was happening on the ground. He continued to advise on likely strategy of the military from his own experiences, particularly on intelligence and communications. He guessed that at this stage the army would have a central role in strategy and therefore there should be a careful eye on their movements particularly when the IRA were planning an ambush.

He predicted that there would not be any simple targets in the future and all movement would be rehearsed and reinforced. He also advised that the army would endeavour to inflict a knock-out blow to the main column and they would try to outflank an IRA ambush. The IRA should be aware that the army might lure them into a trap by sending in a regular patrol with a contingent or contingents well back to move into a flanking position if an attack occurred.

Unlike the IRA they have equipment which enables them to scout a greater distance out than the IRA and their armaments are superior to those of the IRA. While Joe said that all of this would not be unfamiliar to Sean it was nevertheless important to repeat it as in a moment of perceived opportunity decisions might be taken where the enemy was merely lulling you into a false sense of security.

Joe's fiancé's family home was also a target and because of the old man's past Land League/IRB associations it had been searched inch by inch a number of times. Again, there was no evidence found there and consequently no arrests were made. For that Joe alone was thankful, although he hated the trauma he had put others through. While he was welcome there, he refused to visit the house as he worried it would put the safety of its residents, the old man's in particular, in jeopardy. His neighbours, including a retired colonel living in the big house close by, posed a constant threat.

Chapter 44

Geoffrey had gone back to England for Christmas and the New Year. He was quite pleased about this as, with conditions as they were, he would have had to spend most of that time confined to his barracks. In addition, he would not have been able to see Julia as Alastair was not working away from home at that time and also because they had travelled to Dublin for the New Year and were remaining there for a week.

Geoffrey was very pleased to be again with Nannie Kate, who, although retired some time, was still resident in his parents' house and by now an extended member of the family. His mother, as he expected, lost interest in him after the first night of his arrival and was too preoccupied with her plans for a New Year's party in the house. His father showed more interest and there were a number of conversations about the situation in Ireland. He told him that there was a great deal of unease among certain establishment figures in England about the whole affair.

"I was speaking to the former Prime Minister, Lord Asquith, recently who is very concerned about the situation. He said that he had given his promise that the issue would be dealt with after the war and now this. The Unionists and friends of the Tories are blocking the stated will of Parliament and what is happening in our name in Ireland is outrageous. We fought the Great War for democracy and the freedom of peoples in Europe.

"How now can we refuse to accept the democratic will of the overwhelming majority in Ireland? When America entered the War on our behalf, it did so as Woodrow Wilson left us in no doubt that they would not tolerate colonialism after the war. I am now told by my friends in America that there is much annoyance at the way we are behaving in Ireland. Lloyd is paying too much attention to the hardliners in his coalition, such as Bonar Law and Winston Churchill."

Geoffrey, addressing his father in the aristocratic mode, "Well Sir, the situation in Ireland is far from being ameliorated. In fact, in my opinion, it is getting worse. I have noticed a sharp rise in its vehemence. I wish I could say that the blame rests entirely with the other side. It has to be said that the army and indeed the police are not equipped to deal with the type of disturbance and violence occurring in Ireland. Most of the security forces in Ireland whether army or the paratroopers attached to the Royal Irish Constabulary are former veterans from the war and so have a great deal of army experience and training. They are trained to fight an enemy on open ground face to face or at least that is what is said.

"The Irish are fighting from behind ditches and walls in remote countryside where there is an amount of cover and so they are difficult both to see and fight. We say it is unequal and unfair. Not what armies are supposed to do. However, it could very well be argued that we have all gone beyond how armies confronted each other in the past. After the Great War all has changed. No longer do you meet your enemy face to face. Now he is hidden in a hole in the ground while you are marching towards his highly sophisticated weapons which mow you down in the field like a harvesting scythe.

"In Ireland the enemy is concealed but luckily does not have over-sophisticated weapons. They are also on foot, while we are motorised. He knows his terrain backwards as we do not. That terrain is mainly hilly, boggy, misty, sometimes inaccessible, which makes it easier for guerrilla warfare. He does have moreover, the zeal and commitment of one fighting for his rights. The combination can be lethal if your only cause is to subdue him."

"And what about this business we hear in the newspapers of retaliations by the armed forces? Is that correct? Can they be justified? Many of us were appalled by the news seeping back of Cork city centre being burned down by our forces. Surely that is not accurate?"

"I fear it is Sir. It was merely in retaliation against an ambush that occurred earlier in the day in another part of the city and the ambush which took place days before at a place called Kilmichael. However, the burning was against the business areas of the city and it itself was unprovoked. There have also been other cases of which I am not proud as a soldier."

"Surely your senior officers can prevent all of this. Is there no discipline in these forces?"

"The problem Sir is the latitude afforded by the Government for this activity. Not only is it condoned but in many cases, it is encouraged. It is allowed in the mistaken belief that it will turn the population against the insurgency. Regrettably I believe from my experience in Cork that it is very much having the very opposite effect."

"Then what if anything, in your opinion, is the solution to all of this?"

"There are two ways of dealing with the problem. The government could send about 250,000 troops to Ireland and with the martial law we now have in place we could then saturate the countryside with troops, particularly in the areas where the IRA are strongest, and ruthlessly eliminate or imprison all those whom we even suspect are involved.

"Of course, in doing so the majority nationalist population in the south of the country, even those who now do not support violence and I believe most of them don't, would not accept this and the place would become ungovernable. Without further draconian legislation in place and a willingness to treat Ireland like we did India during the insurrection there, we will lose total control.

"The problem with this position is: would the Government be willing to introduce the necessary legislation to bring this about? From what you say I suspect the informed international community and particularly America would be very loud in their protests against such a policy. Can we afford that, as we are struggling to emerge from a world war that has inflicted on us enormous economic problems? Would the population in England accept it?

"The government could of course alternatively attempt to negotiate with Sinn Fein to find an acceptable solution. It would not be easy because the unionists are vehemently opposed to having a majority nationalist parliament in Ireland. Because of historic reasons they have had a privileged position in Ireland, which they see as disappearing if Home Rule were to be introduced for the whole island.

"The new Government of Ireland Act which has just been passed would probably be acceptable to the unionists in the north of the country because they have a majority there. However, in the south, where they are a very small minority, the unionists feel very vulnerable. The current hostilities have exacerbated that. I suppose the two proposed parliaments could work if the unionists in the north and the nationalists in the south can accept it. The minority unionists are not strong enough to oppose it.

"The problem, as I see it Sir, is that I do not expect the nationalists to accept the new arrangements and Sinn Fein have already rejected them outright as not only too little too late but an abnegation of the Act already signed into law. Even that now if it were introduced would not be enough. Sinn Fein are seeking full separation from Britain. Accordingly, the government will have to go further if it wishes to solve the conundrum."

"What a mess. We had all hoped for a modicum of peace and quiet after the tumult of what we all hoped would be a war to end all wars. As you said we are facing an extraordinary time of economic hardship and deprivation as a consequence of the war. Many of our young men, to whom we owe so much, are unable to find work after returning from the war. The Whig/Liberal Party, which you know I have always supported, is in decline—blamed for the deprivations of the war and the consequential rise of a new social order.

"The Labour Party is fast gaining ground with the working class who now have the vote. I can see a time when it will challenge for government. That would certainly be at the Liberals expense. The Labour Party is known not to favour our behaviour in Ireland and can you blame them? Lloyd is conceding principles for short term gain. Better to be on the right side of history even if it means you lose.

"We were on the right side of history immediately after that awful war—have we not learned that in the 20th century sending gun boats to resolve political matters is passe? Woodrow Wilson is seeking a League of Nations to ensure that such wars will be averted in the future. I cannot see how countries can refuse to join such a body. How then do we account for our behaviour with nations who do not want us?"

After that conversation he found his father much more open to him, but because of his father's many commitments, even during the holidays, they never had the privacy of such a frank and uninhibited conversation again. When Geoffrey reflected on this on his return to Ireland after the leave ended, he felt a closeness to his father he had not before experienced but very much regretted all the years before when this opportunity had never shown itself. *Such is the penalty we pay for our inability to communicate: out of sight and out of mind.*

Chapter 45

Joe, who had always had a good relationship with his protestant neighbours was very concerned by the reprisals taken by the IRA against the unionists. While he understood the need to exorcise the informers from the community, he was not happy that they were executed if found guilty. *Just because the security forces had introduced a vicious policy into their behaviour did not mean we should.*

He was also unhappy that many of these executions were carried out after the victim had been tried in absentia and consequently had no means of defending himself. He believed that while unfortunately it was impossible to imprison those who were convicted, because they could not be safely and securely held, they should have been told to leave the country as a penalty, as indeed were the families of women and children who were found to be informers.

Most of the unionists were very moderate in their politics and merely wished to be allowed to get on with their lives as ordinary members of the community in which they lived. Their differences were mainly expressed in the difference of their protestant religion to that of the majority local catholic population. Unfortunately, these differences over many generations had been used as barriers between the communities resulting in cultural polarisation.

Children from one side did not normally mix with children from the other, at school nor at play, and so it led in adulthood to a natural divergence in ethos and understanding.

Joe knew well and could appreciate the fears of some of these unionists, even those who had played no act or part in the conflict. When he visited some of the big houses in the countryside, he found those who confided in him were very anxious to know how they would be treated if Ireland was separated from Britain and what would be the attitude of a catholic run government to protestant owners of larger holdings. Would such a government seize their properties on the basis that their English ancestors had taken these properties from the native Irish hundreds of years previously?

These fears were further exacerbated by the burnings of some mansions of the local loyalist gentry as reprisals for the security forces burnings of nationalist homes.

Joe argued with Sean Hales at times about this and how the IRA could convince the unionist population that they would be treated equally and fairly in a new Ireland. He knew from his many conversations with his fiancé's father that this was always an issue even in past times. He even said that when his young family were in poor circumstances during his time in jail for his anti-British behaviour it was the local parson rather than the local priest who showed practical Christian charity to his wife and children. He with the other Fenians were threatened with excommunication by the Catholic Church.

Sean admitted that IRA policy in relation to this went further than what he would wish, but unfortunately the exigencies of the time were such that the leadership felt there was no other option. *Fire with fire.* They would have to deal with the future when it arrived. They were now fighting for their very existence and they would show no pity for those who supported the enemy. He admitted that there was a danger that mistakes could be made and that the innocent could suffer but he said that was the stuff of war. *Kill or be killed.*

He recounted the deaths of 12 IRA volunteers in the past two weeks. While three were killed at Upton station when a local column attempted to hold up a train, which, to their surprise, carried a large number of heavily armed troops, the others were shot dead, though unarmed at the time. Seven of those killed were teenagers caught in the act of digging trenches in two separate locations. The trenches were being dug in many areas by the IRA to thwart security patrols. He said that they believed informants had been responsible for these events and consequently they were being blamed for these deaths. It was thus a question of survival and the means necessary to achieve that.

Since the killing of the three senior figures by the Essex outside Bandon when they were lulled into a trap set by Percival, Tom Barry wanted to show the security forces in the town that they could not feel entirely safe even in their own citadel. Barry was to have been present that night were it not for a minor heart problem he suffered just beforehand.

In addition, the security forces had been gaining the upper hand through their informers and by follow-up with large forces scouring the countryside and arresting or killing a number of IRA volunteers during the early part of 1921 in

Cork. Because of this, there was a perceived need for the IRA to show that they were still a force to be reckoned with.

Towards the end of February Barry took an expanded column into the town and covered the three barracks occupied by the security services there. After encountering three Black and Tan officers and killing them, they fired on all three barracks, getting a response from each but none of the forces ventured out. After an hour of stalemate, the column left the town having made their point, not only to themselves but also the security forces and, most of all, to the townspeople.

Joe Ryan had been in the town earlier and had sent a message that no unusual security force manoeuvres were taking place. It was now deemed necessary with so many informants, that caution had to be used at every turn. One of the people he saw there, as he furtively skirted the main centres to avoid detection by the security forces or by those he suspected would betray him, was John Flaherty. John invited him to his house on the town's outskirts, which had a large front garden and driveway with a gate so anyone attempting to gain entrance could be observed and give time for escape if needs be. In addition, it had a large garden at the back which gave access to the open countryside.

John was pleased to see him and Joe was not surprised by the relaxed way in which he was received. Over some welcome food and drink (non-alcoholic as Joe did not indulge during his time on the run) they spoke for some hours about events in the town and around the district.

John was quite familiar with the area as he was one of the few who travelled extensively around the country on business and consequently met a variety of people in doing so. His clients were mainly either the wealthy or the agents of large estates. The majority tended to be unionists and so he was well informed about that section of the population's views. However, he also knew some of the leaders of the IRA and in conversations with them they were very open about their aims and determination.

He told Joe that he had been an avid supporter of Home Rule and was very much an advocate of advancing through political means only. He instinctively did not think conflict and violence was the best way forward. He certainly was totally against the 1916 rising and indeed felt the IRA was wrong to have begun the conflict.

However, he was angry about the way in which the security forces had retaliated. In the current circumstances he could not be neutral and while he did not condone some of the actions of the IRA, particularly the executions of unionists and the burning of houses, he understood that the conflict would go on until some solution was found to end it.

"Joe, somehow, I suspect your views are not that different to mine. I do not see you as a zealot. My difficulty is that we will have a bigger problem in the future as a consequence of the Troubles. I can tell you already that the unionists and even Protestants who would have welcomed Home Rule are now fearful about their futures. They believe their properties and businesses and in some cases their lives are at risk if the IRA succeeds. You and I know that will not happen but it is very difficult to persuade them of that when they see some of their fellow unionists being executed, their families being told to leave the country and houses belonging to unionists burned down.

"They do not accept the informer labels that have been put on these victims. They say the evidence against them has been weak or indeed spurious. They are fearful that all that is needed to condemn someone is suspicion. They claim the IRA courts set up for these people are mere proforma exercises to justify the executions. Many of the landholders and even some businessmen would sell out if they could get buyers, who are few and far between in this climate.

"John, I have had the same type of discussion with some of my protestant neighbours who are anything but ardent loyalists. I have tried to reassure them that they are not in danger and that even some people accused of being informers were subsequently cleared by the IRA court. I for one am appalled at the thought of execution. I have seen enough death to be reluctant to take another unless my life or my family's lives are immediately threatened.

"I saw deserters executed during the war by the British army in cases where quite honestly these people should have been sent home to hospital. Once a war begins brutality takes over and hate and fear begets hate and fear.

"The IRA did some dreadful things I would not condone. But by and large the beginning of the conflict was conducted in a gentlemanly way, if you can say that in a war situation. Prisoners who were captured were released by the IRA. But then the British Government sent in those brutal paramilitaries, one worse than the other, and they quite obviously had been given free rein to do as they pleased.

"The Black and Tans have no discipline and are quite often drunk on duty while the Auxiliaries, all former army officers, are exceptionally well disciplined and highly trained. Both forces are ruthless, with little or no regard for the Irish, the Auxiliaries quite obviously are much more dangerous. Unfortunately, some of this malevolence has been adopted by the Essex Regiment here.

"The main culprit for this is Major Percival. He has taken it upon himself to be the driving force behind the elimination of the IRA in this area. He conducts the interrogation of IRA suspects himself and does not refrain from torture to get what he wants from his prisoners. We know he tortured Tom Hales and Pat Harte when they were captured last July. Poor Pat has ended up in Cork psychiatric hospital as a result. Tom is still in gaol.

"As a former army man, myself, I am disgusted by this. I do know however, that Percival's methods do not have the support or approval of a good number of the officers and men of the barracks. One officer we both know, who works closely with Percival on staff matters, has I believe refused to be present at these interrogations.

"The conflict has now escalated to a new level after Tureen and Kilmichael and the security forces are now shooting to kill even when they meet youngsters who are unarmed as we have heard recently. They are now attempting to weaken, if not destroy, the IRA by blanket coverage of whole areas with hundreds of the combined forces to capture volunteers and arms.

"Anyone, even those that in any way fit their profile of the IRA, is taken into custody and interrogated. Unfortunately, some of these raids have been successful and we have lost some valuable manpower and arms have also been recovered. In many ways the arms loss may prove as damaging a blow to the effectiveness of the IRA as the men.

"The success of the raids is put down to the treachery of informers by the leadership of the IRA. From the way that the searches have been conducted and the detailed knowledge of houses where arms and volunteers have been located, that would certainly point to the accuracy of many of these suspicions.

"The IRA of course are not over-exercised by these events and are determined to show that they are very much still in control of the countryside. That is why they have taken a very severe stand against the informers. They mostly wish to send a very strong message back to the unionist community, and indeed to nationalists who might be tempted to sell out their fellow countrymen, that those found to be giving information to the security forces will face the severest penalties without mercy.

"I do not agree with it myself but it obviously will curtail some from coming forward with information on the IRA. I agree however, that it will also negatively affect our relations with the protestant/unionist community and that is really unfortunate. Their main forces are still intact and (thinking but refraining from mentioning the event later that evening in the town) do not be surprised if they show they are still a formidable force able and willing to take the war to the door of the enemy itself."

Joe left early to get clear of the town as he felt there would be a widespread alert in the town next morning after the IRA action.

Chapter 46

Geoffrey found that the flow of information coming in from his sources slowed considerably. He understood this was because of IRA action against informers. Percival reluctantly accepted that this was the case and began to see another way of countering the IRA and hopefully delivering a knock-out blow to their ability to mount a similar operation like Kilmichael or Tureen or indeed the attack on the barracks in Bandon. In many ways the latter was most annoying.

However, he did not believe in confronting the enemy unless he knew his forces were not only superior but strategically at an advantage. He was still of the view that if an opportunity presented itself, they should overwhelm the IRA to the extent that there was no escape.

He had travelled to both his Regimental H.Q. in Kinsale and also to the Army H.Q. in Cork to outline his plan for such a manoeuvre at short notice if the opportunity presented itself. He hoped that such a situation might happen in the Bandon-Kinsale-Cork triangle where they could effectively throw a net around the IRA and wipe them out.

Geoffrey bided his time, hoping that before long the politicians would finally understand that this conflict would not be resolved by a continuation of the war. He understood Percival was not totally oblivious to this but he knew the latter's career and promotion prospects were riding on how it was perceived he performed in this arena. Percival needed at least one substantial success to show that his reputation as a strategist was well deserved.

Geoffrey continued to visit Julia when Alastair was away which was now every week for at least two nights. He was however, conscious of the fast-approaching time when Alastair would be moving to his new position as head of the Cork office. Both of them understood what it would mean for the relationship, but then they had always known that a time would come when their exquisite assignations would no longer be possible.

They did not dwell on it and so every meeting was precious and every moment was to be savoured, to be remembered in the long evenings of their separation. This bitter/sweet affair was made more poignant by the nature of the time and place in which they lived. Each parting as if it was the end and each encounter as if there might not be another, kept their mutual enthrallment as it was on that first exquisite night.

Chapter 47

Tom Barry following up on his attack on Bandon brought his *Flying Column* into a location on the east of the Bandon River and attempted an ambush on the Bandon Kinsale Road. On this occasion, knowing the expanded numbers of the security patrols in the past months he had with him a force of 100 men. He waited for a patrol which regularly arrived along this road. Sometime later his scouts informed him that the patrol had left Kinsale. After some time when there was no show from the patrol, he realised that something had happened.

Sensing that their position may have been compromised by some informant he decided to abandon his position and move eastward. Later still in daylight a scouting military aircraft from Kinsale was seen in the skies above them and from its manoeuvres it obviously was looking for the Column.

While the order had been given to conceal themselves in ditches and hedgerows and any cover, they could find close by, Barry could not be sure they had not been seen and so the Column was moved further east before resting for the night.

Next day he moved again before locating the Column along the Bandon-Cork road at Crossbarry. He was determined to confront the enemy and decided in consultation with other leaders to remain in the area until the opportunity for an attack presented itself. They knew there was a risk involved in being in the one district for too long, particularly now that the security forces were appearing in large numbers when they had word that the IRA were present. The challenge would obviously be far greater but it was felt there was a need to show the IRA was not a trivial group of amateurs and could hold its own even against a superior force.

Early next morning his scouts which were now posted in all directions informed him that lights were seen coming from Bandon but were moving very slowly. It was clear, that the security was searching the areas and houses as they moved along the road. Tom Barry placed his men in sections along the northern side of the east/west roadway well concealed and covering two crossroads and eight roads/laneways leading to that location. He placed two other sections covering their north/west and north-eastern flanks and waited.

Three lorries appeared from the Bandon direction and were fired on. Taken by surprise the troops alighted from the vehicles and attempted to assert themselves but a number having been killed the rest ran and did not stop to reengage. Retrieving the much-needed weapons and ammunition left behind, the section on the northern section was heard to be under fire by troops attempting to outflank the Column and later the section to the east also was being attacked, first from the east and later also from the south.

Both sections held their ground and were reinforced by some from the western sections while the remainder had to engage the second army company coming late to the scene from the Bandon direction to the west. Conceding nothing the volunteers gave more than they received from a vastly larger contingent of the enemy which had obviously been searching in great numbers for the Column since they were spotted by the aircraft near the Bandon River two days before.

The security forces beaten back, the Column, after nearly two hours fighting, were able to retreat unopposed north-westwards before the security forces regrouped and attempted to complete their pincer movement, which they had failed to achieve earlier. On the retreat the Column met and also drove back a large contingent of Auxiliaries approaching from the north. Having cleared potential encirclement and seeing through binoculars from high ground that all was clear they headed west.

They had lost three volunteers in the fighting and three more were wounded. While grieving for their losses the IRA volunteers were proud of what they considered their victory over a force which was at least four times greater than theirs. They had left the scene after beating back the waves of security force attacks and apart from the encounter with the Auxiliaries which were also repulsed, they were never under threat as they retreated.

Knowing that the security forces, incensed that they had failed despite overwhelming odds, would bring even more forces into the area in the hope of cutting off their retreat, the Column moved westward and after tending to the wounded did not stop until they had reached a safe location over twenty miles further on. It was early morning before they could rest.

Back at the barracks in Bandon, Geoffrey, who did not take part in the operation, was the officer in charge. The day before there had been great activity as Percival had arranged a mobilisation of all those troops, he could take from the barracks leaving just a skeleton crew to defend the barracks in case of attack. In addition to those, he had sought and would get R.I.C., Black and Tan support for the operation. The Regiment in Kinsale had informed him that the IRA was seen on the roadway between Kinsale and Innishannon by their spotter plane. They had earlier been informed that the IRA was lying in ambush waiting for the regular patrol from Kinsale.

That had been the trigger that Percival had sought for his plan to attempt to encircle the main IRA column and destroy it. The informer had indicated that the Column lying in waiting was quite large, although no figure was given; it was expected to be more than 50 men. Percival was pleased to hear that because if they could deploy quickly, they might be able to catch them in the area, as a group of such magnitude would be difficult to move without being seen by one of his informants.

He had already deployed scouts to report any unusual movements of groups of more than three people heading away from the area.

Later that afternoon, after speaking with the C.O. in charge of the Auxiliaries in Macroom who would also be involved, Percival travelled to Kinsale to inform his local Regimental H.Q. of his plan, which would also involve contingents from there and the Army in Cork. From Kinsale he would coordinate the operation hoping to ensnare the IRA by closing in on them from all sides of the triangle.

At that stage he had information that one of the principal leaders of the IRA was housed in a location about 4 miles east of Innishannon. He hoped that would indicate that the main group were not far distant and therefore would use that location as the focal point on which to tighten the net.

Geoffrey, in charge after the departure of the raiding group, secured the barracks. Closing the gates and posting extra guards on look-out, he was taking no chances. He had seen what the IRA were capable of and he had no doubt that if they noticed the departure of the main group and had sufficient men available, they would undoubtedly use that opportunity to attack the barracks.

As he lay in his bed alert and fully clothed that night, he had a strange feeling that *while the operation would see action in the coming hours it might not be as easy as Major Percival had assumed. It was becoming obvious now that the IRA* had extremely well-trained soldiers in their ranks and his mind flashed back to Joe Ryan who was a good example of this. They could not have been so organised and so successful with such little resources if they had not been. In a strange way it appeared the more they thought they were successfully dismantling the IRA's effectiveness by the arrests of the men and the capture of their arms and ammunition, the more they appeared to grow stronger.

Like Antaeus they would get their strength from their native earth. But then he felt Percival was no Hercules.

Geoffrey had experienced the same feeling at the Front when they were told that the German lines would be shattered by the continuous extraordinary bombardment for days before the attack and that they would make enormous inroads into German held territory and even turn the war in their favour. Unfortunately, it was they rather than the Germans that were surprised when his men ran into withering fire and were left way short of any gain, with enormous losses as the Germans, in preparation for the shelling, had dug themselves far into the ground and were waiting for them with machine guns to mow them down.

Later in the morning a lorry from the raiding party returned with wounded requesting the dispatch of as many troops as could be spared to reinforce those now fighting the enemy. He was unable to get much information from the NCO who brought the wounded back to the barracks other than that they had run into a large number of the enemy who were putting up a strong opposition. Geoffrey, keeping a minimum of his troops to defend the barracks and keeping his communications centre open, dispatched the others under a Lieutenant and instructed the NCO to lead them to the area as quickly as possible.

It was some hours later that some lorries arrived at the barracks with dead and more wounded. The Sergeant in charge only said they had come under fire from a very large number of the enemy, who were well concealed and extremely difficult to dislodge. He had been instructed to say no more as the fighting was still on-going and taking place at different locations. He had come from the western sector of the battle site and so did not have any information on what was happening elsewhere.

Geoffrey, not questioning the Sergeant further, understood quite well what that meant.

Percival and the commanders of the other contingents were obviously facing very stiff opposition and even from what he had just seen, the losses would be considerable.

It was late evening before Percival and the others returned to the barracks. They had been on duty for over 24 hours by then and needed food and sleep before returning next morning to seek out the enemy. He was reticent about the details of what had occurred but he did say that the IRA had put up a surprising resistance to them and that their numbers were probably equivalent to those of the security forces. They were difficult to dislodge from very well protected cover. They had fought a very effective rear-guard action in difficult terrain for his forces and using their superior knowledge of the countryside were able to escape.

Geoffrey, a veteran of failed certainties, only too well understood the language of palliative embroidery.

Chapter 48

When the official report was made, great pains were taken to suggest that the IRA had suffered a stunning defeat. It was claimed that the IRA had only escaped because of luck in choosing the one escape route not closed by the British forces. However, the reality was that the fighting lasted at least two hours and while the IRA ended up with 3 killed the security forces suffered ten times that amount.

There had been attempts made shortly afterwards to hunt down the IRA Column but by that time it had melted into the west. Percival attempted to suggest that the IRA were greatly weakened by the event but few who knew the real situation were convinced. It did however, ensure that the Army were now more determined than ever to inflict a fatal blow on the IRA, particularly in West Cork. During the successive weeks, they combed the countryside stopping everyone they met and interrogating anyone remotely suspected of involvement with the IRA.

In one major sweep on the entire district a massive operation was launched sweeping the whole area from Cork to the borders of Kerry where those who were not captured would be driven into forces awaiting them there. Barry, using the knowledge of local experts, escaped with his Flying Column in front of the sweep by travelling through normally inaccessible terrain, at times led at night by a rope in single file across bogs and mountain precipices to a secure place.

Boldly, when the security forces ended their search and returned to base, Barry followed soon after and attacked a number of places including Bandon in daylight. During this time, he attacked and destroyed the RIC barracks in Rosscarbery which housed a large number of RIC policemen as well as Black and Tan paramilitaries.

The flood gates were now open to any method to defeat the IRA. As well as capturing IRA suspects, the security forces shot a number of unarmed known IRA volunteers. This led to retaliation by the IRA who targeted security personnel in the towns and villages striking when they were unexpected.

Geoffrey, not having to take part in these operations was free to continue his meetings with Julia whenever the opportunity allowed. At this time his barracks was reinforced by troops for the push against the IRA and it was obvious that while they had captured a number of the IRA members, they were making only dents in that organisation. Something more needed to be done to regain some supremacy. Geoffrey knew that that was indeed possible and if the numbers were forthcoming as requested by the Army, even probable.

However, he also knew that it could not be done without much more violence and disregard for property that would alienate the overwhelming number of the Nationalist population. He believed from correspondence with his father, that scenario would be quite unacceptable to a substantial number of English establishment figures and particularly within the U.S. Congress and amongst Irish Americans, who were fast increasing their political influence in America.

Julia had told Geoffrey at their last meeting that she would be transferring to Cork when her husband would take up duty there in late August. They would however be leaving Bandon finally in early July on an extended vacation before starting the new job in Cork city. They did not dwell on that and understanding from the very beginning that that day would come, they were determined to savour every last moment that was left.

There would be no whimpering or regret. Their time together was a gift freely given with no strings attached and no assurances of how or when it would end. It was and would always be that oasis of desire, visited once but remembered forever.

Meanwhile, the early weeks of spring rolled into summer the Army now in control with more stringent stop and search patrols even in the towns and villages. The Nationalists becoming even more put upon and angry, the Unionists becoming more apprehensive and fearful. Sinn Fein leaders' houses were burned and the IRA retaliated by burning houses of wealthy loyalist landlords. Shootings on both sides against combatants were common.

The IRA continued to carry out executions of informers. The British Army had expanded its force in Ireland and General Wilson, Commander of the Imperial Army, who was an ardent unionist and had mutinied against the Government in 1914 over Home Rule, wanted to increase it further to ensure the annihilation of the IRA.

Joe all this time moved from place to place to avoid the searches by the security forces that were now increasing in intensity and frequency. Following the lead of the IRA columns these were haphazard in nature with no regular pattern and consequently the raids were quite effective. Rarely now did he go into Bandon, as the stop and search procedure made it very difficult to go undetected. Strangely he not only had to fear the security forces but most of the IRA did not know he was on the run and many still believed him to be a loyalist sympathiser. His journeys there consequently were rather fraught.

Speaking to Sean Hales he learned that new tactics were being introduced, including the elimination of informers and the targeting of certain security forces personnel who were regarded as extremely dangerous and central to the operations of the enemy. He was also informed that while Crossbarry was a major success for them it had been reported as a success for the security forces and so the propaganda benefit for them was far less than that of Kilmichael, even though in real terms it was by far their greatest achievement.

He mentioned to Joe that the main target for the IRA in the area was Major Percival, not only because of the torture he inflicts on his victims but also, he is the central strategist in all the operations in the district. In addition, he mentioned other officers in the Army, RIC, and Black and Tans. Included was Geoffrey. Sean told Joe that Percival and Geoffrey separately were seen frequently visiting establishments in the evening in Bandon and orders had been issued for their assassination. Their routes and the times had been noted and instructions had been given.

Joe listened and said nothing. It would have been of little avail. He was of course unhappy to hear Geoffrey's name being mentioned as one of the prime targets. However, it had been noted that Geoffrey was very amiable and had in a short space of time made a great deal of contacts in the town. This of course was taken to mean that he probably was receiving a deal of information which could be dangerous for the IRA.

In any case the IRA were not taking any chances. In addition, Geoffrey had been seen taking a certain route a number of late evenings each week in the past month and by doing so he could be an easy target for someone lying in wait. The order given, would not be countermanded. Still, he could not let this happen.

Joe made his way into Bandon later that day. He would have to make contact with Geoffrey somehow before evening. Unfortunately, he would have to do so in a way that it could never be traced back to him. He could not telephone as this could be listened into either at the telephone exchange or the telephone operator at the barracks. He had thought of getting a street-smart youngster to deliver a message to Geoffrey asking him to meet him, but any civilian going to the barracks these days would be noted and questions might be asked subsequently.

Accordingly, he furtively skirted the town, and tapping into the telegraph wire, he sent a message to Geoffrey in his barracks telling him that Jack Lee wished to meet in the hotel bar in an hour. He knew this would provoke a questioning reaction from Geoffrey who undoubtedly would not have previously received a request from his friend Jack Lee in such a way. He knew Geoffrey would come to check it out: he had to hope that he would not have an escort with him in doing so. It was daylight and Geoffrey, while not foolhardy, would reasonably feel he could handle whatever lay ahead. He also did not wish to show unnecessary force in the town.

Joe, out of sight near a laneway leading to the railway dressed in a railway man's outfit, saw Geoffrey crossed the river bridge from the direction of North Main Street, making his way to the hotel.

Earlier Joe had barely escaped running into a Black and Tan patrol as he came the direction of Ballinadee into Foxes Street.

Just as Geoffrey was passing along Shannon Street at the side-street leading to the railway, Joe hailed him quietly from a doorway. Geoffrey's first reaction was to reach for his pistol, but seeing Joe who was obviously unarmed he quickly ducked into the passageway where Joe was waiting out of sight of anyone passing. There were no niceties passed between them. Joe waited only long enough to say.

"Geoffrey the IRA has seen your movements late evenings over the past month; know which way you travel and probably who you are seeing. You are a target and someone will be lying in wait for you to appear. You will not see anyone; the IRA man waiting for you is an expert at what he does. He, like us, was trained well and honed his sniper skills at the Front. It could happen any evening. Make other plans. Do not go there. If you seek him out, he will be in deep cover and will vanish if he sees a search in progress."

Without waiting for a response Joe was gone, heading back out of town and on the run.

Geoffrey was stunned. Everything was rushing at him all at once. He went to the bar for a drink and to attempt to sort out in his mind the implications of what Joe had just said.

His first concern was for Julia. What implications had this for her? Was she safe? She had to be protected. But that would mean alerting Alastair to their relationship. On rethinking: Joe had not mentioned Julia. He was convinced that if she was in any danger he would have said so. But he had to now assure that she would not be in any way implicated in the future. What would that mean?

He had to take the warning seriously. Joe would not come to tell me unless it was. He had risked everything—he knew that Percival would show no mercy if the army caught him and it must also be a breach of trust with his own side.

What to do? He was to meet Julia again this evening. He understood that if he passed within sight of the sniper Joe described he would undoubtedly be shot. These people do not miss a target in the open. There was also the problem of implicating Julia. That he would not do under any circumstances. There was no other way out. He had to abandon the rendezvous this evening and think out what, if anything he could do in the future. There was so little time left to both of them before Julia departed.

For now, he would have to get word to her that he could not be with her that evening and that a problem had arisen which would also prevent him from seeing her in the days ahead. They had prearranged a system whereby he could send a signal if he was not showing up and he would use that. However, he would have to meet with her at another time to convey the full reason for what had happened. He would not convey that in writing as it might fall into the wrong hands.

Chapter 49

The following weeks moved slowly for Geoffrey. The security forces now only left town in large numbers with slow moving search and destroy patrols. A number of IRA operatives were caught in these operations – although because of intimidation through IRA executions and deportations the informers were far fewer. The main IRA columns avoided confrontation with these larger better armed forces but nonetheless attacked the barracks and harassed the town and villages when it was opportune to do so.

Geoffrey's barracks was by now overfilled with reinforced troops—brought about by the burning by the IRA of a large stand-alone building which was to have housed them. Geoffrey meanwhile, as indeed all of the security forces personnel, had to exercise extra vigilance when alone in the town. The curfew in the town had been increased to run from 7PM. In a strange way Geoffrey felt more vulnerable because of it. It allowed snipers to much more easily pick out security personnel even in mufti.

He had taken Joe's advice over some weeks and had arranged to convey to Julia what had happened when they met at a golf reception in the local hotel. He had ensured that he got an invitation from his friend, Jack Lee knowing she and Alastair would be present. They agreed it would be safer for both of them if they waited. While Julia was very concerned that her husband would discover her dalliance with him, it was the possibility that somehow Alastair as a consequence would be targeted by the IRA as an informer that most worried her.

The Government of Ireland Act of 1920 had provided for two parliaments in Ireland, one in Belfast and one in Dublin. While Sinn Fein refused, the Unionists in the north of the country, understanding that this was their best way for ensuring they would not be subject to a large majority of Catholic Nationalists on the island, were pleased to accept the offer. In the six-county area designated to be subject to the Belfast Parliament the Unionists had approximately a two thirds majority.

Having resolved the problems which Home Rule caused because of Unionist opposition, Lloyd George, who no longer had to contend with the total veto of his pro-unionist Tory Party coalition partner, found that he could find some way out of the current political morass in Ireland. It was realised at that stage that while there might be a military victory over the IRA it would come at a high moral cost for Britain both at home and internationally.

In addition, the Government would have to find a solution that would work in Ireland. It was now clear that he would not receive the cooperation of the elected representatives in southern Ireland for the proposed second parliament in Dublin. In the 20th century in Europe after the Great War it would be extremely difficult to control the country by edict from London. He would have to keep a large standing army in the country to do so.

Accordingly, by the end of June 1921 the British Government offered talks with Sinn Fein to attempt to resolve the problem. This was accepted and a truce was consequently entered into by both sides on 7 July 1921. The talks were held in London during the following months and resulted in a Treaty being signed between both parties on 6 December.

Its terms, which gave the southern part of the country dominion status with an independent parliament, was acceptable to a majority of the representatives in the Dail, but the question of the allegiance to the Crown and the exclusion of the northern six countries from the deal were the main substantial issues, which alienated a large minority of Dail representatives.

The majority agreed to ratify the Treaty and set up a government under its terms. An irreconcilable split developed in Sinn Fein and in the IRA and a civil war resulted.

With the truce in place and hostilities ended in early July, Geoffrey was able visit Julia again without fear of either of them having to worry about the IRA. Unfortunately, there was only time for a few visits before Alastair and Julia moved away.

On their last time together, they did not dwell on their parting. Rather, they wished to ensure that they could both look back on their last evening of intimacy with fond memory, not a wretched regretting of hopeless self-commiseration. On leaving that evening, Julia and Geoffrey embracing for the last time, wished each other future happiness and contentment, carrying away that affection and warmth that came from kindred spirits who met awhile but remembered forever.